Repenting of **Religion**

Repenting of **Religion**

Turning from Judgment to the Love of God

Gregory A. **Boyd**

BakerBooks
Grand Rapids, Michigan

© 2004 by Gregory A. Boyd

Published by Baker Books
a division of Baker Publishing Group
P.O. Box 6287, Grand Rapids, MI 49516-6287
www.bakerbooks.com

Fifth printing, September 2008

Printed in the United States of America

Library of Congress Cataloging-in-Publication Data
Boyd, Gregory A., 1957–
    Repenting of religion: turning from judgment to the love of God /
Gregory A. Boyd.
        p.   cm.
    Includes bibliographical references.
    ISBN 10: 0-8010-6506-2 (pbk.)
    ISBN 978-0-8010-6506-4 (pbk.)
    1. Love—Religious aspects—Christianity. 2. Judgment—Religious aspects—Christianity. 3. Christian life. I. Title.
    BV4639.B69 2004
    241′.4—dc22   200403912

To Gina and Richard Patton

*You rekindled my love for Bonhoeffer
and helped me see the profound antithesis
between love and judgment.*

Jesus calls men,
not to a new religion,
but to life.

DIETRICH BONHOEFFER

Contents

Preface

Very rarely is a connection made between love on the one hand and judgment on the other. In this work I argue that they are as inseparably connected as up and down and good and evil. We love only insofar as we abstain from judgment.

Love is the central command in Scripture and judgment the central prohibition. Indeed, judgment is the "original sin" in Scripture. This is why the forbidden tree in the center of the garden—the prohibition around which life in the garden revolved—was called the "Tree of the Knowledge of Good and Evil."

In my opinion no topic could be more foundational or more important than this one. It addresses the central purpose for which God created humans (to share in his perfect love) and the central obstacle to fulfilling that purpose (our judgment). Yet the connection between these two rarely has been explored. Partly because of this the body of Christ does not consistently love as Christ loves. Indeed, large segments of the body of Christ mistake their judgment—their eating from the Tree of the Knowledge of Good and Evil—to be love! Tragically, they promote the essence of the fall as though it were salvation.

The primary focus of this work is practical. Several thinkers, the most notable being Dietrich Bonhoeffer, have discussed the all-important antithetical relationship between love and the knowledge of good and evil. But the insight has not to date been discussed on a layperson's level with the goal of helping people apply it to their lives. My earnest hope and prayer is that the Spirit of God will use this work to help us acquire a vision for the church as a nonreligious community of outrageous love. I pray that God will use this work to help us free ourselves from our addiction to judgment, experience the unsurpassable love of God, and reflect this Calvary-like love toward all people.

As the numerous quotes and endnotes throughout this work will make clear, my thesis has been greatly inspired by my reading of Bonhoeffer. Indeed, this work can be understood as a consistent interaction with his thought. Bonhoeffer's reflections on love and judgment are highly nuanced, profound, but also difficult for nonacademics to grasp. In this work I try to make the core of his insight accessible to lay readers and academics alike. Toward this end, I have placed much of the more difficult Bonhoeffer material in the endnotes. Lay readers not inclined to wrestle with this material may bypass it and lose nothing of the substance of this work.

At the same time, it needs to be made clear at the start that this work is not intended to be a popularization of Bonhoeffer's theology. Much of what I have to say was never addressed by Bonhoeffer. Much of what Bonhoeffer has to say, even fascinating aspects of his reflections on the knowledge of good and evil, I do not address. Some of what I have to say takes his thought in new directions that I'm sure he did not anticipate and that may not have met with his approval. And despite the profound respect I have for this hero of the faith, some of what I have to say flatly disagrees with what he said. Acknowledging all of this up front hopefully will prevent students of Bonhoeffer from being disappointed and others who have no interest in Bonhoeffer from being put off.

I am indebted to many aside from Dietrich Bonhoeffer for helping bring this work into being. My thanks to Ed Silvoso, who preached a sermon in 1996 at Woodland Hills Church that first opened my eyes to the antithetical connection between love and judgment. I also must express deep appreciation to Woodland Hills Church in Maplewood, Minnesota, for its loyalty in hearing and living out the innumerable messages on "Love and Judgment" that I have given over the last few years. Most of the ideas articulated in this work were first preached to this vibrant congregation, sometimes numerous times. Thanks for your patience!

My covenant brother Dr. Paul Eddy has offered, as usual, outstanding feedback on early drafts of this work. My dear friends Tyler and Chelsea DeArmond selflessly have given much time to reviewing this work, as they did with several previous works of mine. Most of what I have learned about sharing life in community I have learned from my small group of ten years, Greg and Marsha Erickson, Dave and Terri Churchill, and Julie and Alex Ross. I had no idea how profound and beneficial intimate fellowship could be prior to my relationship with these wonderful friends and colleagues in the battle.

As is the case with all my writings and indeed my entire ministry, this work would not have been possible without the constant love and support of my precious wife, Shelley, as well as my three delightful children, Denay, Alisha, and Nathan. Finally, while I had read Bonhoeffer in years past, the profundity of his reflections on the nature of "the knowledge of good and evil" largely escaped me until I met Gina and Richard Patton. They not only reintroduced me to Bonhoeffer but also inspired many of the reflections I offer in this book. The book as a whole has benefited greatly from the many dialogues and debates we have enjoyed on this and related issues over the last several years. It is thus with profound gratitude that I dedicate this work to them.

Introduction

Waking Up to Judgment

And the LORD God commanded the man, "You may freely eat of every tree of the garden; but of the Tree of the Knowledge of Good and Evil you shall not eat, for in the day that you eat of it you shall die."

Genesis 2:16

The knowledge of good and evil seems to be the aim of all ethical reflection. The first task of Christian ethics is to invalidate this knowledge.

Dietrich Bonhoeffer

An Experience of Love

I am sitting in a mall on a Saturday afternoon. As I sip my Coke and relax, I study people. I notice some are pretty and some are not. Some are slender; some are obese. On the basis of what they wear, their facial expressions, the way they relate to their spouses, friends, or kids, I conclude some are "godly" while others are "ungodly." Some give me a warm feeling as I watch their tenderness toward their children. Others make me angry or disgusted.

Then suddenly I notice *I'm noticing all this*. Believing as I do that every activity we engage in, including our thinking, is for a purpose, I begin to wonder what purpose this silent commentary about other people is serving. After a moment's introspection I realize it is on some level making me feel good. It is in a sense feeding me. It's satisfying some need I have to stand in judgment over people. Deep down, I enjoy being the one who at least before the tribunal of my own mind gets to pronounce the verdict: Pretty. Ugly. Good figure. Fat. Godly. Ungodly. Disgusting. Cute. And so on.

With this insight came another, this one, I am sure, prompted by the Holy Spirit. I recalled that Jesus taught wherever we go, our first responsibility is to bless people (Luke 10:5). I recalled Scripture teaches us to think and speak evil of no one (Titus 3:2; James 4:11). Instantly I was convicted by how many nonblessing thoughts—indeed, how many cursing thoughts—I had been entertaining without even being aware of it.

So I stopped. I determined to have one thought, and one thought only, about every person I saw in the mall on that afternoon: it was to love them and bless them as people uniquely created by God who have infinite worth because Jesus died for them. Whatever they looked like, however they were behaving, whatever their demeanor, I simply agreed with God that each of them has infinite worth. I just loved them. I began randomly selecting people in the crowd to love and bless.

As I replaced judgmental thoughts with loving thoughts and prayers of blessing, something extraordinary began to happen. I began to *see* the worth I was ascribing to people, and I began to *feel* the love I was giving to them. As I ascribed worth to people, not allowing any other thought, opinion, or feeling to enter my mind, my heart began to expand. In fact, at certain moments I felt as though I would explode with love. I was waking up to the immeasurable value and beauty of each person in the mall that afternoon.

Sitting in the mall, sipping a Coke, enjoying God's creations, I was experiencing the heart of God. It felt like finding home after having been lost for a long while. It was like waking up from a coma. It was like finding undiluted truth when all you'd known up to that point was the watered-down kind. I felt as though I was remembering something I had long since forgotten or unveiling something I had been covering my whole life. The love, joy, and peace I was experiencing as I dwelt in this place—and it did seem like a mental and spiritual "place"—was beyond description.

Yet I also was filled with a profound sense of compassion for people. In waking up I saw not only the God-given illimitable worth of people but also the many ways this worth is suppressed in our lives. Leaving judgment behind, I sensed on a profound level the loneliness, the fear, the pain, and the emptiness of many people I observed. I recalled the Gospels speak of Jesus' compassion toward the multitudes that followed him, and I felt I was beginning to see what Jesus saw that evoked this emotion (Matt. 9:36; 14:14). As I reflect on this experience, I believe I was in my own way participating in God's seeing and God's feeling for people. I believe I was participating in his love.

Since then I have become convinced that the central goal of the Christian walk is to learn how to abide in this place, to remain awake to this truth, to walk in this experience. Indeed, as I shall argue in the chapters that follow, I am convinced that this was the purpose of creation from the start. It is the most fundamental reason why each of us exists. Scripture calls it "abiding in Christ" (John 15:4; cf. 1 John 4:16). God's desire is for us to participate in his own eternal love and life and therefore in his own eternal joy and peace by dwelling in the Son. We are to dance with the Father, Son, and Holy Spirit in the joyful celebration of their eternal love and life.

I confess that I have not yet learned to dwell permanently in this place, though I am learning how to visit it more frequently and for longer periods of time. The central goal of this book is to help others learn along with me to abide in this blessed place as well.

The Central Commission

As we shall see more fully in the chapters that follow, nothing is more central to the Christian walk than love. Scripture repeatedly and emphatically commands us to live in love (Eph. 5:2) and to put love above and before all things (Col. 3:14; 1 Peter

4:8). It tells us that if we love, we fulfill everything else the Lord requires of us (Matt. 22:39–40; Rom. 13:8, 10; Gal. 5:14) but that if we don't love, nothing else we do is of any value (1 Cor. 13:1–3). Most remarkably, Jesus prayed that his disciples would replicate the loving union he has with the Father by participating in the eternal union he has with the Father. And he prayed that the world would believe in him on this basis (John 17:20–26). It is by our love—by our "abiding" in the Father's love for the Son and the Son's love for the Father—that the world is to know we are Christ's disciples (John 13:35). Our God-like love is to be the distinguishing mark of the believer, the proof that God is real and that God is love (1 John 4:7–5:2).

Yet, if we are honest, we must confess that we do not usually live like this. Whatever else Christians are known for, they are generally not known for their distinctive love. Rarely are people drawn to the conclusion that Jesus is Lord simply because of the radical, God-like love they see among Christians and experience from Christians.

Why is this? What keeps us from living in the place I described above? It is, I submit, the very thing that originally kept me from it while at the mall. In a word, we like to pass verdicts. To some extent, we get our sense of worth from attaching worth or detracting worth from others, based on what we see. We position ourselves as judges of others rather than simply as lovers of others. Our judgments are so instinctive to us that we usually do not notice them. Even worse, they are so natural to us that when we do notice them, we often assume we are righteous for passing judgment! Because of this, it is easy to overlook the fact that our judgments are blocking our love, keeping us asleep, preventing us from living in the truth God created us to live in.

The Nature of the Forbidden Tree

Another way of saying this is that we fail to abide in love because we choose to live from our knowledge of good and evil. This, I shall argue, is why the Bible depicts the origin of our separation from God as eating from the Tree of the Knowledge of Good and Evil, which was in the middle of the garden (Gen. 3:1–9).

Consider, why was the fruit of the forbidden tree a fruit that was said to give the knowledge of *good* as well as evil? Isn't the "knowledge of good" a good thing? Aren't we Christians supposed to be promoting "the knowledge of good"? Isn't following God all about increasing our "knowledge of good and evil" so we can side with "the good" and resist "the evil"? And yet, whether it fits our preconceptions or not, in the Genesis narrative the nature of the sin that separates us from God is said to be the "knowledge of good and evil."

What is it about eating fruit from the Tree of the Knowledge of Good and Evil that warrants its depiction in Scripture as the source of original sin? How does living with our knowledge of good and evil separate us from God? These questions are rarely asked and even more rarely investigated with any thoroughness.[1] It is largely for this reason, I shall argue, that the church has failed so miserably at loving the way Christ commands us to love.

We have failed to understand and internalize the biblical teaching that our fundamental sin is not our evil—as though the solution for sin was to become good—but our getting life from what we believe is our knowledge of good and evil. Our fundamental sin is that we place ourselves in the position of God and divide the world between what we judge to be good and what we judge to be evil. And this judgment is the primary thing that keeps us from doing the central thing God created and saved us to do, namely, love like he loves.

Because we do not usually understand and internalize the nature of our foundational sin, we usually think our job as Christians is to embrace a moral system, live by it, and thus to be good people in contrast to all those who are evil. In fact, I shall argue, God's goal for us is much more profound and much more beautiful than merely being good: it is to do the will of God by being loving, just as God is loving. More specifically, I shall show that God's goal for us is to discover a relationship with him and thereby a relationship with ourselves and others that returns us to a state where we don't live by our knowledge of good and evil. Indeed, the goal is nothing less than for us to participate in the very love that the Father, Son, and Holy Spirit share throughout eternity.

Walking in obedience to God, we are still to detect good and evil, of course. Living in love in no way implies moral relativism. As we shall see in chapter 12, there are selective contexts in which it is appropriate and necessary to share with others and even confront others with our detection of the impact of evil in their lives. But we are not to derive any worth from our detection of good and evil. Nor are we to draw conclusions about people on the basis of it. We are to derive worth from God alone and to love without judgment and without conditions on the basis of the unsurpassable fullness of life we get from God. Our only job is to love, not judge.

As we do this, the love that God eternally is abides in us, and the world sees it and is drawn to it. Whatever good we need to do and whatever evil we need to avoid is done as a result of this. The goal of this work is to help us all move toward and eventually live in this place.

Outline

This understanding of the nature of sin and the goal of life represents a paradigm shift for many if not most Christians. Not only are we trained to live in judgment, but as fallen creatures we all instinctively get life from living this way. To call our lives of judgment into question is therefore difficult on both an intellectual and spiritual level. For this reason I will develop my thesis slowly and in a somewhat nonlinear fashion, explicating my thesis from a variety of angles.

The thesis of this book is that love is the central goal of creation and thus of the Christian life, and that its main obstacle is our getting life from our knowledge of good and evil—from our judgment. The thesis is developed in four parts, each consisting of three chapters.

Part 1 lays out the scriptural teaching on the goal of creation (chapter 1) and discusses how this is achieved in Christ (chapter 2). I then examine how this requires that the commandment to love be seen as the all-important and all-inclusive command of the Christian life (chapter 3).

Part 2 focuses on the nature of the forbidden tree. I first discuss the forbidden tree as the all-important boundary between

us and God and the center around which life in the garden revolved (chapter 4). Utilizing many insights from Bonhoeffer, I
then analyze how living out of the knowledge of good and evil
is antithetical to living out of love (chapter 5). Following this,
I examine how the foundational prohibition against judging—
against eating from the forbidden tree—is repeated in diverse
ways throughout the New Testament (chapter 6).

Part 3 examines the Genesis story of the fall of Adam and Eve
to reveal how it profoundly tells the story of how the accuser
makes us accusers instead of lovers (Rev. 12:10). The process is
founded on a lie about God (chapter 7), which necessarily entails
a lie about us (chapter 8), which results in a merciful curse from
God (chapter 9). Throughout all of this I shall show how Christ
reverses these lies and this curse on the cross.

Finally, part 4 explores the implications this has for our understanding of the Christian life and for the church. I discuss
first how the church is to be a community that embodies Christ's
reversal of the curse (chapter 10). I then discuss how this lifestyle
of outrageous love necessarily confronts all who obtain life from
their religious knowledge of good and evil (chapter 11). And I
conclude by discussing how the church is to grow in holiness,
even while (and precisely because) it is accepting everyone unconditionally, without judgment (chapter 12).

As suggested above, it may be difficult for some to think of
sin as getting life from our knowledge of good and evil. It is like
becoming aware of the air that you've breathed all your life. It
is much easier and initially more self-rewarding to view sin in
terms of evil that is "out there." Yet our failure to become aware
of the root of our separation from God keeps us from living in
the place of outrageous love and joy that God wants us to live
in. This failure is what keeps us from experiencing the life of
Christ fully and is largely responsible for our inability to bear
the kind of witness to which God calls us.

I thus encourage the reader to combine his or her consideration of this book with much thought and prayer. My hope and
prayer is that we all will grow increasingly free from our enslaving addiction to the forbidden tree. In this newfound freedom
we can joyfully participate in the eternal love that God is.

Part 1

The Trinity and the Goal of Creation

chapter 1

Dancing
with the Triune God

As you, Father, are in me and I am in you, may they also be in us, so that the world may believe that you have sent me. The glory that you have given me I have given them, so that they may be one, as we are one, I in them and you in me, that they may become completely one, so that the world may know that you have sent me and have loved them even as you have loved me. . . . I made your name known to them, and I will make it known, so that the love with which you have loved me may be in them, and I in them.

John 17:21–23, 26

Love . . . is the revelation of God. And the revelation of God is Jesus Christ.

Dietrich Bonhoeffer

Jesus calls men, not to a new religion, but to life.

Dietrich Bonhoeffer

The Love God *Is* and the Love God *Gives*

Four Kinds of Love

This is a book on love and its main obstacle—the "original sin," the "knowledge of good and evil." We will do well, therefore, to start by defining what we mean by *love*. This is especially important because contemporary Western people tend to define *love* in a way that is quite at odds with the way the Bible defines *love*.

Unlike English, which has only one word for *love*, ancient Greeks had four different words that could be translated "love," and each had a different meaning.[1] *Storge* generally referred to a person's affection for something. When we say we love our car or a person's smile or another's ability to sing, we are using *love* in this sense. *Eros* was usually used in reference to romantic or sexual love. This is the sense that is usually meant when people today speak about "falling in love" or "making love." *Phileo*, on the other hand, is used most commonly of friendship. When we tell a best friend we love him or her, we don't mean it romantically (*eros*), nor do we mean only that we have an affection for something about that person (*storge*).

Each of these senses of love involves an emotional feeling we have toward another person or thing. For this reason these first three kinds of love are neither universal nor unconditional. We cannot have an affection for everyone and everything (*storge*); we cannot have romantic feelings toward everyone (*eros*); and we cannot experience personal friendship with everyone (*phileo*).

There is a kind of love that is universal and unconditional, however. It is the kind of love referred to by the word *agape*. This love is not a feeling one has, though certain feelings often follow from it. It is rather a commitment one makes, a stance one takes toward another, and an activity one does. It should be present in each of the first three senses of love but also when those forms of love are absent. *Agape* is a kind of love you can have when there's nothing about the other that you like, when you have no romantic interest in the other, and even when the other is your enemy rather than your friend.

As revealed through Jesus Christ, *agape* is most fundamentally the kind of love God had for us while we were yet sinners and the kind of love we are commanded to have toward all others. It is the kind of love God was aiming at in creating the world and thus the kind of love we shall be concerned with in this book.

God's Love Is Jesus Christ

The Bible doesn't give us an abstract definition of *agape* love. It rather points us to its perfect expression in the person of Jesus Christ, dying for us on the cross. "We know love by this," John tells us, "that [Jesus] laid down his life for us—and we ought to lay down our lives for one another" (1 John 3:16). "God so loved the world," he says elsewhere, "that he gave his only Son, so that everyone who believes in him may not perish but may have eternal life" (John 3:16). In the words of Paul, "God proves his love for us in that while we still were sinners Christ died for us" (Rom. 5:8). *This* is what *agape* love looks like. As Bonhoeffer put it, "Love . . . is the revelation of God. And the revelation of God is Jesus Christ."[2] Love, as defined by the one who is love, lays down its life for another, however undeserving. As such, it always manifests Jesus Christ.[3]

The thing about God's sacrifice on Calvary that makes it a perfect expression of *agape* is that it demonstrates God giving that which had unsurpassable worth—his Son—on behalf of a people who had no apparent worth. This is the nature of *agape* love. It is the act of *unconditionally ascribing worth to another at a cost to oneself.*[4] God expresses this love in its most perfect form. And we are called and empowered by God's grace to replicate this love in our relationships with God, ourselves, and all other people.

God Is Love

The most profound truth of the Bible is that "God is love" (1 John 4:8, 16). This is the most fundamental thing to be said about God, for it encompasses everything else. Peter Kreeft expresses the profundity of this passage when he writes:

Love is God's essence. Nowhere else does Scripture express God's essence in this way. Scripture says God is just and merciful, but it does not say that God is justice itself or mercy itself. It does say that God *is* love, not just a *lover*. Love is God's very essence. Everything else is a manifestation of this essence to us, a relationship between this essence and us. This is the absolute; everything else is relative to it.[5]

As Father, Son, and Holy Spirit, God eternally exists as perfect love. Each divine person within the godhead ascribes ultimate worth to the others. In doing this God is not being conceited but simply accurate. For as the one eternal uncreated reality, the triune community is the ultimate value, if you will, from which all created things derive value.

While we cannot clearly conceive of what the fellowship of the Father, Son, and Holy Spirit looked like prior to creation, we can discern its basic nature from the way God reveals himself to us in the person of Jesus Christ. In Christ, and throughout the New Testament, we learn that the fellowship of the three divine persons consists of mutual submission. The triune fellowship is Christ-like. The Father, Son, and Holy Spirit ascribe ultimate worth to one another without any competition.[6] Their eternal life together consists in the divine joy of expressing the absolute value each has for the other.

The essence of this triune love is revealed in God's love for humanity. The eternal other-orientated love of the Father, Son, and Holy Spirit is revealed outside of God, as it were, in his love for humanity. God's own inherent worth is expressed in the worth he ascribes to humanity, and it is truly breathtaking.

God didn't just send us a holy book or commission an angel to die for us. We were worth more than this to God. While we were yet sinners, Christ—who is God himself!—died for us (Rom. 5:6–8). God took on our humanity, our sin, and the just punishment that sin deserves, dying a God-forsaken, hellish death on the cross, because only this could rescue us from our self-chosen destruction. God expresses unsurpassable love for us and ascribes unsurpassable worth to us by sacrificing the One who has unsurpassable value on our behalf! And this unfathomable expression of love to us displays the perfect love that the three divine persons have for one another. God is toward us as he eternally is within himself: God is love.

Our Unsurpassable Worth before God

In fact, there was nothing more that God could have done for us beyond that which he did. God himself went to the farthest extreme, even taking upon himself that which is antithetical to himself (sin), in order to express his love for us and reconcile us to himself (2 Cor. 5:21). This is why we can say that the worth God ascribes to us, which is to say the love God has for us, is *unsurpassable.* And precisely because it is unsurpassable, the act of God ascribing worth to us reveals the perfect, eternal love of the Father, Son, and Holy Spirit. The quality of love revealed in Christ dying for sinners reveals the quality of love within the triune fellowship. It is, quite simply, unsurpassable. A greater love cannot be imagined.

The love demonstrated on Calvary is the center of the gospel, for it reveals the beauty of God himself. Despite our sin, God deemed us worth all this! "For the sake of the joy that was set before him," Scripture says, Jesus "endured the cross, disregarding its shame" (Heb. 12:2). What was this joy? It was the joy of sharing the ecstatic love that God eternally is with you and me, throughout eternity. The cross was the price he was willing to pay to make this happen, and this speaks volumes about the worth he ascribes to you and me. The joyful, worth-ascribing submission that characterizes the Trinity throughout eternity is expressed outwardly in Christ's joyful, yet anguished, submission to a God-forsaken death on the cross—"while we were yet sinners" (Rom. 5:8 KJV).

We are invited to receive the worth God ascribes to us in Christ and are called and empowered to extend this worth to ourselves and all others. Out of the fullness of life and love we freely receive from God, we are commissioned to love God and freely love our neighbors as ourselves (Matt. 22:37–40). This, we shall see in the next chapter, is the central goal of creation and therefore the central mandate of the Christian life.

Dancing in the Triune Fellowship

That They May Be One

Love is the reason anything exists. God created the world out of love—to express his love and to invite others to share in his love. "Since God is the Creator and since creation reflects and reveals the Creator," Kreeft writes, "all creation somehow reflects and reveals love. . . . The universe is a hierarchy of love."[7]

The central goal of creation is succinctly summed up in a profound prayer Jesus said just prior to his crucifixion:

> For [the disciples'] sakes I sanctify myself, so that they also may be sanctified in truth. I ask not only on behalf of these, but also on behalf of those who will believe in me through their word, that they may all be one. *As you*, Father, are in me and I am in you, may they also *be in us*, so that the world may believe that you have sent me.
>
> John 17:19–21, emphasis added

Let's examine this carefully. Jesus prayed that his disciples would be one *just as* he and the Father are one. The loving oneness of the church is to reflect the loving oneness of the Trinity. Indeed, the loving oneness of the church is to *participate in* the loving oneness of the Trinity: "As you . . . are in me and I am in you, may they *also be in us*." As we participate in God's loving oneness, we replicate this loving oneness among ourselves. And as we replicate this loving oneness among ourselves, the world sees and believes that Jesus Christ is sent from the Father. The world knows the reality of the triune God because they encounter the love of the triune God in us.

This prayer expressed not only God's goal for the church but the goal of all creation. Indeed, Jesus prayed that his church would be "sanctified in truth" (John 17:19)—the truth that they are called to be one in the Father and Son—*so that* the world would believe in him and thus become part of the church. The church is to be set apart (sanctified) not by possessing a special religious piety but by participating in and manifesting the perfect eternal love of God. As Bonhoeffer said, "Jesus calls men, not to a new religion, but to life."[8] This participation in God's life distinguishes disciples from others only so disciples can invite all others to share in it.

In other words, as paradoxical as it sounds, the church is to be *set apart* in order to become *all-inclusive*. God's goal for the church is God's goal for the whole world. God wants every human being to become a participant in his divine nature (2 Peter 1:4; 3:8–10).

Expanding the Glory of God

Visual aids might help illustrate this point. The Trinity can be depicted as a triangle (fig. 1). God's essence is the eternal, unsurpassable, infinitely intense love of the Father, Son, and Holy Spirit.

The Trinity created humans not out of need but out of abundance. To use a metaphor from the great Puritan theologian and preacher Jonathan Edwards, God's love "overflows" in creation. It is as though the unsurpassable intensity of the triune love could not be contained, so it burst forth in creation.[9]

The people God creates can also be depicted as a triangle (fig. 2), for we are made in the image of God (Gen. 1:26–27). The threefold nature of this *imago dei* (image of God) is evidenced in many ways, but the aspect that interests us right now is the fact that every human being is created with a God-shaped vacuum in his or her inner being. We are created with a hunger that only the triune God can satisfy. We are created with a nonnegotiable need to be filled with the infinite love that God eternally is. God created us this way because he wants to express the love that he eternally is to us, in us, and through us. God wants to be the source of our *life*—our worth, our sense of fullness, our signifi-

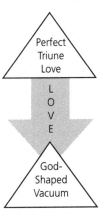

Figure 1: The Trinity   **Figure 2: God's Perfect Love Fills Our God-Shaped Vacuum**

cance. Indeed, he wants us to participate in his own eternal life, which is his triune love.

God's goal is that humans, when filled with God's unsurpassable love and eternal life, would replicate God on an individual level and overflow with love back to God, to themselves, and to their neighbors (fig. 3). As God gives his life to us, we manifest the fullness of this life in ascribing infinite worth to God as our source (worship); we affirm the infinite worth we ourselves have because of what God has done for us in Christ (self-love); and we affirm the infinite worth others have because of what Christ has done for them (neighbor-love). In other words, as a result of God ascribing unsurpassable worth to us in Christ, we affirm God's infinite worth as the source of all life. We therefore agree with God in affirming the derived worth of everyone to whom he ascribes unsurpassable worth, namely, ourselves and all others. Hence, God's love for us generates our love for God, for ourselves, and for all others.

It is important that we never separate our love for God from our love for others. For loving our neighbors as ourselves is one central way we love God. It is impossible to ascribe ultimate worth to God while refusing to ascribe worth to those whom God ascribes worth. Hence, Scripture says that those who claim they love God but refuse to love their sister or brother are liars (1 John 4:20). Moreover, since we are to love our neighbors

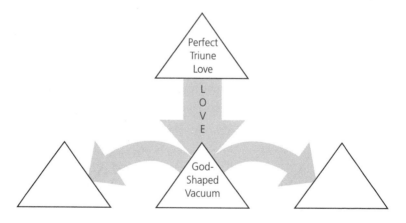

Figure 3: The Triune Love Overflowing to and through Individuals

as ourselves, we may conclude that those who claim they love God but hate themselves are also deceived. They simply are not participating in the love of God.

In God's plan, each created individual would receive God's love and life, filling the God-shaped vacuum in the core of his or her being. Every person would therefore replicate God's loving overflow by ascribing infinite worth to God as source and to themselves and others as people who have infinite worth because of who God is. In this way the human community would replicate the perfect love that God eternally is.

Indeed, the relationship of God to creation and of humans to each other would display in a new way the perfect love of the Trinity. It would form, as it were, a new, enlarged triangle (fig. 4). As Edwards put it, the perfect love of God would be expanded.[10] To be sure, God's own love isn't improved upon, for that is impossible. As the Trinity, God eternally is *unsurpassable* love. But through humans, this eternal love is reflected in new ways. The perfect community of the Father, Son, and Holy Spirit opens itself up for others to participate in it. And as we participate in it, we reflect it to God, each other, and the world.

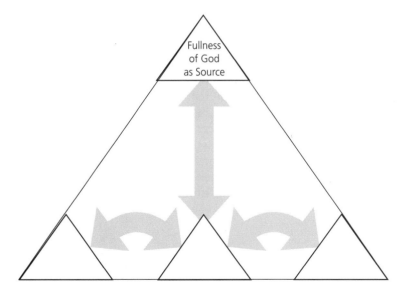

Figure 4: The Expanded Triune Community of Love

Another way of saying this is that the goal of creation is to "glorify God" (Ps. 86:9; John 12:28; 17:1). God's glory is the radiant display of the divine nature. As God's life is poured into individuals and flows through individuals to other people, we individually and collectively "image" God. Like prisms in the noonday sun, we refract light in novel ways by participating in it. We glorify God—we display his perfect love—by receiving it, reflecting it back to God, and reflecting it to ourselves and one another. Individually and collectively we display the radiant beauty of God.

This is the goal of everything. It is the reason why anything other than God even exists. As God is the one being who exists in and of himself, so God's love is the one reality that is an end in and of itself. We might say that the goal of every individual, and of humanity in general, is to dance the eternal dance of the Trinity, to participate in and glorify this unsurpassably loving fellowship. We do this by receiving and reflecting the unsurpassable love that God is.

A more beautiful vision of creation is not imaginable.

Conclusion

How are we to participate in this dance of the Trinity? People often assume that they get closer to God through working hard at overcoming faults or producing positive habits in their lives. Exercises in spiritual discipline have an important role to play in our growth, but we are putting the cart before the horse if we think they actually get us closer to God. The spiritual disciplines help us *experience* this closeness to God, and this is of inestimable value, but they can never *constitute* our closeness with God. As we shall see in the next chapter, our participation in the dance is founded exclusively on our union with Christ by faith.

chapter 2

Life "in Christ"

He is the source of your life in Christ Jesus, who became for us wisdom from God, and righteousness and sanctification and redemption.

1 Corinthians 1:30

Love is the reconciliation of man with God in Jesus Christ. The disunion of men with God, with other men, with the world and with themselves, is at an end. Man's origin is given back to him.

Dietrich Bonhoeffer

The man whom God has taken to Himself, sentenced and awakened to a new life, this is Jesus Christ. In Him it is all mankind. It is ourselves.

Dietrich Bonhoeffer

In the last chapter we depicted the goal of all creation as the glorification of God, which is the expansion and display of his loving, triune nature. God wants a people, a "bride" (Eph. 5:21–33; cf. Matt. 25:1–10; John 3:20; Rev. 19:7; 21:2, 9; 22:17), to whom God expresses himself and who as a result express who God is by how they relate to him, to themselves, and to others. In this chapter we shall flesh this out by discussing how all of this is in principle achieved in Jesus Christ.

Everything we have said thus far is contained in the observation that God created the world *for Jesus Christ*. Quoting a hymn of the early church, Paul proclaims that in Christ "all things in heaven and on earth were created, things visible and invisible, whether thrones or dominions or rulers or powers—all things have been created *through him* and *for him*" (Col. 1:16, emphasis added). God's plan to display his triune love to, in, and through a people is achieved *in Christ*. This is essentially what Paul means when he declares that the "mystery of [God's] will" was "set forth in Christ" and "carried out in Christ Jesus" (Eph. 1:9; 3:11). The means of creating the world and the goal of the world is Jesus Christ. This, we shall now see, is simply another way of saying that God wants to glorify himself by expanding his triune love to include others.

We begin to understand *how* God's plan is achieved in Christ by noting that everything God is *for us*, everything we are *before God*, and everything about our life *in God*, takes place in Jesus Christ. In this chapter we shall explore these three "everythings."

God for Us

In the last chapter we saw that the supreme definition and example of love is Jesus Christ. "We know love by this, that he laid down his life for us" (1 John 3:16). In the person of Jesus Christ, especially in his dying for us on Calvary, we see what true love is like, for here we see what God is like.

Though it may conflict with many frightful preconceptions people have of "the Supreme Being," Jesus reveals that God sacrifices himself for sinful humanity. By sacrificing himself for us, God ascribes unsurpassable worth to people who in and of themselves have little apparent worth. In doing this, God reveals his nature, which is eternal, unsurpassable love.

You'd never know this about God, however, unless your eyes were fixed on Jesus (Heb. 12:2). Jesus completely abolishes all ordinary ideas and expectations people have of a Supreme Being. The Bible says that Jesus is the image of God (Col. 1:15; cf. 2 Cor. 4:4). Hence, every mental picture we have of God must be centered on him. He is also called the Word of God (John 1:1); when

God expresses himself, *he is Jesus*. Hence all other expressions of God must be understood in the light of this one.

Along the same lines, Jesus is called "the reflection of God's glory and the exact imprint of God's very being" (Heb. 1:3). We therefore must not try to make our own imprint of God by projecting onto him conclusions about what he is like deduced from our own life experiences, conceptions, and expectations.

Philip once asked Jesus to show him the Father. Jesus responded, "Have I been with you all this time, Philip, and you still do not *know me*? Whoever has seen me has seen the Father. How can you say, 'Show us the Father'?" (John 14:9, emphasis added). The only place where we see the Father is in the One who is his image, his Word, his exact imprint—his Son, Jesus Christ. To know the crucified Christ is to know all we need to know about the Supreme Being.

As we shall see in chapter 7, the root of all sin—the beginning of the knowledge of good and evil—is entertaining a lie about who God is. If our mental picture of God is skewed, our relationship with God, with ourselves, and with others will be skewed as well. Conversely, the root of all healing and growth in life is found in being rooted and grounded in the truth of who God is, and this truth is decisively disclosed in the One who is "the way, and the truth, and the life" (John 14:6).

Us before God

The New Reality in Christ

Jesus isn't only *God for us*. As amazing as it sounds, he is also *us before God*. With astounding boldness, Scripture declares that when anyone says yes to God's invitation, whenever anyone places his or her trust (faith) in Jesus, he or she is placed "in Christ Jesus." This isn't just a nice figure of speech—*it describes a change in reality*. God transposes us from one domain—our identity "in Adam" (1 Cor. 15:22) and in the kingdom of darkness—to another domain—our identity in Christ (Col. 1:13). When God does this, all that belongs to Christ by nature is given to us by grace. "When a man encounters Christ," Bonhoeffer writes, "everything that Christ is and has is made the property of this man . . . he possesses everything. He lives before God."[1]

The whole of the Christian identity is found *in Christ*. To give but a sampling of the scriptural teaching on this, every person who is in Christ is:

- redeemed and reconciled to God (Rom. 3:24; 2 Cor. 5:19)
- given the free gift of eternal life (Rom. 6:23; 2 Tim. 1:1)
- freed from condemnation, given grace, and forgiven by God (Rom. 8:1; 1 Cor. 1:4; Eph. 4:32; cf. 2 Tim. 1:9)
- set free from "the law of sin and of death" by "the Spirit of life in Christ Jesus" (Rom. 8:2)
- one who has God as the "source of [his or her] life" (1 Cor. 1:30)
- set apart and called a holy one (1 Cor. 1:2)
- established—set on firm ground (2 Cor. 1:21)
- enabled to see the glory of God in the face of Jesus (2 Cor. 3:14–4:6)
- "a new creation" (2 Cor. 5:17)
- given the blessing promised to Abraham (Gal. 3:14)
- made a child of God (Gal. 3:26)
- one who has "obtained an inheritance" that is "imperishable, undefiled, and unfading" (Eph. 1:11; 1 Peter 1:4)
- blessed "with every spiritual blessing" (Eph. 1:3)
- raised up and seated "in the heavenly places" with Christ (Eph. 2:6)
- given "the immeasurable riches of [God's] grace" (Eph. 2:7)
- "brought near" to God, however far off he or she once was (Eph. 2:13)
- called to God's "eternal glory" (1 Peter 5:10)
- made a participant "of the divine nature" (2 Peter 1:4)

When people enter into a relationship with Christ, this is how they truly are. Everything God is toward them and everything they are before God is found "in Christ."

The point is powerfully expressed in Isaiah 42 when God prophesies of the coming Messiah, "I have given you as a covenant to the people" (v. 6; see also Isa. 49:8). God does not say that Jesus will simply *make* a new covenant with God's people. Rather, the passage prophesies that Christ will actually *be* God's covenant with people. As both God and man—God toward us and humanity before God—Jesus literally *is* the new covenant between God and humanity. As the one and only God-man, Jesus reconciles God and humanity in his very being.

The Love of God in Christ

Everything that has been said thus far about our identity in Christ is covered by the truth that in Christ *we participate in God's own eternal love*. God "chose us *in Christ* before the foundation of the world to be holy and blameless before him *in love*" (Eph. 1:4, emphasis added). From the beginning, God chose to have a people who would be the object of his eternal love, as Christ is the object of his eternal love, and who would therefore be "holy and blameless before him" as Christ is holy and blameless before him. God sought to acquire a "bride" for Christ who would receive and reflect the love of the triune community (Eph. 5:25–32; Rev. 19:7; 21:2, 9). And the only qualification for being incorporated into this radiant bride, and thus for being loved by God with the same love he has for Christ, is simply that one is willing to let God do this!

The very same love that the Father has for the Son is now given to us, for we are, as a matter of fact, *in* the Son. The point was made perfectly clear in the prayer of Jesus that we reviewed in the last chapter. Jesus prayed that his disciples, and thus all the world, would know that the Father has "loved them *even as you have loved me*" (John 17:23, emphasis added). Again, several sentences later, he said to the Father, "I made your name [character] known to them . . . so that *the [very same] love with which you have loved me may be in them*, and I in them" (John 17:26, emphasis added). The perfect love that defines God throughout eternity—the ultimate, worth-affirming, mutually submissive love that eternally unites the Father, Son, and Holy Spirit—is now directed toward every person who is "in Christ."

This means that as you read this sentence you could not be more loved than you are right now! The love that God eternally *is* burns toward you with the same unimprovable, passionate intensity that the three divine persons have for each other. The perfect love that God eternally *is* is directed toward you, right here and right now. It is not a secondary, compromised, watered-down, or derivative love. It is one and the same love that is shared by the Father, Son, and Holy Spirit. In the very act of loving Christ, God loves you (fig. 5).

Figure 5: The Father Loves Us, the Bride, in Loving the Son

Participating in the Divine Nature in Christ

In the previous chapter we noted that the goal of creation is for people to participate in the eternal love of the triune God, and now we are beginning to see how we do this. It is not by performing good deeds, successfully conquering certain sins, holding all the right theological opinions, or becoming "religious" people. These may be *by-products* of the change in reality that takes place in us, but they are not the *cause* of the change. We participate in the eternal love of the triune fellowship by allowing ourselves to be placed in Christ by faith. It is simply a matter of saying yes to God's desire to relate to us in the process of relating as the triune community.

This of course doesn't mean that we *become God*. Indeed, the beauty of God's plan for us, and for God's own glory, is achieved precisely because the distinction between God and humanity is preserved. It is in dying for those who are not God, indeed, those who are in and of themselves sinners, that God's own eternal love is displayed outside of himself, and the Trinity is glorified. It is as God crosses the infinite gulf that distinguishes and separates God from fallen humanity that God expresses the infinite intensity of his own eternal triune love.

Precisely in doing this, God ascribes a worth to humanity that mirrors his own worth—*it is unsurpassable*. And it is unsurpassable precisely because we humans are not only not God, we are sinners. Through the act of Jesus becoming a man and dying a God-forsaken death on the cross, and through the act of the Father incorporating all who say yes into the Son, the Trinity opens up the perfect, triune love and allows undeserving sinners to share in the dance of eternal love and glory.

Peter expressed this point well when he wrote, "[God] has given us . . . his precious and very great promises, so that through them . . . *[we] may become participants of the divine nature*" (2 Peter 1:4, emphasis added). We *really do* participate in the triune love that is the "divine nature." Similarly, as we have seen, Jesus prayed that his disciples

> may all be one. *As you*, Father, are in me and I am in you, may they also be *in us*. . . . I *in them* and *you in me*, that they may become *completely one*, so that the world may know that you have sent me and *have loved them even as you have loved me*. . . . I made your name known to them, and I will make it known, so that *the love with which you have loved me may be in them, and I in them.*

John 17:21, 23, 26, emphasis added

We see that our union with the Father reflects and participates in the union of the Father, Son, and Spirit. We participate "in the divine nature." This is why Jesus goes on to pray, "The glory that you have given me I have given them, so that they may be one, as we are one" (John 17:22). The *same glory* that the Father ascribes to the Son is now given to all who are in the Son, which is to say, we participate in the glory of God. Indeed, God is glorified—his love is displayed—precisely in this act of incorporating us into the divine fellowship.

Again, we are not God, but we nonetheless share in the eternal love that *is* God. Our glory doesn't compete with God's glory; it reflects it, and it does so by participating in it. God is always the Source; we are forever the recipients. God is forever "the sun"; we are forever the prisms that refract the light of the sun. The glory is all God's, for it is his alone by nature, but we are allowed to participate in it by grace, through faith. And we do this by being placed in Christ. The Father's glorious, loving relationship with the Son in the power of the Spirit now encompasses a glorious, loving relationship with the Son's bride in the power of the Spirit.

In the Power of the Spirit

A brief word should perhaps be said about the role of the Holy Spirit in incorporating us into the triune dance. One might wonder why Jesus' prayer for his disciples in John 17 to be "completely one" only mentioned his relationship to the Father. Why did he not include the Holy Spirit?

While a great deal could be said about this, I believe the shortest answer is that the Holy Spirit is very much included in our participation in the Father and Son's love for one another, but he is so as a "silent partner." The particular way the Spirit lovingly and submissively participates in our dance with the triune God is by working behind the scenes, as it were, to make it all happen. The Spirit is not the explicit object of the dance but the one working on the inside to open the dance up for us to participate.

The Holy Spirit brings us into the triune dance by working in our hearts to open us up to trust in Christ (John 3:5; 1 Cor. 12:3; Gal. 4:6; Col. 1:8). Through the regenerating power of the Spirit, we are reconciled to the Father through Christ (Eph. 2:18). The Holy Spirit then abides in us (1 John 3:24), teaches us (John 14:26; 16:13), transforms us (2 Cor. 3:17–18; Gal. 5:17–22), empowers us (Acts 1:8; Rom. 8:13), leads us (Rom. 8:14; Gal. 5:18; cf. Acts 10:19; 13:2; 15:28; 16:6–7), sets us free from the law (Rom. 7:6; 8:2–4; 2 Cor. 3:3), and mediates the abundant life of the Trinity to us (John 7:38–39; Rom. 8:14, 16, 26–27).

Moreover, the Holy Spirit immerses us (baptizes us) into the body of Christ and into Christ himself (1 Cor. 12:13). The Holy Spirit further mediates our relationship to the Father through the Son, just as he mediated the Son's relationship to the Father when Jesus was on earth (Rom. 8:26; 1 Cor. 2:10–11; cf. Luke 4:14, 18; 10:21; Acts 10:38; Heb. 9:14). For this reason Scripture teaches that it is the Holy Spirit who causes the love the Father has *for* us to abide *within* us and flow *through* us (Rom. 5:5; Col. 1:8). Hence the unity of the body of Christ—our being one as the Father and Son are one—is construed as a unity in the Holy Spirit (2 Cor. 13:13; Eph. 4:3–4; cf. Rom. 15:30).

We see that our participation in the love of the Father for the Son and the love of the Son for the Father *is* a participation in the Holy Spirit, for the Holy Spirit is the Spirit of both the Father and the Son (Rom. 8:9–11). The Holy Spirit works and abides within us, pointing us to Christ, placing us in Christ, all the while causing us to participate in and be transformed by the love the Father has for the Son and the love the Son has for the Father.

Our Being in Christ

We Are Participants, Not Just Recipients

Thus far we have shown that we are loved by the Father with the same love he has for the Son. Yet we are not just recipients of the love of the Trinity—we are *participants*. When the Father incorporates us into the triune fellowship by placing us in Christ through the power of the Spirit, this doesn't just change how God views us and relates to us. *It changes who we really are.*

We *really are* in Christ, and, through the Spirit, Christ *really is* in us! A great deal of harm has been done by teachers who stress how our union with Christ changes how God *sees* us without emphasizing how this union really *changes* us. The Father doesn't just view us "with Jesus spectacles," as some popularizing teachers have said. Rather, the Father *re-creates* us in Christ, through the Spirit. We are "*created* in Christ Jesus for good works" (Eph. 2:10, emphasis added). "If anyone is in Christ," Paul says, "there is a new creation: . . . everything has become new!" (2 Cor. 5:17). To be sure, God *declares* us to be righteous (he "justifies" us; Rom. 3:21–26; 5:1). But as with the original creation, when God speaks, *reality comes into being* (Gen. 1:1–28; cf. 2 Cor. 4:6).

United with Christ's Death and Life

When God *says* we are righteous, holy, and blameless in Christ, we *are* in fact righteous, holy, and blameless.[2] This point is powerfully expressed by Paul in Romans 6. In this chapter Paul was addressing believers who had responded to his message of grace by asking, "Should we continue in sin in order that grace may abound?" (Rom. 6:1). The idea is that if God's love is displayed by his graciously forgiving us and making us blameless in Christ, why should we not continue sinning so God's grace and forgiveness can be displayed all the more? Whenever the grace of God is preached uncompromisingly, we should expect people who have a fleshly mind to have this misunderstanding (Rom. 8:6–7; 1 Cor. 2:14). But it *is* a misunderstanding!

Paul's answer was profound and to the point. Expressing almost a sense of horror, Paul replied, "By no means!" (Rom. 6:2). He then went on to explain what really happened when they were united with Christ by reminding them of their baptism.

> Do you not know that all of us who have been baptized into Christ Jesus were baptized into his death? Therefore *we have been buried with him* by baptism into death, so that, *just as* Christ was raised from the dead by the glory of the Father, *so we too* might walk in newness of life. . . . We know that *our old self was crucified with him* so that the body of sin might be destroyed, and we might no longer be enslaved to sin. For whoever has died is freed from sin. . . . We know that Christ, being raised from the dead, will never die again; death no longer has dominion over him. The death he died, he died to sin, once for all; but the life he lives, he lives to God. So you also must consider yourselves dead to sin and alive to God in Christ Jesus. Therefore, do not let sin exercise dominion in your mortal bodies, to make you obey their passions.
>
> Romans 6:3–4, 6–7, 9–12, emphasis added

According to Paul, our union with Christ isn't a fictitious thing—it is real. We *really do* participate in Christ's crucifixion and burial. And we *really do* participate in Christ's death and resurrection life. As Bonhoeffer says, in the incarnation Christ took on "our being, our nature, ourselves. . . . Now we are in him. Where he is, there we are too, in the incarnation, on the Cross, and in his resurrection. We belong to him because we are in him."[3]

Moreover, since "the life [Christ] lives, he lives to God," freed from sin, we "must consider [ourselves] dead to sin and alive to God *in Christ*" (Rom. 6:10–11). Our thinking should line up with the truth of *who we really are*. Every thought must be brought "captive to Jesus Christ" (2 Cor. 10:5). We must be "transformed by the renewing of [our] minds" (Rom. 12:2).

It is because we know who we are, owing to the fact that we know the One *in whom* we now exist, that we are to "*therefore . . .* not let sin exercise dominion in [our] mortal bodies" (Rom. 6:11, emphasis added). Our new identity must give rise to a new way of thinking about ourselves, which in turn gives rise to our new way of behaving. Notice that Paul doesn't command us to behave a certain way in order to become something we're not. Rather, he commands us to remember who we *already are* in Christ and to think and live accordingly. Paul is not giving people a new set of ethical rules; he is calling people to live out a new identity.

The life believers now live is no longer a life of their own efforts; in Christ, this old life is dead and buried. Being incorporated into Christ, the life we now live is the life that Christ himself lives, and his life is eternally toward God. In sum, just as we participate in the love and life Christ receives *from* the Father, so we participate in the love and life Christ lives *to* the Father.

Christ is God for us, and us toward God. In Christ, we receive unsurpassable worth, and because this reception is not a fictitious thing—we *really do* have this worth from God!—we also participate in Christ's overflowing of life and love to God and to others. The perfect love that God *is* is directed to us, abides in us, and therefore flows through us—and all of this takes place only as we are in Christ. The love of the Father for Christ is ours, and so is the love of Christ for the Father and for all others (fig. 6).

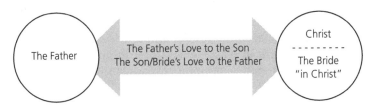

Figure 6: We Participate in the Love of the Triune God

The Lingering Old Self

Of course, as Paul recognized throughout his epistles, we still struggle with "the old self." The habits of our mind and body, programmed as they are by the pattern of the world (Rom. 12:2), continue in force.[4] They have been crucified with Christ—they are in fact "old"—yet we play an important role in recognizing this and thus in discarding them. Growth in the Christian life is primarily a matter of "put[ting] away [our] former way of life, [our] old self" and "be[ing] renewed in the spirit of [our] minds . . . [clothing ourselves] with the new self, created according to the likeness of God in true righteousness and holiness" (Eph. 4:22–24). But this discipline is predicated on knowing who we already are in Christ. It is because of who we already are that we have the assurance of what we shall eventually become.

As we put off the old self and put on the new, as we come to see ourselves as we really are (in Christ) and no longer as we once were in the lie of the old self, we increasingly conform to the image of Jesus Christ (Rom. 8:29; Col. 3:9–10). When we yield to the Holy Spirit within us and are transformed by the renewing of our minds (Rom. 12:2), Christ is increasingly "formed in" us (Gal. 4:19; cf. Eph. 4:7–9).[5] We progressively see ourselves as we are in Jesus and thus increasingly look and act like Jesus. And *this* is how the world comes to know the reality of Jesus Christ and through him the reality of the triune God. They see him in us and experience him through us.

The Community of the Body of Christ

We glorify God—put his love on display—as we grow in conformity with Christ (John 15:5, 8–9). But as with everything else about the Christian life, God didn't intend to be glorified primarily by individuals. He is a social, triune God, and thus he created a world in which everything humans do works effectively only when it is done in relationships.[6] God's witness to the world, therefore, is not just individual Christians but the body of Christ as a whole.

When all who are in Christ live out who they are in Christ in relationship with one another, we display a love that replicates the love of the triune God. This cannot be fully accomplished with isolated individuals. As the disciples of Jesus become "completely one" as the Father and Son are one, the love of the eternal God is glorified, and the world comes to know that Jesus Christ has been sent from the Father (John 17:20–26; cf. 13:35). No one can see God as he is in and of himself, the Bible says. But all are supposed to see God *as his love is displayed in the body of Christ* (1 John 4:12). Through the church, the world is supposed to literally witness and experience the perfect love that God eternally is. If the hearts of those in the world are at all open, they acknowledge the reality of the triune God because he is *right there in front of them*—in the loving community of the church! They witness firsthand the reality of Jesus because they encounter "his body."

If the church is to be the witness God calls us to be, we must be ruthlessly honest with ourselves about the areas in which we are *not* where God wants us to be. And it is painfully obvious that one central area in which we are not remotely close to where God wants us to be is in our relationships with one another. Because of the pervasive, individualistic mindset of Western culture, modern Western Christians tend to view their relationship with God strictly as an individual thing. Church is usually thought of as a weekly, large-group gathering of believers who are for the most part strangers to one another. Even worse, we tend to identify the church as a building that simply houses individual Christians once a week for worship.

As we shall see in chapter 12, nothing could be further from the New Testament understanding of the Christian community. The New Testament never considers the possibility of Christians living out their faith in isolation from other believers. The Christian life is meant to be lived in intimate relationships with small groups of other believers.

To be sure, there is a place for large-group gatherings (Acts 2:46; 5:12), but the primary building blocks for the corporate temple of God (Eph. 2:21–22) are covenantal relationships in which believers know one another profoundly, love one another deeply, and care for one another unconditionally. Only in this way do we grow in Christ and display the social love of the triune God.

Conclusion

We must confess that Jesus' prayer for the church to manifest the perfect, loving unity of the triune God has by and large not been fulfilled. Whatever else the church may be known for in the world, it is not generally known for exemplifying a distinctive, radical, self-sacrificial love, either toward those within the body of Christ or toward those without. The church generally has not left people with the impression that we are unique in the way we affirm the unsurpassable worth of each individual, regardless of how immoral and unlovable he or she may be.

If anything, the church today is largely known for its petty divisiveness along denominational, doctrinal, social, and even racial lines. On the whole, it is perceived as being *less* loving and *less* accepting than most other communities. It is often known for its self-proclaimed and often hypocritical alliance with good against evil and for its judgmentalism toward those it concludes are evil. But, tragically, as a corporate body it rarely is known as being distinctive because of its radical love. In contrast to Jesus' prayer, the world is *not* compelled to believe in the triune God on the grounds that his love is undeniably present among Jesus' disciples.

If this is ever going to change, we will have to keenly diagnose what the root of our problem is. It is, I shall argue, found at the point where sin first entered the world. Our primordial parents, Adam and Eve, are the prototypes of each of us. With them, I shall argue, we choose to live from the Tree of the Knowledge of Good and Evil instead of living in union with the Father, through Christ, in the power of the Spirit. Consequently, as was the case with the Pharisees in Jesus' day, the church has to a significant extent become the promoters and defenders of the very thing from which Christ came to free us.

Before we are ready to develop this notion, however, we must understand and feel the full force of the mandate to love that is placed on the church because of its identity in Christ. In the face of the many competing agendas the church has adopted for itself, we have to become convinced that its central agenda is to love as God loves. To this topic we now turn.

chapter 3

The Center Is Love

For in Christ Jesus . . . the only thing that counts is faith working through love.

Galatians 5:6

Love means the undergoing of the transformation of one's entire existence by God. . . . Loving God is simply the other aspect of being loved by God. Being loved by God implies loving God: the two do not stand separately side by side.

Dietrich Bonhoeffer

The first demand which is made of those who belong to God's Church is not that they should be something in themselves, not that they should, for example, set up some religious organization or that they should lead lives of piety, but that they shall be witnesses to Jesus Christ before the world.

Dietrich Bonhoeffer

In the last chapter we saw that the way God displays his perfect love to us, in us, and through us is by placing us in Christ. In Christ we are the recipients of the eternal, unsurpassable love the Father has for the Son, and we participate in the eternal, unsurpassable love the Son has for the Father. As the fellowship created and sustained by the Holy Spirit (2 Cor. 13:13), we are made "participants of the divine nature" (2 Peter 1:4) and are radically transformed by this participation. As we yield to the reality of who we are in Christ, Christ is formed in us individually and collectively, and the community of believers comes to replicate—to display, to glorify—the beauty of the eternal love of the triune God. We are the prism that reflects the radiant light of the Trinity.

Distinguished by Radical Love

This is who we already are in Christ, individually and collectively. We are in fact new creations in Christ Jesus (2 Cor. 5:17). But precisely because it is who we are, this transformation carries with it a divine mandate. It is the command to love as God loves.

This is not a command to *become something* we're not by striving hard on our own effort. Rather, the mandate to love is simply a command to *be who we already are*. We are *in Christ*, so we must put off the *old self* and display the *new self* we already are in Christ by thinking and acting in congruity with it. The reality of our participation in the loving fellowship of the triune God longs for expression, and this longing is only satisfied when our thoughts, words, and actions are in harmony with it.

Everything we are in Christ, and thus everything we are called to be in Christ, is summed up in the word *love*. The central defining truth of the believer is that in Christ God ascribed unsurpassable worth to us, though we did not deserve it. Hence, the central defining mark of disciples of Christ is that they in turn ascribe unconditional worth to themselves and all others, knowing that Christ died for them as well. "We know love by this, that he laid down his life for us—*and we ought to lay down our lives for one another*" (1 John 3:16, emphasis added).

The Distinguishing Mark of the Disciple

Someone once asked Jesus what the greatest commandment was. Jesus answered by giving him two, implying that it was impossible to do one without doing the other. "'You shall love the Lord your God with all your heart, and with all your soul, and with all your mind.' This is the greatest and first commandment. And a second is like it: 'You shall love your neighbor as yourself'" (Matt. 22:37–39).

The implication is that it is impossible to truly ascribe worth to God while refusing to ascribe worth to those to whom the Creator ascribes worth. This is why the second command is "like" the first one; it necessarily follows from it. We love God—we affirm the unsurpassable worth of God—by obediently ascribing unsurpassable worth to those to whom he ascribes unsurpassable worth. We love those whom God loves, and we love them the way God loves them. And, as we have seen, God ascribes unsurpassable worth to *everyone*, as is evidenced by the fact that Jesus died for everyone (2 Cor. 5:14; 1 Tim 2:6; 1 John 2:2). We thus manifest our love for God by embracing *God's* estimation of every single person we encounter. To do anything less is to fail to ascribe to God the authority, and thus the inherent worth, that he has as Creator.

John sums up the matter bluntly. "Those who say, 'I love God,' and hate their brothers or sisters, are liars" (1 John 4:20). To truly love God includes loving others with the same love God has for us and the same love God has for them. This is part of what it means to be a *participant in the divine nature*. It is, in fact, what it means to be Christian (Christ-like). "Whoever does not love," John wrote, "does not know God, for God is love" (1 John 4:8). Our capacity to love—to fulfill the greatest two commandments—is the definitive evidence that we are in fact abiding in Christ and participating in the perfect love of the triune God.

Christians sometimes try to assess how they or others are doing on the basis of such things as how successfully they conquer a particular sin, how much prayer and Bible study they do, how regularly they attend and give to church, and so forth. But rarely do we honestly ask the question that Scripture places at the center of everything: *Are we growing in our capacity to love all people?* Do we have an increasing love for our sisters and brothers in Christ as well as for those for whom Christ died who are yet outside the church? Are we increasing in our capacity to ascribe unsurpassable worth to people whom society judges to have no worth?

If there is any distinguishing mark of the true disciple from a biblical perspective, *this is it!* Let's read a few more passages from the first epistle of John:

> The children of God and the children of the devil are revealed in this way: all who do not do what is right are not from God, nor are those who do not love their brothers and sisters.
>
> 1 John 3:10

> We know that we have passed from death to life because we love one another. Whoever does not love abides in death.
>
> 1 John 3:14

> How does God's love abide in anyone who has the world's goods and sees a brother or sister in need and yet refuses help?
>
> 1 John 3:17

> Beloved, let us love one another, because love is from God; everyone who loves is born of God and knows God.
>
> 1 John 4:7

> No one has ever seen God; if we love one another, God lives in us, and his love is perfected in us.
>
> 1 John 4:12

> God is love, and those who abide in love abide in God, and God abides in them.
>
> 1 John 4:16

> The commandment we have from him is this: those who love God must love their brothers and sisters also.
>
> 1 John 4:21

The point of these teachings is that we know we are participating in the love of God because we are *in fact* loved and love others with the love that God is. The love of God is not merely a theoretical belief we entertain, nor is it a fiction God entertains about us. *It is a reality.* We are in fact *in Christ* and therefore are recipients and participants of the perfect love of the triune fellowship. As we "abide in love" we "abide in God" and "God abides in [us]" (1 John 4:16). God lives in us, not theoretically but really. Because it is real, *it is something that can and should be experienced and witnessed.*

The Distinguishing Mark to the World

Christians are not the only ones who are supposed to witness this distinguishing mark. Non-Christians also are to see it, and this is the main way God intends them to be brought to faith in Christ. It is the central way God's glory is extended to all the earth. Indeed, God leverages the credibility of his salvation plan on Christ's disciples loving as Christ loved! God doesn't depend primarily on the words of his disciples, nor on their clever apologetic arguments, nor on their ability to concoct ingenious marketing techniques. God relies on his disciples participating in the love that he is and thus replicating it toward each other within the body and toward all others outside the body.

"By this," Jesus said, "everyone will know that you are my disciples, if you have love for one another" (John 13:35). Jesus prayed that his disciples would replicate the very same love that he and the Father share "*so that* the world may know that you have sent me and have loved them even as you have loved me" (John 17:23, emphasis added). The thing that more than anything else demonstrates the reality of the loving, triune God is that we embody the reality of the triune God in our relationships with one another and with the world. Nothing less than the credibility of the gospel, the reputation of God, and the salvation of people hangs on our fulfilling the commandment to love.

Consider that Jesus was the perfection of holiness (Heb. 7:26), yet he did not claim that the world would believe in him because of the unique holiness of his followers. Jesus was the very manifestation of the wisdom of God (1 Cor. 1:30), yet he did not claim that the world would believe in him because of the unique wisdom of his followers. Jesus had all the authority of heaven to work signs and wonders (Matt. 28:18), yet he did not claim that the world would believe in him through unique demonstrations of power. Rather, he leveraged everything on love.

Christ is the incarnation of God's love, he brings all who say yes to him into this love, and he claims that the world will be drawn to believe in him through the display of this love in his disciples. As we overflow toward others with the same radical, Calvary-type love God gives to us, others are compelled to believe both that God is real and that he wants to pour this same love upon them.

The All-or-Nothing of the Christian Life

The All-Encompassing Command

Scripture never tires of driving home the centrality of the command to love. "This is the message you have heard from the beginning," John said, "that we should love one another" (1 John 3:11; cf. 1 John 3:23; 2 John 5). This is *the* message! John spoke as though there was no other message. So too, Jesus said, "This is my commandment, that you love one another as I have loved you" (John 15:12; cf. John 13:14). He spoke as though there was no other command because, as a matter of fact, *there really isn't* any other commandment. Every other commandment and every other message is contained in this one.

Hence, after giving us the two inseparable "greatest" commands to love God and our neighbor as ourselves, Jesus added, "On these two commandments hang all the law and the prophets" (Matt. 22:40). Everything in the Old Testament hangs on and is summed up in these two. Paul said, "The whole law is summed up in a single commandment, 'You shall love your neighbor as yourself'" (Gal. 5:14). And again, "The one who loves another has fulfilled the law. . . . Love is the fulfilling of the law" (Rom. 13:8, 10). For this reason, the commandment to love is called "the royal law" (James 2:8).

The point of all such teachings is that if we truly abide in Christ and love God, ourselves, and our neighbors as ourselves, we will fulfill everything else God requires of us. It is virtually impossible to obey this commandment consistently and not fulfill the entire law. This is why Scripture consistently emphasizes that the singular aim of the disciple must be *to love*.

Everything we do, Paul said, is to be "done in love" (1 Cor. 16:14). We should never engage in anything that is not motivated by love and does not promote love. We are to *"live in love*, as Christ loved us and gave himself up for us" (Eph. 5:2, emphasis added). We must not just occasionally ascribe worth to others in a self-sacrificial way; we are called to *live* in love. Love must characterize our lives day in and day out.

Similarly, Paul said, *"Above all*, clothe yourselves with love" (Col. 3:14, emphasis added). Christ-like love is something we are commanded *to wear*. It should envelop us at all times. This command, we must note, is placed *"above all."* Peter agreed when he wrote, *"Above all*, maintain constant love for one another" (1 Peter 4:8, emphasis added). There's nothing, absolutely nothing, that should *ever* displace the command to love as the first and foremost concern of the disciple—no doctrine, no ethical principle, no personal agenda, *and no exceptions*. If our thought, word, or deed doesn't result in ascribing unsurpassable worth to the person we've encountered, it shouldn't be thought, voiced, or acted on. It is that simple; love alone must govern each and every encounter in our lives.

The centrality of love for Paul is reflected in some of his prayers as well as his teachings. Paul's prayer for the Philippians, expressing God's heart for all believers, was that their "love may overflow more and more" (Phil. 1:9). His prayer for the disciples at Thessalonica was that they would "increase and abound in love for one another and for all" (1 Thess. 3:12). Later he wrote to these disciples that his prayer of thanksgiving for them was "because your faith is growing abundantly, and the love of everyone of you for one another is increasing" (2 Thess. 1:3). The central mark of a maturing Christian, and of a maturing congregation, is that they increasingly love others as Christ loves them.

The Universality of the Love Command

While the New Testament certainly emphasizes the importance of believers loving others—for God's glory to the world depends on our replicating God's oneness, as we have seen (John 13:35; 17:20–26)—it by no means restricts the command to love for other disciples. Our love is to "abound . . . for one another *and for all*" (1 Thess. 3:12, emphasis added). Since God ascribed unsurpassable worth to every human being in becoming a human and dying for them, and since we participate in this triune love because we are in Christ, we are empowered to, and commanded to, love without any consideration of how worthy the other person appears. Indeed, it is precisely the radical, unconditional nature of our love that testifies to the world that our love does not originate in ourselves but in God.

This aspect of the command to love is prominent in the teachings of Jesus. While nonbelievers can be expected to love those who love them, disciples are called and empowered to love even their enemies and pray for those who persecute them (Matt. 5:43–44; Luke 6:28). While nonbelievers can be expected to do good to those who do good to them, disciples are called and empowered to do good even to those who harm them (Luke 6:34). As Paul put it, we are to "overcome evil with good" (Rom. 12:21).

Similarly, as God "is kind to the ungrateful and the wicked" (Luke 6:35), and as he allows the blessings of nature to come "on the evil and on the good" (Matt. 5:45), so our love must be given without consideration to the relative merits or faults of the person we encounter. We are to love like the sun shines and like the rain falls: *indiscriminately*. We are to "be merciful, just as [our] Father is merciful" (Luke 6:36). We are to give to beggars, lend to those in need, not resist evildoers, and give without expecting anything in return (e.g., Matt. 5:39–42; Luke 6:31–36). In other words, we are to love without strings attached, without conditions, without any consideration whatsoever of the apparent worthiness of the person we encounter.

Our model in this is Jesus Christ; we are called to imitate him (Eph. 5:1–2; 1 Peter 2:21). Jesus was a scandal to the authorities because of his outrageous love. He loved the unlovable. For example, while the Pharisees scorned a woman of ill repute who was acting inappropriately toward Jesus (judged by their religious standards), Jesus loved her and affirmed her (Luke 7:36–50). Similarly, to the shock of his own disciples, Jesus broke the racial and religious codes of his Jewish culture by talking to a Samaritan woman with a scandalous past (John 4:4–27).

Jesus let her know that he was aware of her five failed marriages and that she was living with a man to whom she wasn't married. He didn't reveal this to shame her but to convince her he was the Messiah, that he loved her, and to offer her eternal life. As a result of this, the woman became a joy-filled outspoken evangelist (John 4:28–29).

It was not without reason that Jesus acquired the scandalous reputation of fellowshipping with the dregs of society (Matt. 9:10–11; 11:19; Mark 2:15–16; Luke 7:34; 15:1). He loved and fellowshipped with prostitutes, tax collectors, and drunkards. He loved, gave attention to, and helped the "unimportant" people as well as the "important" people. Indeed, he even loved those who crucified him to the point of praying for their forgiveness (Luke 23:34).

This is how we are to love, for this is how we are loved! God's love is impartial and universal, and so must ours be (Deut. 10:17–19; 2 Chron. 19:7; Mark 12:14; John 3:16; Acts 10:34; Rom. 2:10–11; Eph. 6:9; cf. 1 Tim. 2:4; 1 Peter 1:17; 2 Peter 3:9; 1 John 4:8). Anyone in need whom we happen to come upon is our "neighbor" whom we are called to love (Luke 10:27–37).

Nothing is closer to the heart of God than this kind of love. Indeed, love *is* the very heart of God. Hence, loving as God loves—manifesting the truth that we are in union with Christ and in fellowship with the triune community—must be the singular concern of the Christian. Whomever we encounter, whatever situation he or she may be in, whatever his or her lifestyle might be, however much we may approve or disapprove of the person's appearance, words, or deeds, our *one and only concern* must be to affirm his or her unsurpassable worth with *our* words and deeds. This is the concern that must be above all other concerns. It is the concern we must wear and live in. With every person we encounter, the only question that should be on our mind is, *How can I, right here and right now, affirm the unsurpassable worth of this person for whom Christ died?*

It's Love or Nothing

Love and Religious Noise

We noted above that the commandment to love fulfills the entire law. If we carry this out consistently, we will fulfill everything else that God requires of us. But even this doesn't fully express the absolute centrality and singular importance of the commandment to love. For not only is it true that if we love we fulfill the law; it is also true that if we don't love, *it doesn't matter what other laws we do fulfill.* Indeed, without love, absolutely *nothing* is of *any* significance. Paul made this point very clearly when he wrote:

> If I speak in the tongues of mortals and of angels, but do not have love, I am a noisy gong or a clanging cymbal. And if I have prophetic powers, and understand all mysteries and all knowledge, and if I have all faith, so as to remove mountains, but do not have love, I am nothing. If I give away all my possessions, and if I hand over my body so that I may boast, but do not have love, I gain nothing.
>
> 1 Corinthians 13:1–3

These are some very impressive religious activities: speaking in tongues, prophetic powers, understanding all mysteries, having all knowledge, mountain-moving faith, giving away possessions, sacrificing one's life. Yet they are all devoid of any real value if they are not done in love. They are nothing more than religious noise—a noisy gong or clanging cymbal.

We have perhaps heard this passage too many times to readily appreciate how utterly radical it is. Try to hear it as though for the first time. Paul was saying that *the only criteria that matters* when assessing the value of any activity is this: Is it done in love? Does it ascribe unsurpassable worth to others, and does it increase people's capacity to ascribe unsurpassable worth to others?

Christians are often impressed by miraculous powers, supernatural gifts, and altruism. And there's certainly nothing wrong with these acts. But if they aren't motivated by love and don't promote love, we are to consider them *altogether worthless.* Even more commonly, Christians are often impressed with great worship music that inspires passionate singing, eloquent sermons that can bring audiences to laughter and tears, grand church buildings that inspire awe, and rapidly growing congregations that defy ordinary statistics. Again, there is certainly nothing wrong with any of these things. We

can praise God for all of them. But if we are thinking biblically, if such things do not flow from and contribute to love,
they are nothing more than an irritating clashing cymbal. They
are "nothing."

For people of the kingdom, participants in the triune fellowship, love and love alone is the bottom line. This is the only thing
that gives value to anything we believe, say, or do. This is the
reason the world exists, and this is the reason the church exists.
Whatever music we play, sermons we preach, churches we build,
people we impress, powers we display, stances we take, doctrines
we teach, things we achieve—if believers are not growing in their
motivation and ability to ascribe unsurpassable worth to people
who have no apparent worth, *we are just wasting time.* We are
not making true disciples.

Indeed, we may actually be doing worse than this. For by
engaging in all these wonderful activities without love—by
making all this "religious noise"—we are actually providing a
distracting counterfeit to the one thing that is needful. How
easy it is to not notice that we are unloving when our religious
activities are going so well! Our religious noise drowns out the
cry of God's heart.

This was the chief error of the Pharisees. As we shall see in
chapter 11, the Pharisees of Jesus' day had a lot of religion but
no genuine love. They carried out the law to a fault, but their
obedience was not motivated by love, and it did not result in
love. Jesus assessed that the "love of God" was not in them (John
5:42). They would "tithe mint and rue and herbs of all kinds"
while "neglect[ing] justice and the love of God" (Luke 11:42).
They did not ascribe unsurpassable worth to God as Creator nor
to those to whom God ascribes unsurpassable worth. To no one
did Jesus speak harsher words than to these loveless religious
professionals.

Do We Need to Be Balanced?

Even as I write these words, I can hear someone saying, "Yes,
we must love. But we must balance love with truth." "Love has
its place, but we must not forget God's wrath." "Love must never
take the place of correct biblical doctrine."

I understand and appreciate the concern for truth, holiness, and correct biblical doctrine, especially in these postmodern times, and I fully agree that we need to be balanced in all our teaching. But the concern to balance love with any competing command is misguided. It is, in fact, *unbalanced*. Two points need to be made.

First, if we take seriously the biblical teaching that the love command is the *greatest* command, that we must put it above all other considerations, that we must clothe ourselves with and even live in love, then there can be no thought of balancing love with any other concern. Nothing can qualify a command that is "above all" other commands. If the command is to love *everyone* as Christ loves us, there simply is no situation in which the command does not apply.

Whatever we do with our concern for truth, holiness, or doctrine, if it isn't done *under* "the royal law" to express unsurpassable worth to others, it is actually worse than doing nothing. As we shall see more fully in the following chapters, when *anything* supplants or even competes with love as our first and foremost concern, it becomes to this degree evil—regardless of how true and noble it may be in and of itself. Because the command to love is the central biblical doctrine, it is the only one we can, and must, hold in an "unbalanced" way. Put differently, the only way to be "balanced" in our understanding and practice of love is to see all other commands as aspects of it, not competitors alongside of it.

We have to wonder where anyone got the idea that love in any way *competes with* truth, holiness, or biblical doctrine. Love *is* the central biblical truth; it *is* the essence of all holiness, as John Wesley saw; and it *is* the most important biblical doctrine.[1] As Bonhoeffer argued, if our definition of love is Jesus Christ, there can be no thought of separating love from truth or ethics. "It is the essence of love that it should lie beyond all disunion."[2] Love is not simply one among many points. It is the point that encompasses, unifies, and gives life to every other point of Christian life and thought.

Hence, if a person is concerned with living in truth, the place to start—and continue and finish—is with the truth that he or she is loved and thus is to love others as himself or herself. If this truth isn't lived, every other truth in which he or she might believe is worthless. If a person is concerned with holiness, the place to start—and continue and finish—is with the command to love. If this all-encompassing dimension of God's holiness isn't lived, being holy in any other respect is simply a Pharisaical smoke screen for the fact that he or she is unholy. And if a person is worried about being biblically correct, this is the place to start—and continue and finish. For if we aren't correct about this biblical doctrine, we are simply wrong on every other point we affirm, even if we happen to be affirming the right doctrine. Every truth, every deed, every teaching is reduced to nothing more than religious noise when it isn't placed under and clothed in the commandment to love.

Second, as we shall see more fully in chapter 7, any attempt to qualify God's love with another attribute—God's wrath, for example—amounts to a fundamental denial of the centrality of the revelation of God in Christ. For Christ reveals God's holiness and wrath against sin precisely as he reveals God's love for sinners. Indeed, God's holiness and wrath are what God's love looks like against sin. Peter Kreeft expresses the point well when he notes,

> What is the wrath of God . . . ? Is it real or not? It is real, but it is not part of God himself. God is not half love and half wrath, or 99 percent love and 1 percent wrath. God *is* love. Wrath is how his love appears to us when we sin or rebel or run away from him. The very light that is meant to help us, appears to us as our enemy when we seek the darkness.[3]

Love defines every aspect of the Christian's life, for love ultimately defines every aspect of God's life. Indeed, we may more specifically say that as Christ defines every aspect of the Christian's life—for Christ is the definitive revelation of God's love—so Christ defines every aspect of God's life. All the attributes of God are to be *defined by Christ*. In the crucified Messiah we see God's just and holy wrath against sin, but we see it as a manifestation of God's love. Out of love for sinners, Christ bore our sin and suffered the wrath of God's punishment on the cross. *All* that God is, dwelt in Christ (Col. 2:9). He is the Word (John 1:1), image (Col. 1:15), and "exact imprint of God's very being" (Heb. 1:3). What this exact imprint reveals is that "God is love"

(1 John 4:8). Everything God does, even his expressions of holy wrath, are done out of love.

Hence, as those who are called to live in such a way that people can know God by knowing us, we are called to love. We are only balanced in our understanding of love when we understand that it is the one thing we must live in—to all people, at all times, in all situations, without exception. If we do this, everything else we need to do will get done. If we don't do this, there's simply nothing else worth doing.

How much harm has been done to the church and to the cause of Jesus Christ because Christians have placed other considerations alongside or above the command to love as God loves? In the name of truth, Christians in the past have sometimes destroyed people, even physically torturing and murdering them. In the name of holiness, Christians have often pushed away and shamed those who don't meet their standard, creating their own little holiness club to which struggling sinners need not apply. And in the name of correct biblical doctrine, Christians have frequently destroyed the unity of the body of Christ, refusing to minister or worship together because of doctrinal differences, sometimes viciously attacking those who disagree with them.

The unsurpassable worth of the person who doesn't share our truth, doesn't meet our definition of holiness, or doesn't agree with our "correct biblical doctrine" has all too often been neglected or denied. Which means that in such cases the truth, holiness, or correct doctrine we have defended was altogether worthless: clashing cymbals, resounding gongs, religious noise, nothing more. Such noise tarnishes the reputation—the glory—of God. It also explains why the church generally has been known for many things other than love and many things that contradict love.

What's the Problem?

So what's the problem? If all who truly say yes to God are already in Christ, participating in the eternal love of the triune fellowship, why doesn't it show more clearly? What is blocking the flow of love that believers already possess by virtue of their union with Christ? Why do we have such difficulty becoming what we already are? Why has Jesus' prayer for the loving unity of his church and for it to be the vehicle for glorifying God fallen so short?

The answer is *not* simply, "Because we aren't trying hard enough." If the issue was merely a matter of our willpower, I don't for a second believe we'd be doing so poorly at overcoming it. As with every other issue with which Christianity is concerned, this is not an ethical problem and does not call for an ethical solution. No, the problem is far more profound, far more subtle, and far more sinister than ethics can address. To understand it, we have to go back to the very beginning of human history and right into the very essence of the fall.

What we shall find is that, as has been the case with almost all religions throughout history, the Christian religion has to a significant extent become the defender and promoter of the fall rather than the proclaimer of the Good News that alone can free us from the fall. As with most religions, it has set itself up as the guardian of the knowledge of good and evil rather than the example of how to transcend the knowledge of good and evil by living in love.

To understand this, we have to take a long, hard look at Genesis 3, where the problem began, and especially at the fruit of the Tree of the Knowledge of Good and Evil, which Scripture specifies as our downfall. This is our task in part 2 of this work.

Part 2

The Forbidden Tree

chapter 4

Becoming the Center

Now the serpent was more crafty than any other wild animal that the LORD God had made. He said to the woman, "Did God say, 'You shall not eat from any tree in the garden'?" The woman said to the serpent, "We may eat of the fruit of the trees in the garden; but God said, 'You shall not eat of the fruit of the tree that is in the middle of the garden, nor shall you touch it, or you shall die.'" But the serpent said to the woman, "You will not die; for God knows that when you eat of it your eyes will be opened, and you will be like God, knowing good and evil."

Genesis 3:1–5

Man took to himself a secret of God which proved his undoing. The Bible describes this event with the eating of the forbidden fruit. Man now knows good and evil.

Dietrich Bonhoeffer

The middle has been entered, the limit has been transgressed. Now man stands in the middle, . . . now he lives out of his own resources and no longer from the middle. . . . Now he lives out of himself, now he creates his own life, he is his own creator.

Dietrich Bonhoeffer

We have seen that we were created for unbroken, loving fellowship with God. God's goal for creation is to have his perfect, triune love displayed to us, in us, and through us. God seeks to be glorified—his triune love expanded and displayed—by how God relates to us, how we relate to God, how we relate to ourselves, and how we relate to others. As we abide in God and God abides in us, we are to participate in the unsurpassable, loving nature of the triune God and love ourselves and our neighbors in the process of loving God, just as God loves us and our neighbors in the process of loving himself. The goal is for humanity to dance with and in the triune God.

Sin ruptured this fellowship and sidetracked the plan. It was restored in Christ, however, and the purpose of the church now is to reexpress the original goal of creation by living it before the world. As the church replicates God's unsurpassable and unconditional triune love within itself and to all others, the world comes to believe that Jesus has been sent by the Father. They come to know that the fellowship has been restored because *they see it!* God is glorified.

Yet, as we also noted in the last two chapters, the church as a whole has repeatedly failed to fulfill this mandate. In part 2 we explore the question, Why is this so? My conviction is that we have neglected the biblical teaching that the origin and essence of sin is rooted in the knowledge of good and evil. Consequently, we have tended to define sin as that which is evil, over against that which is good, rather than defining it more profoundly as *that which is not in union with Christ*, whether "good" or "evil."

Consequently, the church has tended to focus on symptoms rather than on the source of the disease. We have tended to define ourselves as the promoters of good against evil and have often seen ourselves as specialists on good and evil. We have consequently become judges of good and evil rather than lovers of people regardless of whether they are good or evil. As harsh as it may sound, we have sometimes promoted the very essence of the fall—the knowledge of good and evil—as though it were salvation!

To flesh out this thesis, we must go back to the beginning and dig deeply into the origin and essence of sin. In this chapter we shall discuss the significance of the location of the forbidden tree in the center of the garden. In the next two chapters we shall discuss the nature of the forbidden tree. And in chapters 7 and 8 we shall examine the nature of the serpent's lie that persuaded us to eat from this tree.

The "No Trespassing" Sign at the Center

Honoring the Center

The first thing we need to notice about the Tree of the Knowledge of Good and Evil is that it was located in the middle or center of the garden, along with the Tree of Life (Gen. 2:9; 3:3).[1] At the center of the Paradise God provided for Adam and Eve and all their descendants was a *provision* and a *prohibition*. "Upon these two trees," Bonhoeffer noted, "the destiny of man is to be decided."[2] The Tree of Life was God's provision to meet our needs and share his life endlessly. The Tree of the Knowledge of Good and Evil was God's prohibition against humans overstepping their proper domain.

At the center of the glorious life God wants humanity to share in is a "No Trespassing" sign that God graciously gives us to protect us from overstepping our finitude. At the center of the beautiful existence God wills for us is the humble recognition that we are not God and thus must leave to God what God wills to keep for himself, namely, the knowledge of good and evil. Everything else in the garden surrounds this center.[3]

In God's plan, God alone would know good and evil. As Creator, God alone has the right and the ability to define good and evil. Things are good or evil insofar as they align with or oppose *God's* will, not *our* wills. When God administers judgment, knowing good and evil, it serves God's purpose of inviting agents into his love. When humans try to do this, however, it tends to facilitate death for ourselves and others.

Moreover, God alone knows each human heart. God alone knows what each person was originally given to work with in terms of his or her psychological, physical, and even spiritual aptitudes. God alone knows the myriad factors that influence each decision people make. And God alone knows the extent to which people choose what they do out of their own free will and the extent to which their choices are the result of factors outside themselves. Unless we are intimately involved in a person's life, this information is completely hidden from us. Hence, while there are intimate contexts in which we are to hold each other accountable (see chapter 12), Scripture uniformly testifies that God alone is able to judge and warns us not to judge (see chapter 6).

The essence of sin according to the Genesis account is the transgression of this proper boundary. We are not satisfied being God-like in our capacity to love; we also want to become God-like in our capacity to judge, which is how the serpent tempts us. But in aspiring toward the latter, we lose our capacity for the former, for unlike God, we cannot judge and love at the same time.

The essence of sin is that we play God. We critically assess and evaluate everything and everyone from our limited, finite, biased perspective. Instead of simply deriving life from that which is given at the center of our existence, we try to derive our likeness of God, our life and worth, from that which is forbidden at the center of our existence.

The New, Empty Center

When Adam and Eve ate from the tree, they imposed their will into the center of Paradise, and this was the act that destroyed Paradise. They invaded the proper domain of God. Instead of recognizing that they were supposed to derive life *from* the center, they placed themselves *in* the center. They tried to become "like God."

An analogy from architecture might help illustrate the situation. Certain architects speak of living spaces as being composed of "centers" that mutually define each other, and thus collectively define the entire space.[4] Every space that is truly beautiful and "alive" has a center to the space *as a whole*, a *source center* that other centers revolve around and complement. The complementary centers contribute to the life of the space as a whole by being in complementary, noncompetitive relationship to the source center. If there is no source center, however, every center competes to become a source center, and the room is chaotic, ugly, and dead.

We might think of God's original design for creation in terms of a well-designed living space. God is the source center which every other center—every distinct aspect of creation—is to revolve around and complement. Humans in this plan are to derive their life, love, and worth from the source center and reflect it in their own distinct way, thereby contributing to the life of the space of creation as a whole (fig. 7). In other words, we are created to glorify God.

As with all living spaces, the beauty of the space of creation depends on the integrity of the distinction between the complementary centers and the source center. The "No Trespassing" sign placed at the center of the garden represents the warning to preserve this boundary and thus the order, beauty, and life of creation. Everything depends on humans remaining humans and not trying to be God—not trying to be their own source center.

Adam and Eve violated this boundary. They thrust themselves into the center of the garden to try to make themselves "wise like God." They tried to design their own space, as it were, with themselves as the center. And we do the same. We try to make

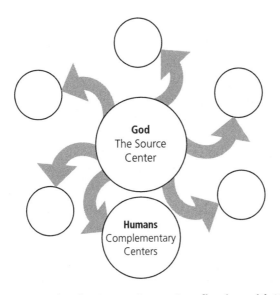

Figure 7: God Is the Source Center Overflowing with Life to Other Complementary Centers

creation—and God—revolve around us. Instead of remaining content being complementary centers, we try to make everything complement us. We attempt to use things and people to derive our worth, meet our needs and expectations, or improve our lives in some way. And we "know good and evil" in the process, for we invariably judge things as "good" or "evil" on the basis of how well they play the idolatrous role we assign them.[5]

Living as the source center means living as judge. But we were not created to function as the source center. We were created to function as complementary centers. We have no life in ourselves to dispense to other centers. Consequently, the center of the room we design is not a center of fullness but a center of emptiness. Without God as our center, we are not a source of life but a vacuum that sucks life. We can't radiate life to other centers; we can only try to draw life from them. In the room we rebelliously design, the world and God revolve around us, and we become a virtual black hole (figure 8). It is out of the depravity of this black hole that we function as a center, playing God, judging good and evil.

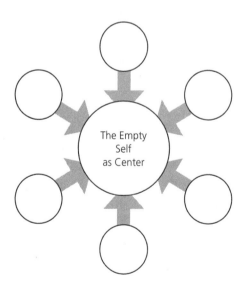

Figure 8: We Become Empty Centers Trying to Derive Life from Surrounding Centers

This is life "in the flesh" or life "in Adam." It is life lived under the serpent's lie and thus life lived *as though* we were the center. This way of life is diametrically opposed to God, for it makes it impossible for the fullness of God's love to flow into us and through us.

In this fallen way of life, people and things have worth only to the extent that they fill us. Instead of simply ascribing unsurpassable worth to others because the Creator does, we ascribe limited worth to people depending on our judgment of them. Do these people love me? Do they please me? Do they benefit me? Do they affirm me? Do they agree with my opinions? *We* are the ones who declare that someone or something is good or evil, for we have set ourselves up as the center around which everything revolves and, therefore, the standard against which everything is measured. "For man in the state of disunion," Bonhoeffer says, "good consists in passing judgment, and the ultimate criterion is man himself. Knowing good and evil, man is essentially a judge."[6]

Every judgment we think, speak, or act upon presupposes that we are in a position of superiority over the person we judge. It presupposes that we are "god" relative to the person or thing we judge. The judgment is illegitimate because in reality we are not god to anyone. We are not the center of anyone's life. Furthermore, the judgment is inaccurate because in reality we are not wise like God. We cannot know what God knows. And the judgment is invariably self-serving, for we are using it to fill the God-shaped vacuum in our lives.

Our judgment cuts us off from our true source of life, and the person we judge becomes a source of life for us. Our condemnation of that person, whether it be about a major lifestyle issue or a minor matter of appearance, gives us a momentary feeling of worth, of superiority, of fullness—of deity. Though we are in fact empty, we can, at least in our own minds, stand over someone for a moment. Though we ourselves are sinners, we can, at least for a moment, drink from the well of believing that at least we are not "like *that* person." However bad we may feel about ourselves, the Tree of the Knowledge of Good and Evil has something to feed us, at least for the moment.

Restoring the Center

If we are to live the life God intends for us, if we are to participate in the ecstatic love of the triune God, God must be restored
as the center of our lives. We must die to ourselves as center, die
to our addiction to idols, and die to the perpetual judgments we
entertain in our minds. God can only be our source of life when
he is the center of our lives. So long as we thrust ourselves into
the center, we will be forced to seek life from idols, judging good
and evil, and thus be cut off from our source center. We will live
a life that is actually death. The only way to discover true life is
to die to the "life" of living as the center and be restored to our
true source center (Matt. 10:39; 16:25; cf. Gal. 2:19–20).

Christ Restores the Center

In a most profound sense, this restoration is already accomplished in Jesus Christ. Christ overcomes our separation from
God and restores God's Tree of Life in the center of our existence.[7]
On the cross, Christ in principle condemned every person as a
rebellious and empty center and reconciled every person to God
by restoring God as his or her true source center.

When we by faith say yes in the core of our being to what God
has already done for us in Christ, we begin our participation in
this new reality. What was true and what is true about Christ
becomes true of the believer. The self that lived as the center,
trying to derive life from the world, judging everything as good
and evil, is crucified in Christ's crucifixion. The self "in Adam"
is now "old," for it no longer has any validity. The believer is
a "new self" that lives in Christ and thus participates in God's
divine nature (Rom. 6:3–10; 2 Peter 1:4).

The Millisecond between the Old and the New

Nevertheless, though the old self is crucified in Christ, its old
ways of thinking, feeling, and acting persist. It is *in fact* dead, yet
we continue to think, feel, and live in it *as though* it were not. How
is this possible? If our reality has changed, why is it not instanta-
neously manifested? How can we still continue to think, feel, and

act as though we were the center instead of God? Why do we still have to resist urges to get life from sources other than God?

The questions are not just applicable on an individual level; they have cosmic significance. If Christ in truth defeated Satan and other powers that resist God's purposes when he rose from the dead, why does Scripture still say that "the whole world lies under the power of the evil one" (1 John 5:19)? Why is Satan still called "the god of this world" and "the ruler of the power of the air" (2 Cor. 4:4; Eph. 2:2)? If death has in fact been defeated, why do we still die? If all of creation has been restored in Christ, why is it still under bondage to corrupting powers?

The answer is that there is a gap between the *victory* Christ accomplished on the cross and its *manifestation* in our lives and throughout creation. All things have been subjected to Christ and to those who are in Christ, according to the author of Hebrews. But *"we do not yet see* everything in subjection" to Christ and to his church (Heb. 2:8, emphasis added; cf. 1 Cor. 15:23–28). So too John writes that "we *are* God's children now"; but *"what we will be* has not yet been revealed." The only thing we know is that "when [Christ] is revealed, we will be like him, for we will see him as he is" (1 John 3:2, emphasis added). The whole creation "waits with eager longing for the revealing of the children of God" (Rom. 8:19) when Christ's victory over creation's bondage will be perfectly manifested.

This is the gap between the "already" and the "not yet." It is the interval between the death of the old and the manifestation of the new. We might think of it as the split-second interval between a bomb exploding and the full impact it makes on its environment. Or we might think of it as the millisecond that exists between a light bulb being turned on and the disappearance of darkness from the room. The impact of a bomb is *in principle* made the moment the bomb explodes, and the room is *in principle* lit the moment the bulb goes on. Yet there is an interval between what happens *in principle* and what is *manifested* as fact. So it is with all that Christ accomplished on the cross and its manifestation throughout creation and in our lives.

Of course from our perspective the explosion of a bomb and the force it makes on its environment are one event. So too from God's perspective, and therefore as a matter of fact, the work of Christ and its impact on creation are one event. For a being like

God who had no beginning and has no end, the two thousand years that have passed thus far between "fact" and "manifestation" is less than a millisecond. Indeed, if ten thousand more years pass before the Christ-event is fully manifested, it will still be less than a millisecond from God's perspective. The delay only seems long for finite creatures like us who physically live for less than a fraction of eternity (see 2 Peter 3:8–10).

The central goal of the Christian life is to yield to the truth of who we already are in Christ and thus manifest this truth in the context of a world that still lives as though it were not true. We are to manifest "the already" in the midst of the "not yet." The goal is to align ourselves with the new reality God has created in Christ. The goal is not to become something we are not already. It is, rather, to simply manifest what we already are because of Christ. The bomb of Christ's work has gone off; we must simply allow its impact to be felt fully. The light of Christ's life has been turned on; we must simply allow the darkness to flee. And as we do it in our lives, we extend the influence of the bomb and spread the light of Christ throughout the world. God's will is accomplished "on earth as it is in heaven" (Matt. 6:10).

Dying to Life in the Center

Though we participate in the life of the triune God by faith, we only *experience* and *manifest* this participation to the extent that we put off all ways of thinking, feeling, and acting that are inconsistent with this divine life. We are already new creations in Christ Jesus (2 Cor. 5:17). Yet we must "put away [our] former way of life, [our] old self, corrupt and deluded by its lusts, and . . . be renewed in the spirit of [our] minds" (Eph. 4:22–23). As we renew our minds and come to truly see ourselves as we are in Christ (cf. Rom. 6:11; 12:2), we "clothe [ourselves] with the new self, created according to the likeness of God in true righteousness and holiness" (Eph. 4:24; cf. Col. 3:7–9).

The old self is corrupted and deluded by its lusts, as Paul says, for it lives under the lie that life is to be found by violating God's prohibition and by living out of its own empty center. It is deluded into thinking that life can be found in what we do and what we get. This lie is what we must put off if we are to experience the fullness of life that defines our new self. And we do it by bringing our thoughts, and thus our feelings and actions, into alignment with the truth of who we are in Christ.

To the extent that we continue to identify ourselves with the old self, we experience this "putting off" as death. The Bible calls it "repentance" (*metanoia*). Though the term has come to mean feeling remorseful for our sin, it actually means "to turn around." We turn from our old self that has lived as the center of everything, the judge of everything, and therefore as needing things as a source of life.

The prospect of living life with God as our only source center and, therefore, as the one judge of everything, is threatening to the old self. The prospect of living without the perpetual need to achieve one's ultimate worth by striving is impossible for the old self. Yet this is what must be done if we are to experience life in Christ. We must repent.

This death experience is what Jesus was referring to when he taught, "Those who find their life will lose it, and those who lose their life for my sake will find it" (Matt. 10:39; see also 16:25). When we die to the self-centered existence of the serpent's lie, we find what real life is. When we crucify the self that compulsively tries to fill its own emptiness by striving, we find our true self that receives fullness from God for free and that joyfully overflows with this fullness toward others. When we slay the accuser within ourselves, we are freed from the bondage of the Accuser and manifest the life of unconditional love that our Creator always intended for us and that our Savior died to restore to us.

We are to crucify ourselves daily so that, with Paul, we may say, "It is no longer I who live, but it is Christ who lives in me" (Gal. 2:20). We are to experience our true self that is united with and participates in the life of Jesus Christ. Indeed, we are to experience Christ *as* our life (Col. 3:4). This is life lived from our true source center. It is life lived as God intended it to be lived. It is living from the source center in the place that is free from judgment and therefore free to love. It is what it means to be truly human, truly alive, truly awake, and truly free. But it is only found by dying to oneself as the center.

chapter 5

Love and Religion

For the whole law is summed up in a single commandment, "You shall love your neighbor as yourself." . . . Live by the Spirit, I say, and do not gratify the desires of the flesh. . . . But if you are led by the Spirit, you are not subject to the law.

Galatians 5:14, 16, 18

The wise man is aware of the limited receptiveness of reality for principles; for he knows that reality is not built upon principles but that it rests upon the living and creating God.

Dietrich Bonhoeffer

It is not by ideals and programmes or by conscience, duty, responsibility and virtue that reality can be confronted and overcome, but simply and solely by the perfect love of God.

Dietrich Bonhoeffer

What is religionless Christianity?

Dietrich Bonhoeffer

We have seen that the life God created humans to enjoy is centered on a provision and a prohibition. At the center of the garden was a Tree of Life and a forbidden tree. Our lives are meant to be centered on the confidence that God will share his eternal life with us as well as on the reverent acknowledgment that we are not to seek that which God reserves for himself. We are not to try to be God. We are to leave to God the knowledge of good and evil.

The fundamental cause and evidence of our separation from God, and thus the fundamental cause and evidence of our inability to receive and give the fullness of God's love, is that we violate this prohibition. We transgress the boundary God set between God and humanity. We assert ourselves as a source center instead of being content as a complementary center that receives everything it needs from the source. In doing this, we cut off our lifeline to our true source, become empty, and then try to fill the vacuum we have created with sources other than God. The world becomes a stage of idols from which we desperately and futilely try to get the fullness of life God has already offered us for free.

When we live this way, we are living from the fruit of the Tree of the Knowledge of Good and Evil. The act of invading the center is the act of assailing God as the only rightful judge of the world. For, as Bonhoeffer notes, to live as the center is to live as a judge. Instead of getting fullness of life from the love that God is, we attempt to get life from being wise, knowing good and evil. We live in judgment rather than love.

We need to clearly understand why love and judgment are opposed to each other. To understand this is to understand why the forbidden tree is termed a Tree of the Knowledge of *Good* and Evil rather than simply the Tree of Evil. What is it about this knowledge that severs our union with God? What is it about living from the fruit of the Tree of the Knowledge of Good and Evil that is so diabolical that Scripture depicts it as the root of all that is wrong with humans?

Social and Spiritual Pathology

An Ethical Marriage

The antithesis of love and judgment, and thus the significance of the forbidden tree being a Tree of the Knowledge of Good and Evil, can perhaps best be explored through an analogy. What would we think of a husband who continually lived in the question, "What is the ethical thing to do?" regarding his relationship to his wife? Wouldn't the question itself be evidence that this man was *not* living in loving union with his wife? In healthy marriages in which the husband and wife live in a one-flesh, loving union, each person operates out of love, not a list of ethical principles.

To be sure, the loving husband and wife do many good things for one another, but they don't do these things *because they're good*. They do these things *because these things express love*. Chores and child-rearing responsibilities are shared, flowers are bought, cards are given, sexual intimacy is shared, long conversations are enjoyed, and conflicts are resolved not because there is an ethical rule about each particular activity that specifies what is "the right thing to do." These activities are done out of a fullness of love that is shared, not out of a desire to "be good." True, it may be that the couple had to learn how to express their love toward one another. But to the degree that they are living out of love, they follow principles of loving behavior not as abstract ethical mandates but as loving guidelines.

Scripture teaches that God's goal for humanity is something like a marriage. God aims at, and in Christ achieves, a one-flesh and one-spirit relationship with us (Eph. 5:21–32; cf. 1 Cor. 6:17). God is not first and foremost interested in acquiring a people who happen to believe all the right things and act in all the right ways. God's first concern, and really his only concern, is to have a people who are united with him in love. Indeed, as we have seen, God's goal is to have a people who participate in the same love that the Trinity enjoys eternally.

Out of the fullness of life and love we receive from him as source, God calls us to believe certain things, do certain works, and make many sacrifices. But God doesn't call us to do these things because they are ethical. God calls us to do them because he has made us participants in his love. Everything hangs on our understanding the difference between living out of love, which then produces good results, and living out of goodness as an ethical goal in and of itself.

The Sociopathic Husband

We can perhaps make the distinction between living in love and living in ethical principles clearer by expanding the analogy of a husband and wife. Imagine a husband who is a sociopath. He operates only with a self-centered motivation and is incapable of genuinely loving his unfortunate wife. He understands only behavior, not the inner emotions of other people. Yet let us suppose, for whatever reason, it is in this man's self-interest to appear to be an ideal husband. It is the way he thinks he can get his own needs met.

Thus, to meet his own needs, the sociopathic husband reads books on being a good husband and intensely studies those he perceives to be ideal husbands in order to learn how they behave in their marriages. He records, memorizes, and learns to mimic every aspect of a good husband's external behavior down to the slightest detail. He becomes a virtual expert on "good and evil" in marriages. He could tell us and even model for us all the right things to do and all the things to avoid to be a "good" husband. He could formulate a rule about what a husband ought to do for almost every conceivable situation.

Moreover, because it fits his strategy for getting life, the sociopathic husband is always assessing himself and other husbands. Part of his strategy for convincing himself he's okay is to compare himself favorably to other husbands whose behavior doesn't measure up to his own. Yet the self-centered motivation of the sociopathic husband isn't apparent, precisely because he has become an expert on how good husbands behave—and good husbands always appear to put their spouse's needs above their own.

Despite this man's impeccable ethical exterior, we would all agree that this man is not someone any woman would ever want to marry. *For the man in fact does not know how to love.* Indeed, though he himself is unaware of it—being a sociopath, he isn't aware of the inner reality he lacks—his perfect exterior is actually a mask for his lacking the only reality that makes a good marriage good, namely, the reality of love.

While outside observers would undoubtedly be impressed with this man, the sociopath's wife would eventually see through the façade. On the one hand, her husband's performance is *too per-*

fect. It lacks the dimension of flexibility, playfulness, spontaneity, and human imperfection that is an essential part of real life and love. Despite the good behavior, the wife would sense that there is no genuine intimacy, no touching of souls, no shared life with this man. The wife would sense that her husband is always one step removed from an *actual relationship* with her. She would sense that her husband is in fact relating to a set of rules, not to her. She would come to realize that she is married to an ethical abstraction, not a real, living, loving person.[1]

On the other hand, the wife would surely notice that her husband's performance is at crucial times far short of perfect. For real life is not the kind of thing that can be captured in a manual of dos and don'ts. Every concrete situation in life, and therefore every actual situation in a marriage, is unique in its own way, and this uniqueness can never be fully anticipated or handled by a set of rules. Only love can live fully and effectively in the concrete here and now. Only love can effectively relate to *this particular person* in *this particular situation*. Hence, as Bonhoeffer brilliantly makes clear in his masterpiece, *Ethics*, only love knows how to live in the actual world instead of an abstract world of ethical principles.[2]

Undoubtedly, everything the sociopathic husband would do toward his wife would be "good" by abstract ethical standards. These would generally be the behaviors in which healthy, loving husbands engage. He smiles when she walks into the room. He laughs when she laughs, looks concerned when she's worried, puts his arm around her and looks sad when she's sorrowful, and so on. But the only reality the sociopathic husband is aware of in doing all this is the reality of behavior, not the reality of empathetic emotions that lie behind this behavior when healthy people engage in it.

The well-behaving sociopath lives in the world of ethical rules, not the world of love.

Spiritual Pathology and the Knowledge of Good and Evil

In our fallen state we are not unlike the sociopathic husband in our relationship with God. Our separation from God is a separation from our source of life, which is God's love. In placing ourselves at the center of the garden, we become a self-centered vacuum perpetually trying to suck life from our environment. Thus, like the sociopathic husband, we become self-appointed "experts" on knowing good and evil.

In our fallen condition, our assessment of good and evil never shuts off, for the void in our spirit that drives us to look for and evaluate idolatrous sources of life never goes away. We are addicted to judgment, for we are addicted to idols.

Lacking the reality of God's love flowing in us and through us, we become spiritually pathological. As the husband was dead to his wife in terms of genuine love, in our fallen state we are dead in our sin and dead to God (Eph. 2:1, 5; Col. 2:13). In trying to be the source center of our world, we are cut off from our true source center, and everything we do is directly or indirectly related to a strategy for filling the resulting emptiness.

Consequently, we lack real life—the full life of God—but unknowingly try to mask it and compensate for it by our external behavior. We critically assess behavior, things, and people in terms of *good* and *evil*, depending on what they can do for us and depending on how well they conform to our standards. Our judgment is both the result of our seeking to feed ourselves with idols as well as an idol with which we feed ourselves.

Self-serving Religious Pathology

In our fallen state, separated from our true source center, we live from the knowledge of good and evil regardless of the particular idols from which we try to get life. Some people choose secular idols and thus adopt a corresponding set of criteria of what is good and what is evil. Money, prestige, security, pleasure, and so forth are good, while financial burdens, being overlooked, insecurity, discomfort, and so forth are evil. Religious people, on the other hand, choose religious idols and thus set up a different set of criteria for what is good and evil. Religious people's beliefs, rituals, and behavior are good, while those of other people, insofar as they are different from their own, are evil.

Religious Pathology

Religious idolaters of course don't recognize their idols as such. On the contrary, part of their religious strategy for getting life is to contrast their "true" beliefs and ethical behaviors with the idols to which secular people cling. But as a matter of fact, religious idols are just as idolatrous as secular ones. Indeed, this is the most prevalent and enslaving form of idolatry throughout history.

From the perspective of those inside religion, getting life from the rightness of one's beliefs and the purity of one's behavior looks much better than getting life from things such as money, pleasure, and prestige. But in fact, people are not closer to the true source of life because their idols look better from their own perspective. The sociopathic husband who mimicked good behavior is no closer to genuine love than the uncaring husband with bad behavior. Another way of saying this is that even the truest beliefs and the most righteous deeds are devoid of any value unless they arise out of a fullness of love (1 Cor. 13:1–3).

Because it is part of their strategy for getting life, religious idolaters—like the Pharisees of Jesus' day—tend to be vigilant in assessing beliefs and behavior for just the same reason that the sociopathic husband was vigilant at assessing marital behavior. Because they are focused on their own behavior, they are fine-tuned in noticing others' behavior, and they assess these behaviors by the same standards they assess their own. The standards used to judge others invariably favor the religious people doing the judging. These standards are, after all, part of *their* strategy for getting life. Hence, the sins a particular religious community is good at avoiding tend to be the ones identified as most important to avoid in the mind of that community, while the sins a community is not good at avoiding tend to be minimized or ignored altogether—regardless of what emphasis the Bible puts on those sins.

Gluttony and Homosexuality

To give one example, few churches target overeating as sin. Yet the Bible has a good deal to say about the sin of overeating (gluttony). In the Jewish culture of Jesus' day, the inability or unwillingness to control one's eating was viewed as being on a par with the inability or unwillingness to control one's sex drive. Lust and gluttony were two major evidences that a person was undisciplined, governed by "shameless passion" (Sir. 23:6; 4 Macc. 1:3, 27).

This attitude toward overeating is generally reflected in Scripture. Proverbs warns that gluttony as well as drunkenness can lead to poverty (Prov. 23:21). It depicts gluttony as breaking God's law, to the point of warning that those who are "companions of gluttons shame their parents" (Prov. 28:7). Paul speaks against people whose "god is their belly"—their lives are centered on the pleasure of eating (Phil. 3:19). And Ezekiel proclaims that the sin that led to the destruction of Sodom was that its citizens were prideful and enjoyed "excess of food" but "did not aid the poor and needy" (Ezek. 16:49). When one considers that over 60 percent of Americans are overweight and 20 percent are obese, together with the fact that the amount of food Americans consume beyond what they need could feed the 30 percent of the world that is starving, one wonders why the sin of gluttony isn't portrayed as the sin that makes America a modern Sodom and Gomorrah!

On top of this, everything the Bible says about greed—the most frequently mentioned sin in the Bible after the sin of unbelief—applies to food as much as it does to possessions and money. It is the sin of hoarding more than you need for yourself. Similarly, everything the Bible says about the call for believers to walk in freedom, not being controlled by anything (e.g., 1 Cor. 6:12; Gal. 5:1), applies to food as much as it does to addictive substances. And the call for believers to honor their bodies as the temple of God (1 Cor. 6:19), though often applied to unhealthy habits like smoking, certainly has a far more significant application when it comes to food. More people suffer and/or die from health issues related to being overweight than suffer from illness and/or die from smoking! Indeed, medical professionals now consider obesity a national epidemic.

Despite this, conservative evangelical churches and religious organizations do not generally consider overeating to be a significant sin. No one questions the genuineness of the faith of overweight people. On this issue, we all tend to acknowledge that we have faults of our own and thus can't judge overweight people just because their fault tends to be more visible. We are widely inclined to acknowledge that, despite the Bible's strong teaching on this sin, eating disorders are actually rather complex.

Most people who cannot or will not control their eating are using food to medicate pain or inappropriately address other issues in their lives. We thus are rightfully inclined to acknowledge that there are issues deeper than food that need to be addressed. We graciously give space to obese people to grow in Christ at their own pace. They have to answer to their Master on their own terms as we do on ours (Rom. 14:4). And we understand that simply saying, "Stop eating so much," isn't likely to be a loving and helpful way to address their situation.

What is more, we understand that overweight people need to gradually grow in being disciplined about food out of the fullness of life that they have been freely given in Jesus Christ. If they try to lose weight to get God or others to accept them—engaging in this program out of an empty center—they're not likely to be successful. And even if they were successful, the worth they acquired would attach to their *doing*, not their *being*. Their weight loss would thus leave intact the most fundamental question gluttony and all other forms of sin point us toward—the question of where we find our life for free, unconditionally, apart from our doing.

In any event, while there is a significant amount of judgmentalism and discrimination against overweight people in American society, as a whole Christians tend to exercise compassion toward them. A few even see the merit of fighting against the social trend of discrimination on behalf of our overweight brothers and sisters. Most Christians wisely recognize that one would have to be on the inside of an overweight person's story to know how to apply the biblical teaching about food control to his or her life in a loving way. On this issue we concede that if biblical truth is applied in unloving ways, it is simply religious noise and may actually be damaging.

Because of this, overweight people are generally welcomed into church fellowships without any suspicion. We may be thankful for this. No one accuses churches of compromising the Word of God because they accept overweight people into fellowship. Indeed, few would think of questioning the commitment even of churches that have an obese pastor.

Consider then, why is this same gracious mindset not extended to gays for instance? The mindset of most conservative Christians is that this sin is a deal breaker. It defines who is "in" and who is "out." In conservative Christian circles, the genuineness of the faith of a gay person is usually suspect if not outright denied. On this issue there is no allowance for God to work with people in an individual manner. The assumption is that we all answer to the same Master using the exact same criteria (contra Rom. 14).

Hence, most conservative churches and religious organizations do not accept gays as part of their organization, and they judge churches and organizations that do as compromising the Word of God. In contrast to their treatment of people who overeat, conservative Christians usually do *not* acknowledge that one has to be on the inside of a gay person's story to know how biblical teachings can be applied in a loving way. On this issue, the only thing a person needs to know and proclaim is that homosexuality is wrong. The assumption is that saying, "Just stop your activity," *is* enough to address their situation. Again in stark contrast to our view of believers who overeat, with regard to homosexuals, conservative Christians are generally unwilling to grant that we are all sinners and thus are in no position to judge.

What is more, far from seeking to ascribe worth to gays by siding with them against discrimination, many conservative churches and organizations consider it righteous to take a hardline stance against this sin not only in the church but in society. In the name of not compromising the Word of God, they feel the need to protect society from this "perversion" by working to make sure gays *don't* have the same employment, housing, or social benefits as nongays (cf. Matt. 25:34–46). In fact, often the rhetoric of conservative Christians against gays is positively hateful. Yet we would never dream of acting this way or speaking this way toward people who habitually eat more than they need. There are no antiobese churches. But it is rare to find a conservative evangelical church that is *not* antigay, at least in its attitude if not in its explicit ministry.

Why does this radical contrast between attitudes toward overeaters and gays exist? Is it because homosexuality is emphasized more in Scripture than gluttony? This is far from true, especially if one considers the sin of greed to include food as well as money and possessions.[3]

Is it because homosexuality is more harmful to society? It is not clear what distinct social harm homosexuality causes, if any. But whatever one thinks it to be, it certainly wouldn't rival a sin that is one of the leading causes of death in America! When one further considers that a third of the world is malnourished while we Americans consume massive amounts of excess food (that we as a nation directly parallel Sodom in this area!), the claim that homosexuality is more harmful than gluttony rings hollow. Add to this the enormous medical expenses obesity produces, using up precious resources that could be spent fighting other illnesses and diseases, and the claim becomes positively absurd.

But even if homosexuality *were* more harmful, why should this warrant any Christians concluding that this is the behavior that determines whether one is "in" or "out" of the Christian faith? Who authorized us to rank sins in this fashion?

Is this inconsistency due to the fact that homosexuality is a choice one makes and is less complex than overeating? In point of fact, the causes of homosexuality are at least as complex and painful as the causes of habitual overeating, and the ambiguity of how much free will is involved is the same. If ever there was a behavior one needed to understand from the inside to discern how biblical principles can be applied in love, it is this one.

To be sure, both overeating and homosexuality involve people's free will. And one can find examples of both types of people who overcame their struggle. But why do conservative Christians not hold up examples of people who lost weight to indict those who continue to overeat, while we routinely do this with people who are gay? Why do we rightfully acknowledge that not all overweight people are the same but do not acknowledge this with gays? Why do we graciously allow for distinctions between people and degrees of culpability with overeaters but make no such allowances with gays (e.g., the radical difference between being promiscuous or living in a lifelong, covenantal, monogamous relationship)? Why do we exercise compassion toward overeaters and allow them space to grow in Christ at their own pace but do not extend this same compassion to gays?

Could it be that if conservative Christians treated overeaters the way they treat gays—forcing them to have their own "obese churches" the way gays have to have their own "gay churches"—conservative churches might be 20 to 60 percent less full? By contrast, only about 1 to 2 percent of the population is gay. If a community wants to feel righteous by targeting a sin to define itself against, it clearly needs to be a sin of which the majority of its own members are not guilty! Homosexuality makes for a very good target.

This seems to be a classic case of a religious community using its knowledge of good and evil in service to itself, parasitically feeding itself worth by extracting it from an arbitrarily selected group from which it separates itself. It's a classic case of getting life from judging others. Toward these people the church has failed in the one thing for which the body of Christ is called to be known: outrageous, self-sacrificial love. We have not ascribed the worth God ascribes to them by dying for them. We thus do not fellowship with these sorts of sinners on the fringes of society the way Jesus did. We are of course confident "that God's judgment on those who do such things is in accordance with truth" (Rom. 2:2). Yet God judges us as hypocrites, for we do the very same kind of things, though we will not acknowledge it (Rom. 2:3–4).

The point is that the exercise of a community's knowledge of good and evil is invariably self-serving. Religious idolaters *need* to believe that the sins they commit are not as bad as the ones they avoid. Though they of course must acknowledge that they are not perfect, they need to be convinced that at least they are not like *those* people—the targeted group of sinners they tend to avoid.

This contrast is a central aspect of the strategy for getting life that their religious idol demands. It defines the way they eat of the Tree of the Knowledge of Good and Evil. This idolatrous way of living becomes so ingrained in an idolatrous community that they do not notice that the distinctions and rankings they make and feed from are perfectly arbitrary—except for the fact that *they* created these distinctions to feed themselves. They simply assume that *their* distinctions are *God's* distinctions, so to violate any of these distinctions is to violate God himself. However imperfect they may be, at least they are not like *those* sinners. In the words of Bonhoeffer, those who get life from the knowledge of good and evil are fully conscious of [their] own faults and of [their] duty of humility and thankfulness towards God. But, of course, there are differences, which for God's sake must not be disregarded. . . . If anyone disregards these differences, . . . he sins against the knowledge of good and evil.[4]

The self-serving strategy of discriminating between greater and lesser sins, and thus between those who are in and those who are out, is so ingrained in the idolatrous form of religious life that those who feed off it sincerely believe they are simply reflecting the mind of God in their distinctions.

In point of fact, their distinctions reflect the original sin that sets people apart from God.

The Emptiness of Religious Idolatry

As said earlier, striving to get life from religious idols is just as spiritually pathological as is striving to get life from secular idols. If anything, Jesus suggested that those who strive to get life from religious idols are actually *further* from the true source of life precisely because religious idols don't appear to be idols to those who get life from them. Those who know they are sick are more likely to receive a physician, while those who mistakenly think they are healthy ignore him (Matt. 9:12). How it must have shocked the religious establishment of his day to hear Jesus proclaim that the prostitutes and tax collectors would enter the kingdom of God before the Pharisees (Matt. 21:31).

The real issue is not what *kind* of idols people embrace but whether they are trying to fill the void in their souls with an idol at all. So long as people strive to get life from an idol of any sort, they block themselves off from their true source of life.

Since the religious idol usually requires that their sense of worth is associated with their religious performance, they usually *look* good. Indeed, in all likelihood, they will look *better* than those who have a genuine relationship with God for the same reason the above-mentioned sociopathic husband would look better than most truly loving husbands. Looking good is the religious idolaters' way of life. Like the sociopathic husband, they are vigilant about their own beliefs and behavior as well as those of other people. The Pharisees looked better than Jesus' disciples, and the Pharisees knew it.

In fact, however, this hypervigilance is evidence not of genuine spiritual health but of an inner emptiness and sickness. It is evidence of a spiritual pathology. The very attempt to fill the emptiness of their lives by their beliefs and behaviors rather than God prevents them from ever getting their emptiness *really* filled.

Not that the emptiness cannot be placated for periods of time; it can. If people's idolatrous religious strategies for getting life are successful, as they were with the Pharisees, these people will derive some surrogate life by believing they do all the right things, embrace all the right interpretations of Scripture, hold to all the right doctrines, engage in all the right rituals, and display the right spirituality. They will get even more surrogate life by looking down on those who don't do and believe all the right things as they do. Indeed, they may experience even more surrogate life by entertaining a "holy anger" toward those who do not conform to their way of thinking and behaving (a fact that perhaps explains the remarkable divisiveness within Christianity). But the positive feelings offered by religious idols are fleeting. The emptiness returns, driving religious idolaters to further futile attempts to get life by their religion.

Love and the Law

The Impotence of the Law

Consider Paul's view of the law. On the one hand, Paul believed that the Old Testament law is good and holy (Rom. 7:12). On the other hand, Paul said that it only serves to expose and even increase sin (Rom. 5:20; 7:5–11). On a deep level, Paul wanted to carry out the law, but on another level, Paul found himself unable to do this consistently (Rom. 7:9–24). The result was that the law brought Paul to the point at which he proclaimed that he was a "wretched man" and cried out for someone who "will rescue me from this body of death" (Rom. 7:24).[5]

Of course, the "someone" Paul found was Jesus Christ, who set Paul free from the condemning bondage of the law and thus

from the "body of death." "There is therefore now no condemnation for those who are in Christ Jesus" (Rom. 8:1). Moreover,
in Christ, Paul received the Spirit of God, who empowered him
to live as God wanted him to live, not because there was an
external law hanging over his head, but because it was in his
heart to fulfill the law.

> For the law of the Spirit of life in Christ Jesus has set you free
> from the law of sin and of death. For God has done what the law,
> weakened by the flesh, could not do: by sending his own Son in
> the likeness of sinful flesh, and to deal with sin, he condemned
> sin in the flesh, so that the just requirement of the law might be
> fulfilled in us, who walk not according to the flesh but according
> to the Spirit.
>
> Romans 8:2–4

Paul discovered an entirely different way of living. Life in
the flesh is characterized by striving to get something you don't
already have. It is living out of an empty center, eating from
the Tree of the Knowledge of Good and Evil, perpetually trying
to fill the void in one's soul. In its religious form, living in the
flesh includes trying to feel right with God on the basis of the
rightness of one's beliefs and behaviors. It is epitomized by living under the law.

By contrast, life in Christ is living out of a fullness of life and
love you have for free, for in Christ we are filled with God's own
Spirit and are made a participant in God's own triune fellowship.
Life in Christ is a life that is free from condemnation from God
and therefore free from any condemnation of ourselves or others.
It is life that empowers us to do the right thing because it frees us
to do the loving thing, precisely because we are no longer trying
to get life from doing the right thing. In Christ, we die to the law
as a way of getting life and thereby come alive to God as the only
source of life. In Christ, we are freed from our religious pathology
because we are filled with the love that is God himself.

The Law Leads Us to Christ

From the perspective of his life in Christ, Paul perceived that
one of the reasons God gave the law in the first place was to

lead us to Christ (Gal. 3:17–24). The law leads us to Christ both by showing us what love for God and others looks like and by showing us how we can never be united with God through the law. "No one is justified before God by the law" (Gal. 3:11; cf. 2:16).

We can no more arrive at union with God through the law than a sociopathic husband can become a loving husband by trying to do everything a loving husband is supposed to do. As with the sociopathic husband, the fact that we even have to strive to get right with God on the basis of our ethical behavior simply shows that we lack the one thing that is necessary for a genuine relationship to exist: love.

The law is, in a sense, a classic Catch-22. Our very effort in striving to get life precludes our ever getting life. And that is exactly the point! Through the law, God actually intensifies our need to get life from the Tree of the Knowledge of Good and Evil—the law increases sin (Rom. 5:20; 7:7–8)—in order to break us from the illusion that we can ever get life from our knowledge of good and evil.

The only way we can get life is by being united with God, as he always intended. And the only way to be united with God is to receive it as a gift. We must die to ourselves as centers, abandon attempts to get life by anything we do, receive God's mercy and love freely given to us in Christ, and make him our one and only source center. In other words, a life-giving relationship with God can only be entered into when we stop trying to establish it on the basis of our knowledge of good and evil. It can only be entered into by placing our total confidence in God's ability to make us good and abolish our evil in Jesus Christ. The only way we can be freed from our spiritual pathology is to recognize the carnality and futility of our knowing, performing, and judging on the basis of the forbidden tree and to receive God's forgiveness and healing as a free gift.

Another way of saying this is that the only way to get life is to have it freely infused into us by the Spirit of God. As we learn to walk in the Spirit and not in the flesh, all that belongs to God by nature begins to be evidenced in us by grace. When we abide in love—in the One who is love—the evidence of love is manifested in our lives. It is the fruit of the Spirit. Without striving to acquire something we don't yet have—precisely *because* we don't strive to acquire something we don't yet have—we manifest love, joy, peace, patience, kindness, generosity, faithfulness, gentleness, and self-control in our lives. There is no law against such things (Gal. 5:16–23), and there is no law that can get us such things.

When people have died to themselves as center and live in their identity in Christ, their actions do not spring from an abstract ethical system. In the words of Bonhoeffer, they rather spring "from joy in the accomplishment of the reconciliation of the world with God; they spring from the peace which comes with the completion of the work of salvation in Jesus Christ; they spring from the all-embracing life which is Jesus Christ."[6]

Such people do not filter the world through their knowledge of good and evil. They do not relate to others through an ethical system. They do not define themselves as those who are "in" over and against others whom they judge to be "out." Instead, they filter the world through their concrete relationship with Jesus Christ. They relate to themselves and others in the light of the worth God has ascribed to them in Christ. Because of this, they are empowered to experience and overflow with the scandalous love of Jesus for sinners.

Ethics and the New Testament

It is crucial we remember that the New Testament's behavioral injunctions are predicated on the new life and identity believers have in Jesus Christ. When this point is forgotten, the New Testament's behavioral injunctions are mistaken to be ethical mandates after which people are encouraged to strive. In this case, we are adhering to the letter of the New Testament but not to its spirit, and our thinking is bringing about death rather than life (2 Cor. 3:6).

For example, Paul teaches that love is not rude (1 Cor. 13:4–5). If we forget what the New Testament is about—the new life given us in Jesus Christ—we easily misinterpret this teaching to be an ethical injunction. We read it as saying, "Thou shalt not be rude." So in sincere obedience we set about doing our best to avoid being rude. We will tend to feel good about ourselves when we are avoiding rudeness, and we will feel bad about ourselves when we find we are rude. Moreover, given this focus, we will invariably notice the rude behavior of others and judge them accordingly, just as we judge ourselves.

Of course, it is not always easy to differentiate between having healthy personal boundaries that sometimes tell people to go away, on the one hand, and actual rudeness, on the other. So to fulfill this ethical mandate, we may have to think earnestly and debate long on what exactly constitutes rudeness and the specific conditions under which a behavior might look rude but not actually be rude. If there are situations in which people disagree, we might find ourselves planting ourselves on one side of the debate or the other. Indeed, if it is important enough to us, our posturing could result in factions of Christians arguing with one another—often very rudely!

Now we must notice in this scenario that we are entirely focused on our behavior, centered on ourselves, and living out of our knowledge of good and evil. We are living out of our heads, filtering everything through what we think we know about rudeness. Most significantly, we have *entirely missed the point of Paul's teaching*. For Paul's point was not that we should try hard to avoid rudeness but that we must *live in love*. If you are living out of the love of God, you won't be rude. Indeed, you will fulfill all the law. Conversely, you can strive to obey a hundred rules you've created to define rudeness in particular situations but be completely devoid of love.

As with all of his behavioral injunctions, Paul was not giving us a list of do's and don'ts in 1 Corinthians 13. He was rather describing what life in Christ, life in love, and/or life in the Spirit looks like. His purpose was not to get us to *act* different; his goal was to help us to *be* different. In telling us love is not rude, for example, Paul was giving us a flag to help us notice when we are acting out of love and when we are not—that is, when we are acting out of the old self and when we are acting out of the new. Paul's behavioral injunctions are not things we are supposed to strive to perform, nor are they new universal ethical rules by which we are to try to motivate all people to live. They are evidences that disciples are participating in the abundant life Jesus came to give.

Similarly, when Paul told us that "the fruit of the Spirit is love, joy, peace, patience, kindness, generosity, faithfulness, gentleness, and self-control" (Gal. 5:22–23), he was not telling us to *try to act* loving, joyful, peaceful, and so on. If we could simply will these things into existence, they would hardly be the fruit *of the Spirit*. Paul was rather encouraging us to live by the Spirit, not the flesh (Gal. 5:16). He was pointing us to a radically new way of living, one that places God rather than ourselves at the center of our lives. He was helping us get free from our spiritual pathology.

Jesus did the same thing throughout his ministry. He was not calling people to a new religion or a new ethical system; he was, as Bonhoeffer says, *calling people to life*. Hence, Jesus consistently evaded the standard ethical issues of his day. When someone wanted him to settle an inheritance dispute with a brother, for example, he responded, "Friend, who set me to be a judge or arbitrator over you?" (Luke 12:14). He was telling the man that he did not come to give definitive answers to our many difficult ethical questions. He rather came to offer an alternative way of living to all ethical systems. Hence, he simply reminded the man that "one's life does not consist in the abundance of possessions" (Luke 12:15). Jesus was offering this man, and all people, real life. Life from God, not idols; life lived in fullness, not emptiness; life lived in celebration because of a fullness one has for free, not in a desperate attempt to get full by striving. Possessing such life would not resolve this man's ethical dilemma, but it would put it into a new perspective.

In the same way, Jesus systematically cut through ethical disputations about the *proper* grounds for divorce (Matt. 19:3–12), the *proper* attitude toward the government (Matt. 22:17–22), the *right* way to handle adultery (John 8:2–11), the *right* rules to keep on the Sabbath (Luke 6:1–11; 13:10–16), and a host of other dilemmas that characterized life in the first century. With unprecedented wisdom, Jesus turned such disputes into occasions to show those who would presume to be judges in these dilemmas that they were themselves guilty of sin and thus in no position to judge. In doing this, he showed people an alternative way of living—one that didn't center on getting life from resolving all life's issues or from the rightness of their views but rather centered on loving God, self, and others. He revealed himself to be "the centre of life," Bonhoeffer said. "In no sense did he come to answer our unsolved problems."[7] Neither he nor any New Testament author did what ethical systems are designed to do.

Jacques Ellul summarizes this perspective in powerful terms that warrant a lengthy quote.

> The revelation of God in Jesus Christ is against morality. Not only is it honestly impossible to derive a moral system from the Gospels and the Epistles, but further, the main keys in the gospel—the proclamation of grace, the declaration of pardon, and the opening up of life to freedom—are the direct opposite of morality. For they imply that *all* conduct, including that of the devout, or the most moral, is wholly engulfed in sin. . . . As Genesis shows us, the origin of sin in the world is not knowledge . . . it is the knowledge of good and evil. . . .
>
> In the Gospels Jesus . . . gives as his own commandment "Follow me," not a list of things to do or not to do. He shows us fully what it means to be a free person with no morality, but simply obeying the ever-new word of God as it flashes forth. . . . We are as free as the Holy Spirit, who comes and goes as he wills. This freedom . . . is the freedom of love. Love, which cannot be regulated, categorized, or analyzed in principles or commands, takes the place of law. The relationship with others is not one of duty but of love.[8]

The New Testament is not about ethical behavior; it's about a radical new way of living. It is about life lived in surrendered union to God through faith in Jesus Christ. It is about experiencing the transforming power of God's love flowing into and through a person. It demands a form of holiness that is far more exacting than any ethical or religious system. It demands a holiness of the heart that does not feed the fallen self by distancing itself from sinners but rather sacrifices itself to unite with sinners.

This kind of holiness can never be achieved through behavior. It has to be received by grace. Jesus' ministry and the whole New Testament undermine our ethics and religion in order to position us to humbly receive this empowering and life-transforming grace.

Conclusion

The church as a whole has not failed to preach the message that salvation is by grace, not by works. Generally speaking,

Christians don't try to be saved by meticulously carrying out the Old Testament law. Yet we must wonder if we have adhered to the letter of Paul's teaching and missed its spirit (2 Cor. 3:6). For as much as we claim that our relationship with God is based totally on the work of Christ, it seems that many of us nevertheless continue to try to get life from the rightness of our beliefs and goodness of our behavior. We continue to eat of the Tree of the Knowledge of Good and Evil, which the law, leading us to Christ, was meant to abolish.

The church as a whole often seems to function like a sociopathic husband. The evidence is pervasive. The fact that the collective body of the church is known more for its declarations of good and evil than for its outrageous love is telling. We often do good things (at least as *we* define good), but something is often lacking—and it happens to be the one thing that is needful. The church as a whole does not look like the body of Christ, whose outrageous love attracted people who would otherwise have had nothing to do with a "religious establishment" or "ethical system." We don't generally have tax collectors, prostitutes, and other sinners (not *former* tax collectors and *former* sinners) in our company (Mark 2:16). Rather, despite our own insistence that it is not so, we often look like a body of Pharisees whom sinners—people with *certain kinds* of sin we've identified as more serious than our own—avoid at all costs.

Another evidence of our spiritual pathology is that at both an individual and corporate level Christians often lack the freedom, flexibility, joy, boldness, and playfulness of a real lover. The abundant life and reckless love Jesus exemplified and came to bring is often replaced with a hypervigilance on what people ought to believe, how people ought to behave, and how the church should appear. We live out of our ethical maxims and religious ideas rather than the vibrant, concrete life and love of God. We live in the abstract, not the concrete.

In a proper context, of course, there is nothing wrong with concerns about right belief and proper behavior. But it is evidence of spiritual pathology when these concerns dominate our individual or collective lives and are not rather merely by-products of what ought to dominate our lives: the outrageous, freely given, unsurpassable love of God to us and through us.[9]

Similarly, though it is rarely noticed, most Christians tend to walk more in judgment than they do in unconditional love. When we view those in our culture who have the religious status that tax collectors and prostitutes had in first-century Jewish culture, is our first thought to bless them and ascribe to them unsurpassable worth? When we encounter a drug addict, a homeless person, a hooker, a racist, a promiscuous gay person, a transvestite, a heretic, or a murderer, do we not usually first form a judgment about him or her? Are we immediately reminded that we are sinners on the same level as them, saved only by God's grace? Do we not often on some level contrast ourselves with them and place ourselves over them? Do we not sometimes think that however imperfect we may be, at least we are not like *those* people? Do we not sometimes think we must first fix them—or at least pronounce our opinion about their lifestyle—before we can fully embrace them as close friends?

If we are honest, we must admit that this tends to be the conservative Christian mindset. Even more disconcerting, however, is the fact that we usually do not notice that we are judging and that this is sin. To the contrary, we often assume that our ability to judge *is part of our godliness!* It proves to us that we are not like *those* people. To some extent, our sense of being right with God is rooted in the delusion that we are standing up for holiness, truth, and God by mentally or verbally passing judgment on others. We are inclined to pronounce, "We know that God's judgment on those who do such things is in accordance with truth" (see Rom. 2:2), without realizing that in this very act of judgment we expose ourselves as being at least as guilty as those we judge. Unlike *those* people, we believe *we* are on the side of the good and the side of God.

In contrasting ourselves with others in this way, we are eating from the Tree of the Knowledge of Good and Evil. And in so doing, we are forsaking the most fundamental job description God gave us: to love others as he has loved us.

So long as we strive to get life from the rightness of our beliefs and behaviors, so long as we live in the flesh and persist in religious idolatry, we will be spiritually pathological and will judge rather than love. We cannot correct this situation simply by trying hard any more than the sociopathic husband could become loving by working harder at perfecting his behaviors.

Spiritual pathology can only be cured when we wake up to the futility of our idolatry and realize God's love is the one thing that can ever fill the void in our souls. Only when we receive God's love, given to us in Christ, as an unconditional, free gift can we ever love others in an unconditional and free manner.

chapter 6

Love and Judgment

If you judge the law, you are not a doer of the law but a judge. There is one lawgiver and judge who is able to save and to destroy. So who, then, are you to judge your neighbor?

James 4:11–12

Bearing within himself the knowledge of good and evil, man has become judge over God and men, just as he is judge over himself.

Dietrich Bonhoeffer

Every day man dies the death of a sinner. . . . He cannot raise himself up above any other man or set himself before him as a model, for he knows himself to be the greatest of all sinners. He can excuse the sin of another, but never his own.

Dietrich Bonhoeffer

A Dysfunctional Bride and Witness

Christ's Dysfunctional Bride

Because we have rarely taken seriously the specific nature of our separation from God as depicted in the Genesis narrative, we have often trivialized sin by understanding it merely as that which is evil rather than as disobeying God by trying to get life from knowing good and evil. Consequently, the church has to a large extent continued to eat from the Tree of the Knowledge of Good and Evil without realizing it.

Indeed, sometimes we have been guilty of unwittingly promoting the fruit of the forbidden tree *as though it were salvation*. We have too often defined ourselves as the practitioners and defenders of the good, the judges and conquerors of evil, and the saviors of people and society. We churchgoers not only eat of the Tree of the Knowledge of Good and Evil, we do it *better* than others!

The result is that God's goal of acquiring for himself a bride who knows what it is to joyfully receive, rejoice in, and mercifully display God's unsurpassable love has been hindered. God's bride does not adequately know or experience the joy of living in union with God, loving people unconditionally and outrageously, free from all judgment. Rather, to a significant degree, God has a bride who is like the sociopathic husband, mentioned in the last chapter, trying to do all the right things to fill a hole in his soul while lacking the one thing that makes a husband truly good. To a significant degree, God has a bride who squelches the free love and abundant life that could flow to her and through her, for he has a bride who to a significant degree lives off the goodness of her morals and rightness of her theology.

The extent to which we live off the fruit of the knowledge of good and evil—even an orthodox, "saved" version of this fruit—is the extent to which our participation in the triune dance is suppressed.

Christ's Dysfunctional Witness

The extent to which we live off the fruit of the knowledge of good and evil is also the extent to which we fail to invite others into the dance, for by God's design, the invitation was to be extended primarily by our love. Perhaps the greatest indictment on evangelical churches today is that they are not generally known as refuge houses for sinners—places where hurting, wounded, sinful people can run and find a love that does not question, an understanding that does not judge, and an acceptance that knows no conditions.

To be sure, evangelical churches are usually refuge houses for *certain kinds* of sinners—the loveless, the self-righteous, those apathetic toward the poor and unconcerned with issues of justice and race, the greedy, the gluttonous, and so on. People guilty of *these* sins usually feel little discomfort among us. But evangelical churches are not usually safe places for other kinds of sinners—those whose sins, ironically, tend to be much less frequently mentioned in the Bible than the religiously sanctioned sins.

It is rare indeed that a drunkard, drug addict, or prostitute would think of going to church because he or she just needed to feel loved and accepted. These people may go to bars, fellow addicts, drug dealers, or pimps to find refuge and acceptance, but they would not go to a church. In fact, as with the Pharisees in Jesus' day, the church has generally represented everything people with these kinds of sins want to avoid at all costs. It has most often represented nothing but condemnation for these people. Indeed, churches frequently cultivate a reputation for "cracking down" on sins that fall into their "unsanctioned sin" category. To fail to do this, many have assumed, is to compromise our reputation for being set apart for holiness.

I submit that, despite being carried out with utmost sincerity, the desire to acquire a distinctive "holy" reputation is inevitably hypocritical. As we saw in the last chapter, the sins we declare ourselves to be against are invariably selected to *not target ourselves*. If we were consistent in cracking down equally on *all* sins, we'd be cracking down on ourselves more than on those outside the church. And if we retained a system of evaluating sin at all, sins such as impatience, unkindness, rudeness, and self-righteousness—all indications that love is absent (1 Cor. 13:4–5)—as well as prevalent "church" sins such as gossip, greed, and apathy would rank higher on our list than sins such as homosexuality or heterosexual promiscuity.

Striving for a holy reputation is also self-serving because the whole enterprise is unconsciously designed as a strategy for getting life for ourselves. Though it is mostly unconscious—indeed, though we uniformly deny it—we are feeding ourselves with our devised sin lists. We feel righteous and secure that we are "in" while others are "out" as we compare ourselves favorably with others who don't measure up (according to our own biased measuring device).

Most fundamentally, the quest for a holy reputation is sinful, for it cuts to the heart of God's goal for creation and the central call of the church to be a community that receives, lives in, and recklessly shares the unsurpassable love of the triune God. *Above all else*, this love is that for which the church is called to be known. Sadly, in the name of acquiring for ourselves a reputation of holiness, we have often compromised the one reputation God calls us to have. Jesus was willing to forsake any possibility of having a holy reputation for the sake of loving those who were unholy.

To be sure, Christians are called to be a holy people, set apart by their good works. This is what transforming love looks like as it takes hold of people. But this is not a reputation we should *seek to acquire* or *protect*. The one reputation we are called to acquire is identical to the one reality we are called to live in: We are to be, and to be known as, a people who receive and give love in an outrageous, impartial, unconditional way.

If we simply seek to be who we are in Christ, to love without judgment, everything else we need to do will be done. If we don't manifest this reality, however, it doesn't matter in the least what else we do and are known for. Another way of saying this is that the only thing that gives any value to our holiness is our love (1 Cor. 13:1–3).

The Root of the Problem

The fundamental problem behind the church's dysfunction as a bride and as a witness is that we have not adequately understood and internalized the Bible's teaching that the root of our separation from God is not merely evil as such, but it is the fruit of the Tree of the Knowledge of Good and Evil. We have selectively declared war on one aspect of the forbidden fruit (evil) in the name of eating from another aspect of the forbidden fruit (good), when God has told us not to eat of the forbidden fruit at all. The religious and ethical version of the forbidden fruit is just as prohibited as a licentious or hedonistic version. In either case, we are caught up in trying to be the center, trying to fill our own emptiness, and thus trying to live by judging what is good and evil. We are thereby blocking the flow of love and thwarting God's purpose for creation and the church.

How can the church begin to acquire the reputation of love it is supposed to have? It is not by devising more loving programs, for this would be just another form of us trying to *do the good thing.* Rather, the way to acquire a reputation for being loving is to simply *become loving.* As we love God, ourselves, and others out of the fullness of our participation in the triune God, the world will see that Jesus Christ has been sent by the Father (John 17:20–26).

To be clear, this isn't to suggest that we should engage in loving activity *to get* a reputation. It is simply saying that we are called to live in outrageous love and that when we do this, it impacts the world. To engage in loving activity for the purpose of accomplishing something else (e.g., gaining a certain reputation) is to continue to eat from the Tree of the Knowledge of Good and Evil. We are still placing something above love. Love is reduced to a means to a higher end. We are still living out of emptiness, trying to feed ourselves, rather than out of the fullness we already have in Christ. Instead, we are to manifest God's love simply because we *are in* God's love. Our reputation is simply the impact this new identity makes on the world when we live in congruity with it.

In short, the greatest need of the church is simply to be the church, which is the collective body of people who submit to God and participate in God's eternal love. When we try to be the church by doing good things, we cease manifesting who we already are. The greatest need, therefore, is for Christians individually and collectively to simply *stop trying to get life from knowing good and evil.* Our one need is to simply be people who are loved for free, who are filled with love for free, and who therefore love all other people for free. Our one need is to join in the dance of the triune God, to celebrate in God's triune self-celebration, and thus to live and love in the fullness of the triune love.

The root of our separation from this, we have seen, is our judgment. It is both the fundamental cause of our separation and the chief evidence of our separation. Because this concept is so foundational and yet so foreign to our usual ways of thinking, it will be helpful to examine passages outside of Genesis 3 in which the prohibition at the center of the garden is articulated. What we will find is that the commandment not to judge—not to eat of the forbidden tree—is emphatically repeated in the New Testament.

I shall structure our exploration around four key passages. Each one of them is, in its own way, a call to stop eating from the forbidden tree and to live in the union with God that our Creator created us and redeemed us to have.

Matthew 7:1–5

Do not judge, so that you may not be judged. For with the judgment you make you will be judged, and the measure you give will be the measure you get. Why do you see the speck in your neighbor's eye, but do not notice the log in your own eye? Or how can you say to your neighbor, "Let me take the speck out of your eye," while the log is in your own eye? You hypocrite, first take the log out of your own eye, and then you will see clearly to take the speck out of your neighbor's eye.

Appropriate and Inappropriate Judgment

The root for the word *judgment* in Greek (*krino*) literally means "to separate." The English word *critic* comes from this word. A movie critic, for example, is one who helps us separate good movies from bad movies.

As we shall discuss more fully in chapter 12, there is a positive way Christians are supposed to be "critics" or "separators" on behalf of one another. In intimate contexts in which people have invited one another into their lives—contexts such as the small house churches all first-century Christians participated in—helping people separate good and wise actions (for example) from bad and unwise actions plays a crucial role. We are to help those with whom we are close and about whom we have some intimate knowledge to discern matters in their lives. In love, we are to offer feedback and even confront one another if necessary in order to help each other grow to be conformed to the image of Jesus Christ.

What is more, as disciples live in union with God through Christ Jesus, they are empowered to distinguish between life that manifests reconciliation with God and life that manifests alienation from God. They are enabled to discern the difference between living in the knowledge of good and evil and living in love. They are freed to walk in the Spirit, not in the flesh, and to know the difference between the two. And, in appropriate contexts, they will be led by God to proclaim this distinction as a means of freeing people enslaved to forbidden wisdom. This is essentially what Jesus did when he confronted the Pharisees (see chapter 11).[1]

However, this sort of discernment and loving feedback is obviously not what Jesus is referring to in Matthew 7, for this loving type of *krino* is commanded, while the type of judgment Jesus is speaking about is forbidden. What is the difference between the two? Most fundamentally, the judgment Jesus prohibits is not about distinguishing between good and bad behaviors or between life in union with God versus life in separation from God—it is about *separating people*. "Judgment passed on another man," Bonhoeffer wrote, "always presupposes disunion with him; it is an obstacle to action."[2]

More specifically, the one doing the judging is separating himself or herself from and placing himself or herself above the one being judged. The judgment Jesus prohibits is not about ascribing worth to others by helping them be free from things in their lives that suppress their worth. It's about trying to experience worth *for oneself* by *detracting* it from others. It is not about noticing the difference between good and evil and giving feedback out of love. It's about eating from the Tree of the Knowledge of Good and Evil to get life.

This type of judgment is antithetical to fulfilling the command of God to love. As Bonhoeffer put it, "When we judge other people we confront them in a spirit of detachment, observing and reflecting as it were from the outside. But love has neither time nor opportunity for this. If we love, we can never observe the other person with detachment, for he is always and at every moment a living claim to our love and service."[3]

The only conclusion about people God allows us and commands us to embrace is the one given to us on Calvary: People have unsurpassable worth because Jesus died for them. The judgment that Jesus prohibits is sin precisely because it goes beyond what God allows, violates what God commands, and therefore transgresses the proper boundary between us and God. This judgment enthrones the judging person as the center around which others revolve and causes the judge to parasitically feed off the worth of the one he or she judges. Every judgment of this sort repeats the original rebellion of Genesis 3. And every judgment blocks the flow of God's love through us, for we cannot *ascribe* worth to another while we are *detracting* worth from him or her in our thoughts, words, or deeds.

While we are able to assess the healthy and unhealthy impact of behaviors, and while it is in certain contexts appropriate to share our assessment with others, as we have said, only God can fully know a person's heart. Only the omniscient God can know the innumerable physical, social, mental, and spiritual variables that have played a role in shaping people to be who they are. Hence, only God can know the extent to which people choose their courses of action out of the center of their morally responsible freedom and the extent to which their behavior is the result of influences outside of their control. Only God knows the complete story of a person's life; hence, only God can accurately judge that person.

Standing in the Place of God

When finite humans draw conclusions about people other than the one God commands us to embrace (that people have unsurpassable worth because Jesus died for them), we are rebelling against God by acting as though we are God. We are living out the serpent's deception: "You will be like God, knowing good and evil" (Gen. 3:5). The point is poignantly illustrated in the life of Joseph.

Because of their jealousy, Joseph's brothers turned against him and sold him into slavery. As a result, Joseph was separated from his father, who loved him, and was unjustly imprisoned in Egypt while being forced to work as a slave for many years. Later, when God had raised up Joseph to a high-ranking political position within the Egyptian government, his traitorous brothers begged him for food, for there was a famine throughout the land.

The brothers were understandably concerned that Joseph would seek retaliation for their harsh treatment of him. They would have considered Joseph gracious and forgiving if he simply spared their lives and made them all slaves (Gen. 50:15–18). But Joseph went far beyond this. He said to his terrified brothers,

> Do not be afraid! *Am I in the place of God?* Even though you intended to do harm to me, God intended it for good, in order to preserve a numerous people, as he is doing today. So have no fear; I myself will provide for you and your little ones.
>
> Genesis 50:19–21, emphasis added

Despite the cruel treatment he had received from his brothers, Joseph refused to stand in the place of God and condemn them. Instead, with eyes of love he hid their sin (1 Peter 4:8) and directed their attention to how God used it to further his own divine purposes.

When we judge others negatively, we stand in the place of God. We leave the proper domain given to us, with its vocational description to be God-like in how we love, and move to the center to carry out a job that belongs only to the One who rightfully occupies the center. We eat of the fruit of the Tree of the Knowledge of Good and Evil and thus do not love.

Jesus commands us not to violate the prohibition at the center of life. Surrendering all judgment to God, we are to look past people's sins. We are to believe and hope for the best in others (1 Cor. 13:7). In fact, when the sin is against us, our focus should be on how God can creatively use this offense to further his good purposes for our lives, just as Joseph did.

Tree Trunks and Dust Particles

We cannot judge others because it is not our place as humans to function as the center and judge of other people. But we also cannot judge others because we ourselves are sinners who deserve judgment. If we don't want to be judged, Jesus says, we must not judge. The measure of the judgment we give is the measure with which we shall be judged. When we eat of the forbidden tree, we are judged by the forbidden tree. "The sword wherewith they judge their brethren will fall upon their own heads," Bonhoeffer wrote. "Instead of cutting themselves off from their brother as the just from the unjust, they find themselves cut off from Jesus."[4]

This is why human judgments are always hypocritical. The act of judging others subjects us to the same judgment we apply to them. The hypocrisy of our judgment is manifested in the fact that it is always selective and self-serving, as we noted earlier. Our knowledge of good and evil is always bent in our favor. Because we are trying to fill the vacuum in our spirit with our judgments, we amplify the sins of others while minimizing our own sins.

In Matthew 7, however, Jesus teaches us to do the exact opposite. We should consider our own sins to be *logs* and other people's sins to be *specks!* The picture of people with tree trunks sticking out of their eyes looking for dust particles in other people's eyes is absolutely ludicrous—and that is the point. We are finite, sinful human beings, and as such, we have no business setting ourselves up as the moral police of others, acting as though we know the state of other people's hearts and concluding that we are in any way superior to them. While we can discern the impact of behavior, the only conclusion we are allowed to know about a person's heart is that he or she has infinite worth before God.

Now it may sometimes happen that the destructive impact of a person's behavior has to be stopped out of love for the person and for those he or she would harm. But we cannot move beyond this intervention to a judgment about the person. For our own sake, the Lord forbids us to draw conclusions about others. This is God's job. Our one and only job is to ascribe unsurpassable worth to them, however destructive their sin may be. To keep us on the right track, the Lord instructs us to see their sin, whatever it may be, as a mere dust particle.

If one struggles in this area, it may help to imagine a life-story that puts a person's sin in a context in which it is rendered into a dust particle, even when it's destructive and must be stopped. Perhaps the person was abandoned or abused as a child. Perhaps the person has a brain defect that causes sociopathic behavior. Perhaps the person has never been loved or was psychologically damaged by other means. Perhaps, along with all this, he or she is undergoing terrible demonic attacks. Unless we have taken the time to incarnate ourselves into the person's life, we cannot know. And even when we know his or her story intimately, there is still much we cannot know.

What we can know is that we have tree trunks in our own eyes that keep us from seeing accurately, so we must, on the authority of Jesus Christ, view the person's sin as mere dust particles in comparison to our own. And we must do so while ascribing to him or her the unsurpassable worth Christ ascribes to us.

Giving and Receiving Judgment

In Matthew 7 Jesus is doing nothing less than contrasting two mutually exclusive ways of living. We either live in love, or we live in judgment.[5] The extent to which we do one is the extent to which we do not do the other. If we eat of the Tree of the Knowledge of Good and Evil, then we are judged by the Tree of the Knowledge of Good and Evil. If we stand in judgment and do not forgive, we ourselves will be judged and not forgiven (Matt. 6:14–15). If we do not show mercy, we will not be given mercy (James 2:13). If we condemn others, we will stand condemned (Luke 6:37). "If I . . . subject [a person] to human judgment," Bonhoeffer wrote, "I bring God's judgment upon my head, for I then do not live any more on and out of the grace of Jesus Christ, but out of my knowledge of good and evil which I hold on to."[6]

Conversely, if we die to ourselves as center and thus die to ourselves as judge, we will receive the life of one who will never be judged. If we accept Christ's reconciling act and simply have faith that God is who he says he is in Christ, that we are who God says we are in Christ, and that all others are who God says they are in Christ—in other words, if we simply abide in love—then, in fact, *all we are is defined in Christ*. In Christ there is no judgment (Rom. 8:1), for we have entirely opted out of the judgment game created when we lost Paradise. Recognizing that we can only lose in this game, for we are ourselves sinners, we no longer try to get life by critically evaluating ourselves or others before God. We simply receive, live in, and give the love and mercy of God that has triumphed over judgment (James 2:13).

"The source of the disciple's life lies exclusively in his fellowship with Jesus Christ," Bonhoeffer wrote. And he continued,

"He possesses his righteousness only within that association, never outside it. That is why his righteousness can never become an objective criterion to be applied at will. He is a disciple not because he possesses such a new standard, but only because of Jesus Christ, the Mediator and very Son of God."[7]

Love and judgment represent two antithetical ways of living. We either live out of union with God, and thus with our fellow sisters and brothers, or we live out of ourselves as center, in separation from our sisters and brothers. We either live by God's righteousness or by our own.[8] Which way we live ultimately comes down to this decision: Shall we eat of the Tree of the Knowledge of Good and Evil or not? Shall we live in grateful dependence on God or not? Shall we let God be judge, or shall *we* try to be judge? Shall we live in God's mercy and thus give God's mercy, or shall we pass judgment as though we were God and thus live under God's judgment? In short, shall we let God be God and honor the boundary he set between us, or shall we try to stand in the place of God?

Living in the garden in which God intends us to live is determined by our response to this central question. The decision we make at the core of our being either loops us into a cycle of God's eternal love, in which case we find we don't need to judge, for we are full of life from God; or we get looped into a cycle of our emptiness, in which case we can't help but judge, for we are always trying to fill the vacuum created by our lack of life from God. If we don't want to be judged, the only thing we can do is repent of our judgment and helplessly and joyfully receive the nonjudging mercy and love he has given us in Christ. It is only if we abide in love and allow God's love to be perfected in us that we can "have boldness on the day of judgment" (1 John 4:17).

Romans 2:1–4

You have no excuse, whoever you are, when you judge others; for in passing judgment on another you condemn yourself, because you, the judge, are doing the very same things. You say, "We know that God's judgment on those who do such things is in accordance with truth." Do you imagine, whoever you are, that when you judge those who do such things and yet do them yourself, you will escape the judgment of God? Or do you despise the riches of his kindness and forbearance and patience? Do you not realize that God's kindness is meant to lead you to repentance?

The central point of Romans 1–2 is that humans all have enough revelation of God to live right with God, *but none of us do*. Hence, when any of us set ourselves up as judge of others, we bring judgment upon ourselves, for we ourselves are guilty. Whoever says he or she is not guilty of sin is a liar (1 John 1:10). No one measures up favorably against the standard of God's perfection revealed in creation (Matt. 5:48). No one has had every one of his or her actions flow out of faith in God. Yet Paul said that "whatever does not proceed from faith is sin" (Rom. 14:24). No one has altogether avoided careless thoughts and words. Yet Jesus says each of us will give an account of these on the day of judgment (Matt. 12:36). Everyone has at some point said, or at least thought, of someone in slanderous terms. Yet Jesus says our doing so makes us "liable to the hell of fire" (Matt. 5:22). Few have completely avoided having lust in their hearts, even if they've refrained from actual fornication or adultery. But Jesus teaches that the former is as much a violation of God's ideal as the latter (Matt. 5:27–28). All of us have done these kinds of things, and much more.

Paul summed up the dire state of humans before God apart from Christ by saying, "There is no one who is righteous, not even one; there is no one who has understanding, there is no one who seeks God. All have turned aside, together they have become worthless. . . . All have sinned and fallen short of the glory of God" (Rom. 3:10–12, 23). Though we rarely evaluate ourselves this harshly, for we measure ourselves by self-serving standards according to a forbidden knowledge we were never meant to have, the fact of the matter is that on our own, apart from Christ, we are all condemned.

We are thus in no position to judge others. It is so easy for believers to justify their judgment of others with the reassurance, "We know that God's judgment on those who do such things is in accordance with truth" (Rom. 2:2). But this slogan, according to Paul, offers no assurance because it cuts both ways. Precisely because God's judgment is "in accordance with truth," it stands over *us* as much as *them*. In point of fact, our judgment is never really "in accordance with truth," for we don't know the whole truth of any person's story, and we are self-serving sinners who are trying to scrape up a morsel of worth by placing ourselves above others. God's judgment is true, but for just this reason we can never identify *our* judgment with *God's*. Indeed, as finite and fallen human beings, we have no business entertaining judgment over others in the first place.

When we place ourselves in the center instead of confessing our own sin and receiving mercy and life from the One who is the center, we bring condemnation on ourselves. In the act of judging, we are despising the riches of God's "kindness and forbearance and patience" (Rom. 2:4), for we are acting as though we don't need it. This, Paul warns, is disastrous. "In passing judgment on another you condemn yourself" (Rom. 2:1). As Jesus said, the measure of judgment we give is the measure of judgment we will receive. The strong words of Paul, like the strong words of Jesus, are spoken in love to keep us respecting the "No Trespassing" sign that signifies the boundary between us and God. God is God; we are not. God is all holy; we are not. God is judge; we are not.

Against all this, Paul wanted us to "realize that God's kindness is meant to lead [us] to repentance" (Rom. 2:4). Rather than being concerned with playing God over others, we must be concerned only with repenting before God for our own sins. Our sins should be to us tree trunks we confess and seek to get rid of, while other people's sins should be to us dust particles we seek to hide with love.

Bonhoeffer expressed the perspective of the true penitent when he wrote:

> Wherever there is still a weighing up and calculation of guilt, there the sterile morality of self-justification usurps the place of confession of guilt. . . . What does it matter to you whether others are guilty too? I can excuse any sin of another, but my own sin alone remains guilt which I can never excuse. It is not a morbidly egotistical distortion of reality, but it is the essential character of a genuine confession of guilt that it is incapable of apportioning blame and pleading a case, but is rather the acknowledgement of one's own sin of Adam.[9]

To live with an accurate, Christ-centered assessment of oneself is to live with the awareness that each of us is in desperate need of God's mercy and is thus obligated to extend mercy to all others. It is thus to live with the awareness that none of us is in a position to weigh the sin and calculate the guilt of others. The biblical warnings about judgment are God's gracious and stern way of keeping us mindful of our true situation and thus mindful of what is and is not our proper duty. We are called to walk in merciful love, not judgment.

Romans 14

Who are you to pass judgment on servants of another? It is before their own lord that they stand or fall. And they will be upheld, for the Lord is able to make them stand. . . . Why do you pass judgment on your brother or sister? Or you, why do you despise your brother or sister? For we will all stand before the judgment seat of God. . . . So then, each of us will be accountable to God. Let us therefore no longer pass judgment on one another, but resolve instead never to put a stumbling block or hindrance in the way of another. . . . The faith that you have, have as your own conviction before God. Blessed are those who have no reason to condemn themselves because of what they approve. But those who have doubts are condemned if they eat, because they do not act from faith; for whatever does not proceed from faith is sin.

Romans 14:4, 10, 12–13, 22–23

The Strong and the Weak

In this chapter Paul addressed how Christians were to live in harmony with one another when they had differing ethical convictions. Some Christians were vegetarians; others thought it was okay to eat meat (Rom. 14:2, 21). Some thought it fine to eat meat that had been dedicated to idols, while others deemed this sinful (1 Cor. 8:4–11). Some thought they should abstain from all alcohol; others thought it okay to drink freely (Rom. 14:21). Some thought certain days were special holy days; others thought every day was alike (Rom. 14:5). How are Christians to live in harmony when they hold these differing convictions?

It was a question Paul frequently had to confront in his new congregations (Rom. 14; 1 Cor. 8; Col. 2:16–23). It is certainly a question that is relevant today.

Paul's teaching, in a nutshell, is that Christians should act in love, not in judgment. Those who have a robust faith (with whom Paul himself clearly sides, cf. Rom. 14:2, 14; 1 Cor. 8:4–13, 10:25–30) and thus have no conviction about eating meat, drinking wine, or not honoring special days, should not despise their weaker sisters and brothers by arrogantly flaunting their freedom before them. Paul's position was that Christians are in fact free on matters such as these. But we must live out our liberty on such matters in love (Gal. 5:13; cf. Rom. 14:19–21; 1 Cor. 8:1–3, 9).

This means that those with a robust faith must be willing to forgo privileges that may cause others with whom they are in relationship to stumble. "If your brother or sister is being injured by what you eat, you are no longer walking in love" (Rom. 14:15).[10] When Christians refuse to do this, they are in effect judging those who don't share their freedom rather than loving them. In their freedom they are standing over and despising those who don't yet enjoy their freedom.

Conversely, Paul tried to bring the weak along in their faith by showing them that their convictions are personal, not universal. They must follow their conscience without judging others who don't share their convictions. It is okay to hold to stricter convictions on matters as an expression of their faith in Christ, Paul was saying, but they must not *equate* their stricter convictions with faith in Christ and thus judge others who don't share them.

Paul's teaching, we see, has both an individual and communal application. Individually, Paul sees a person's own faith as the ultimate criteria for whether he or she should eat meat, drink alcohol, or engage in certain activities. There is no absolute right or wrong on these matters. Each person must hold to his or her own faith "as your own conviction before God" (Rom. 14:22). People are blessed if they have no pain of conscience about a particular matter, Paul said. But they condemn themselves if they have doubts and yet engage in an activity, for "they do not act from faith; for whatever does not proceed from faith is sin" (Rom. 14:23).

The conclusion Paul leads us to is that each believer should focus on his or her own relationship with God. Rather than being concerned with whether others are walking in faith, we each should be concerned with whether we ourselves are walking in faith. At the same time, as an aspect of our own concern with walking in faith, we must be aware that we do not live or die to ourselves (Rom. 14:7). Our attention to our own walk includes a concern for others, not in terms of evaluating them, but in terms of whether we express love to them in our walk.

Answering to One's Own Master

Just as important as the question of whether we are individually acting out of faith on a particular issue is the question of whether we are acting out of love for others on a particular issue. Just because I can eat meat or drink alcohol in faith does not mean that I should do it, for it may not be a loving thing to do as I live in relationship with another for whom this freedom is a possible stumbling block.

Both aspects of Paul's teaching are captured in saying that we are to live in love, not judgment. Our one concern should be to live in faith and to act in love. Indeed, the only thing that matters within the Christian community is "faith working through love" (Gal. 5:6). All judgment is to be left to God.

Paul emphasized this point by depicting each person's relationship with God as the relationship between a servant and master. No one has the right to judge another person's servant, Paul said, for that servant answers only to his or her own master. "Who are you to pass judgment on servants of another?" Paul asked. "It is before their own lord that they stand or fall" (Rom. 14:4).

We are thus to regard each person's relationship to God as *sui generis* (literally "a unique genre," or "one of a kind"). It is as though each person has his or her own God before whom he or she stands. Our task in relationship to others is to simply trust that the Lord is working in their lives and that God is able to uphold them and "make them stand" before him, on the terms he stipulates (Rom. 14:4). With the awareness that "we will all stand before the judgment seat of God," we are to be concerned only with the fact that we ourselves "will be accountable to God" (Rom. 14:10, 12).

Hence, whether Paul would classify us as among the strong or the weak, we are to "no longer pass judgment on one another" (Rom. 14:13). When we judge each other, we deflect our attention away from our one task of walking before our Lord and instead act as though *we* are the Lord. In judging we act as though we are the other person's master and thus as though he or she has to answer to *us*. We are attempting to stand in the place of God.

Indeed, even if we refrain from judging others but yet judge ourselves in ways that are contrary to God's judgment at Calvary, we are still playing God. This is why Paul said that so far was he from worrying about being judged by others, he didn't even judge himself (1 Cor. 4:3). All judgment, including self-judgment, must be surrendered to the One who is the only judge of the earth.

Forgoing Privileges While Standing Firm

Paul's instruction to stronger Christians not to flaunt their freedom before weaker Christians raises an interesting question. How could Paul tell the Corinthians that the strong must be willing to alter their behavior for the weak while he told the Galatians to stand firm against altering their behavior for the sake of others (Gal. 5:1–12)? Indeed, he told the Christians at Colossae, "Do not let anyone condemn you in matters of food and drink or of observing festivals, new moons, or Sabbaths. These are only a shadow of what is to come, but the substance belongs to Christ" (Col. 2:16–17).

The answer highlights an important aspect of Paul's teaching on love and judgment. At Galatia and Colossae, certain teachers were trying to require Christians to engage in or abstain from certain activities *as a means of improving their standing before God*. These were not merely personal convictions that certain weak Christians had but doctrines with which certain teachers were burdening Christians, as though simple faith in the work of Christ was not enough to acquire everything we need before God. They were trying to force Christians to supplement their *relationship with* Christ with a *religion about* Christ.

There is a world of difference between abstaining from drink or honoring a day as holy out of love so as not to injure a sister or brother in Christ and doing so as an effort to get something you think you don't already have in Christ. To do the latter is to deny the total sufficiency of Christ's work, to equate faith with the behavior, to eat once again from the Tree of the Knowledge of Good and Evil, and thus to live once again out of emptiness rather than fullness. It is to submit once again to the bondage from which Christ came to free us.

As one who was responsible for these fledgling congregations, Paul had no patience whatsoever with this mindset. Indeed, as was the case with Jesus, Paul's harshest words were reserved for teachers who harmed people by bringing them into this sort of religious idolatry and demonic bondage (e.g., Gal. 1:6–9; 5:1–4, 12; 1 Tim. 4:1–3). Out of love for those being harmed by this teaching, Paul, like Jesus, attempted to put a stop to such teachings.

James 4:11–12

> Do not speak evil against one another, brothers and sisters. Whoever speaks evil against another or judges another, speaks evil against the law and judges the law; but if you judge the law, you are not a doer of the law but a judge. There is one lawgiver and judge who is able to save and to destroy. So who, then, are you to judge your neighbor?

The Bible in general, and the New Testament in particular, places a great deal of emphasis on how we use our words. Words can be a tremendous vehicle of benefiting or harming others. Hence, sins of the mouth (e.g., gossip, slander, reviling) are frequently mentioned in the New Testament's various lists of sins, often in the same context as things such as murder and adultery (e.g., Matt. 15:19; Rom. 1:29–30; 1 Cor. 6:10; 2 Cor. 12:20; Col. 3:8; 1 Peter 2:1).

Of all biblical authors, James has the most to say about the right and wrong use of the tongue, which he likens to the small rudder that guides the whole ship. Control it, and you can control the whole body (James 3:1–4). Conversely, if you cannot control it, the tongue is like a match in a dry forest. Though it is extremely small in comparison, it can nevertheless burn down the entire forest (James 3:5).

The tongue, then, is extremely powerful. For with it, James said, "we bless the Lord and Father, and with it we curse those who are made in the likeness of God. From the same mouth come blessing and cursing." In this light, James's instruction to his audience is simple: "My brothers and sisters, this ought not to be so" (James 3:9–10).

When we speak evil against others, we are judging them. Even more seriously, when we speak evil against others, we are speaking evil against the law and thus judging the law. Consequently, we are "not a doer of the law but a judge" (James 4:11). When we judge others, we are acting as though we were the law to which the others we are judging are accountable.

In judging others, therefore, we are judging as inadequate the law and the God who gives it. In Paul's words, we are denying that "it is before their own lord that they stand or fall." And we are not trusting that "they will be upheld, for the Lord is able to make them stand" (Rom. 14:4). When we judge others we are presuming to help God fix people, as though we had the power and wisdom to do this, and as though God needed our help. Most fundamentally, when we judge others we are trying to *fix ourselves* by desperately filling the vacuum in our lives with a momentary sense of ethical superiority—the vacuum that our standing in the center as judge produced!

This is why when we judge others, and thus judge the law, we are not a "doer of the law." Individually, our only task is to live in union with God. Our only concern should thus be to do his will at all times, in all places, to all people. The "doer" of the law, wrote Bonhoeffer, is

> the man who simply knows of no other possible attitude to the word of God when he has heard it than to do it, who therefore continues to concern himself strictly with the word itself and does not derive from it a knowledge for himself on the basis of which he might become the judge of his brother, of himself, and eventually also a judge of the word of God.[11]

Whatever the particulars of God's Word for us may be in any particular situation, it is most fundamentally to express love out of a fullness of the love we have received. "The one who loves another has fulfilled the law" (Rom. 13:8).

We see, then, that one cannot simultaneously do the law and judge the law. Bonhoeffer again made the point forcefully:

> There are two possible attitudes to the law: judgment and action. The two are mutually exclusive. The man who judges envisages the law as a criterion which he applies to others, and he envisages himself as being responsible for the execution of the law. He forgets that there is only one lawgiver and judge "who is able to save and to destroy" (James 4:12). If a man employs his knowledge of the law in accusing or condemning his brother, then in truth he accuses and condemns the law itself, for he mistrusts it and doubts that it possesses the power of the living word of God to establish itself and to take effect by itself.[12]

When we judge others for disobeying the law, we ourselves disobey the law, for we do not love like the law commands. Our focus shifts off our obligation to carry out God's will and off the tree trunks we have in our own eyes and instead attends to dust particles in other people's eyes that we assess on the basis of our self-serving knowledge of good and evil.

This, in fact, is precisely why those involved in religious idolatry engage in judgmentalism so intently. It is a central aspect of their strategy for getting life. If we live in the knowledge of the forbidden fruit, our awareness of the tree trunks in our own eyes diminishes our sense of worth. Since we are not living by grace, however, acquiring and protecting a sense of worth by our actions is the driving force in our lives. Judging others helps us avoid judging ourselves and thus having our worth diminished. If we are looking for dust particles in other people, we don't have to notice our own tree trunks. Indeed, far from having our worth diminished, our worth is fed as we parasitically suck worth out of those we judge to ascribe worth to ourselves.

This, again, is the opposite of love and the opposite of doing God's will. In judging, we are not doing the one thing the Lord requires of us, for we are trying to do the one thing the Lord reserves for himself and forbids for us. We are thrusting ourselves into the center, violating the proper boundary between us and God, and eating of the Tree of the Knowledge of Good and Evil instead of simply walking with God in love within the perimeters of the garden he set up for us.

Hence, James reminds us, "There is one lawgiver and judge who is able to save and to destroy. So who, then, are you to judge your neighbor?" (James 4:12). Our job is to love our neighbors and leave all judgment to God. We are, therefore, never to speak evil of them (cf. Titus 3:2). Indeed, we are never to *think* evil of them regardless of their treatment of us, regardless of their lifestyle, regardless of their religious beliefs, regardless of their past or present sin. We are to know them only as we ourselves are known and love them as we ourselves are loved—namely, as desperate sinners for whom Christ died. And if they do not know or accept this yet, our Christ-like, self-sacrificial love becomes the means by which God works to influence them to do so. For he desires all to participate in the life and love of the triune fellowship.

Conclusion

Jesus came not to condemn the world but to save the world by loving it despite the fact that it deserved condemnation (John 3:17; 12:47). While Jesus certainly confronted religious teachers who were harming others (see chapter 11), he judged no one (John 8:15). His loving presence brought judgment on those who rejected him (John 9:39), but in his humanity he left the application of this judgment to his Father (John 12:48). In Jesus' view, as in the view of the authors of the New Testament, God alone is judge, for he alone knows the true hearts of people (John 8:50; Rom. 2:16; 2 Tim. 4:8; Heb. 10:30; 12:23; James 4:12). No human knows this, even about himself. Hence, Paul said, "I do not even judge myself" (1 Cor. 4:3). No human, not even Jesus, can "pronounce judgment before the time, before the Lord comes, who will bring to light the things now hidden in darkness and will disclose the purposes of the heart" (1 Cor. 4:5).

The one thing we are created to do, saved to do, and commissioned to do is love. And this, for finite human beings, is the opposite of judgment. We are commanded to embrace all people in love, not separate ourselves from them and place ourselves above them. This is why God, out of his love for us, warned us in the beginning to refrain from eating from the forbidden tree and why this warning is repeated throughout the New Testament.

Part 3

The Lie
and the Curse

chapter 7

The Lie about God

The serpent said to the woman, "You will not die; for God knows that when you eat of it your eyes will be opened, and you will be like God, knowing good and evil."

Genesis 3:4–5

Shall a faultfinder contend with the Almighty? . . . Will you condemn me that you may be justified?

Job 40:2, 8

God sides with the real man and with the real world against all their accusers. Together with men and with the world He comes before the judges, so that the judges are now made the accused.

Dietrich Bonhoeffer

The path that leads to our eating from the forbidden tree is deception. The Accuser lures us to eat of the Tree of the Knowledge of Good and Evil and become judges by deceptively luring us into his judgments. In the Genesis narrative, and in all of life, the foundational judgments that transform us into judges are about God and ourselves. In this chapter we shall discuss our judgment about God, and in the next chapter we shall discuss our judgment about ourselves.

The First Judgment: God Isn't a Reliable Source

An Untrustworthy God

In the Genesis narrative the serpent is described simply as the wisest creature the Lord God made (3:1). However, later revelation identifies him as Satan (2 Cor. 11:3), the "tempter" (1 Thess. 3:5), "adversary" (1 Tim. 5:14; 1 Peter 5:8), and "accuser" (Rev. 12:10) who comes to "steal and kill and destroy" (John 10:10; cf. 1 Peter 5:8). However we understand this, it is indisputable that what the serpent was up to in this passage was killing, stealing, and destroying the harmony of Adam and Eve's relationship with God.[1] He intended to extinguish the flow of God's love to, in, and through the humans God had created.

The method he used was judgment, for when carried out by anyone other than God, as we have seen, judgment destroys trust and squelches love. The Accuser's goal was to introduce a judgment about God that, if believed, would quickly transform creatures of love into creatures of judgment.

Hence, the serpent began with an accusation about God.

> He said to the woman, "Did God say, 'You shall not eat from any tree in the garden'?" . . . The serpent said to the woman, "You will not die; for God knows that when you eat of it your eyes will be opened, and you will be like God, knowing good and evil."
>
> Genesis 3:1, 4–5

The serpent planted a seed of mistrust in the mind of the innocent woman. He accused God of being untrustworthy. Indeed, the serpent gave Adam and Eve a picture of a god who didn't have Adam and Eve's best interest in mind. It was a picture of a god who, far from being capable of providing Adam and Eve with all they need, was himself needy.[2]

Even worse, the serpent implied that God himself only acquired his privileged position by eating of the Tree of the Knowledge of Good and Evil. This is why God now had to secure his position by keeping others from eating of the same tree. God's motive in forbidding the tree, therefore, was not love; it was to protect his own unique status. The serpent presented himself as letting Adam and Eve in on the divine secret. He was going to help Adam and Eve have their eyes opened. If they would eat from this tree, they would attain the same status as Yahweh.

In the context of the Genesis narrative, the story of Adam and Eve's action on the basis of the lie they believed is tragic because it did not have to happen. The Genesis account presupposes that Adam and Eve possessed the power of choice. If their relationship with God was to be *loving* and *obedient*, it could not be otherwise, for love and obedience require choice.[3] Nothing in the passage suggests their rebellion was divinely planned or fated.

Nor does the text suggest that God in any sense set them up to fall by tempting them with an evil tree they had to resist. The passage does not depict the forbidden tree in the middle of the garden as intrinsically evil. It was simply forbidden. It was, as we have said, simply the "No Trespassing" sign that specified the proper boundary between humans and God.[4] It stipulated that we were to live with the awareness that we are not God and that our fullness of life depends on leaving to God what properly belongs to God. But God wanted us to obey this sign out of love and thus as an act of our free will.

Unfortunately, Adam and Eve willfully succumbed to the craftiness of the serpent. They yielded to the lie and agreed with its accusation against God. And the moment they did this, the life-giving flow of love from God began to be blocked. Judgment always severs union.

The Misguided Homing Device

Adam and Eve's story is not just a "once upon a time" story; it is also the story of every human being. The beginning of all sin—the origin of all that is unloving—is a judgment about God. We embrace a picture of God that is less loving, less beautiful, less full of life, less gracious, and less glorious than the true God really is. From this, everything that attaches to sin, everything that characterizes life "in Adam" (1 Cor. 15:22) and life in "the flesh" (Rom. 7:5; 8:4–8) follows. When our picture of God is distorted, we can no longer trust God to be the source of our life. It is impossible to live in God's love if we don't believe God *is* love.

This deceptive picture of God in turn leads to sinful, idolatrous behavior. As we have seen, we are created with a nonnegotiable need for the love, worth, significance, and companionship that only the true God can provide. We are created to have the perfect, triune love (that God is) poured into us and flow through us. This is the abundant life we were created to enjoy and which the Enemy wants to steal and destroy (John 10:10). If the deceiving Accuser is successful in distorting our mental picture of God so that God appears incapable or unwilling to give us life, we invariably look elsewhere to find life, and the abundant life God alone can give us is lost.

We might say that, under the power of a judgment about God, the need-based "homing device" that was intended to drive us to God now drives us to try to fill the God-shaped vacuum in our hearts with other things. Like a starving man imprisoned in a dungeon for whom insects begin to look tantalizing after a while, our hunger for God begins to give other things the illusory appearance of being viable candidates for filling the hole in our soul.

Believing the serpent's lie, Eve "saw that the tree was good for food, and that it was a delight to the eyes, and that the tree was to be desired to make one wise" (Gen. 3:6). Undoubtedly the tree would not have seemed so desirable if Eve had been viewing things accurately. If she had remained yielded to God rather than believing the serpent's accusation about God, the prospect of disobeying God and eating from the forbidden tree—of going beyond the "No Trespassing" sign—would not have been appealing to her. If she had viewed the tree with a full soul rather than a hungry one, she wouldn't have seen it as "good for food," a "delight to the eyes," and "desired to make one wise" (Gen. 3:6). It was only because she was seeing the tree through the filter of her judgment and consequent emptiness that she saw something this life-destroying as life-supplying. In her new perception, violating God's "No Trespassing" sign seemed to offer her something she did not have.

Life "in Adam"

The lie about God that leads to emptiness, which in turn leads to the illusion that the world is viable "soul food," constitutes life "in Adam." The eyes that see aspects of the world as a desirable source of life are the eyes of the "mindset of the flesh," which Paul says is at war with God (Rom. 8:6–7). In our fallen state, we no longer seek union with the loving God as our source of life. We rather live life hungry, seeking what we judge to be *good* for us, avoiding what we judge to be *evil* for us, always futilely believing that if we just had more of the good and less of the evil we would become full. The hunger our disunity with God creates makes people and things in our environment seem like viable food for the soul. Hence, the world becomes a stage filled with surrogate gods that look appealing, and our lives become a perpetual quest to get life from them.

Whereas God intends us to live "in Christ," out of a fullness we freely receive from him, our judgment about God leads us to live "in Adam," out of an emptiness we are forever trying to fill. In other words, the fall (our disunion with God) transitions a life of *abundance* and *celebration* into a life of *hunger* and *desperation*. The natural man is in effect lowered to the level of the animal kingdom, perpetually trying to feed his hunger from his environment, whether that be other people or things. Our lives become lives of assessing good and evil, based on our idolatrous strategy for getting life, rather than lives lived in Christ out of the fullness of God's love.

Everything about life in Adam is rooted in and follows from believing a lie about who God is. Every futile, idolatrous, hunger-driven quest presupposes a false view of reality. It is a lie about what is real, what life is ultimately all about, who we are, and what constitutes "the good life." And at the foundation is an accusing judgment about God and thus an unwillingness to trust that God desires and is able to supply what it is we are questing after.

The Truth: God Is Revealed in Jesus Christ

Uncovering the True God

The foundation of everything that is sin and that blocks love is a false picture of God. Conversely, a true picture of God is the foundation of everything that is life-giving and that promotes love. This is why the revelation of God in Jesus Christ is the absolute centerpiece of God's plan of salvation and thus the center of the biblical witness. If we are to grow in love, Christ must be the central focus of all our thinking and living.

Christ is *the truth* that dispels all lies. Indeed, the root of the word *truth* in Greek (*alethia*) means "not covered." The serpent hid the true God under a deceptive judgmental cloak that has concealed the true God from the minds and hearts of people throughout the ages (2 Cor. 4:4). But by becoming a man and dying on the cross, Jesus removes this cloak and uncovers the real God for us. He *is* the "way, and the *truth*, and the life" (John 14:6, emphasis added). So too, the Holy Spirit is called "the Spirit of truth" because, while Jesus discloses the Father to us, the Holy Spirit enables us to recognize this by opening up our hearts and minds (John 14:17; 15:26; 16:18).

The Central Revelation

The centrality of Christ for our understanding of God cannot be overemphasized. He is the one and only image and Word of God (Col. 1:15; cf. John 1:1; 2 Cor. 4:4–6). On Jesus' own authority, we may trust that seeing him is seeing the Father. There is no place else we can or should look to know what God is like (John 14:7–10). In the words of St. Irenaeus of the second century, Jesus is the "visible of the Father."[5] While "no one has ever seen God," Jesus, who is "God the only Son" and is "close to the Father's heart," has "made him known" (John 1:18). The invisible God is made visible in an image and is spoken as a Word: Jesus Christ.

To be sure, God has been revealing himself in various ways throughout history to all people at all times, but with a particular focus on the Hebrew people through which God hoped to reach the world (Gen. 12:1–3; Isa. 42:1–7).[6] But to the extent that these revelations are authentic, they point to and find their definitive culmination in Jesus Christ. In the words of the author of Hebrews,

> Long ago God spoke to our ancestors in many and various ways by the prophets, but in these last days he has spoken to us by a Son, whom he appointed heir of all things, through whom he

also created the worlds. He is the reflection of God's glory and the exact imprint of God's very being, and he sustains all things by his powerful word.

Hebrews 1:1–3

All previous revelations are surpassed by and find their completion in Jesus Christ. He alone is the reflection and exact imprint of God's very being. It is not as though Christ reveals one aspect of God that stands on an equal footing with previous revelations. He is the *focal point* of all revelation. He is the essence of the revelation given through Moses (John 5:46). He is the wisdom of God fully revealed (1 Cor. 1:24). The *"whole fullness* of deity dwells bodily" in him (Col. 2:9, emphasis added). Whereas previous revelations of God in Scripture, nature, and other religious traditions are partial, Christ is the full revelation of God. And while previous revelations are written, in Christ God is revealed *in bodily form*. He is the living, concrete, embodied picture of God.

The Supremacy of Christ and the Command to Love

We may draw a parallel between the position Christ has regarding God's revelation and the position love has regarding God's commands. We earlier argued that love is the only doctrine that we should hold in an "unbalanced" fashion, for no other commands or concerns can stand next to it in first place to qualify it (see chapter 2). This command is to be placed "above all" others (Col. 3:14; cf. 1 Cor. 13:1–4, 13). All other commands and concerns must be interpreted and lived out *in the light of this one*. We might now say something similar about the revelation of God in Jesus Christ.

The revelation of God in Christ ought not to be qualified by other previous or subsequent revelations, as though it shared its privileged platform with another revelation. Christ is "above all" in just the same way that the love commandment is "above all"—and for just the same reason. Christ is the preeminent revelation of God's unsurpassable love. Indeed, the revelation of God's unsurpassable love in Christ Jesus grounds the preeminence of the command to love.

This is the center and foundation of the gospel. Everything else revolves around this and is built upon it. All growth in the Christian life is predicated on it. Only to the extent that we resolve in our minds and hearts that *God looks like Jesus*—dying a God-forsaken death on the cross in order to open up the fellowship of the perfect, loving, triune community—can we make progress expressing God's love in our lives. As we fix our eyes on the glory of God revealed in the face of Jesus Christ, who is the image of God, we are transformed "into the same image from one degree of glory to another" (2 Cor. 3:18–4:6). As we focus on the One who is the perfect expression of God's love, we increasingly participate in this perfect love.

The Criteria for All Theology

Theology is thinking (*logos*) about God (*theos*). It is a good and necessary discipline, but only so long as it is centered on Christ. All of our speculation and debate about such things as God's character, power, and glory must be done with our focus on Jesus Christ—more specifically, on the decisive act by which he reveals God and redeems humanity, his death on the cross.

The definitive thing to be said about God's character is found here: *God dies for sinners on a God-forsaken cross.* The definitive thing to be said about God's power is found here: *God allows himself to be crucified on a cross for sinners.* And the definitive thing to be said about God's glory is found here: *God dies a horrifying, God-forsaken death upon the cross.* God's character, power, and glory are decisively revealed on the cross.

Though it is "foolishness" to the natural mind, the cross is the power and wisdom of God to all who believe (1 Cor. 1:18–24). If we entertain concepts of God's character, power, and glory that are inconsistent with what is revealed here, our thoughts are outside of Jesus Christ. Every thought about God, every mental picture we entertain about God, every single emotion that is "raised up against the knowledge of God" must be taken "captive to obey Christ" (2 Cor. 10:5).

The true God revealed in Jesus Christ is not at all what the natural mind would expect—it is "foolishness"—for our natural expectations are influenced by our experiences in a fallen world that is permeated with the foundational lie of the serpent. We create a god of our own designs by magnifying our own fallen conceptions of character, power, and glory. Consequently, sometimes God's character, power, and glory are presented in ways that don't even resemble Jesus Christ, even within the Christian tradition. We project onto the screen of heaven a cosmic Caesar, controlling the world through coercive power and intimidation rather than accepting God's definition of himself in the crucified Jesus Christ.[7] Such mental chimeras may inspire fear, but they do not transform us to become outrageous lovers.

The only hope we have of getting out of this fallen condition and walking in the ecstatic love of the triune God is to resolve that God's revelation in Christ is true, however much it may contradict our fallen, worldly expectations. When the deceptive veil over our mind is removed and we see the glory of God shining in the face of Jesus Christ (2 Cor. 3:16–4:6), and when we fix our eyes on Jesus (Heb. 12:2), we find a picture of God that could not possibly be more loving and beautiful. For here we find God going to the greatest extreme possible—suffering a God-forsaken, hellish death at the hands of the very creatures for whom he was dying! God pays the highest price and thus ascribes the highest worth to people who in and of themselves have no worth. This is the greatest expression of love imaginable, and it alone reveals the truth about who the eternal, triune God is. God is *this kind of love* (1 John 4:8; cf. 1 John 3:16; 4:9–10). If we harbor any other estimation about God, it will block the flow of the love that God is to us and through us.

If all this seems too good to be true, that is simply an indication that our thinking is moving in the right direction. If we're thinking accurately, it *should* seem "too good to be true." For the truth is that we can hardly begin to fathom the full depth of the love of the triune God.

Rooted and Grounded in Love

Paul prayed for the congregation of disciples at Ephesus,

I pray that, according to the riches of his glory, [God] may grant that you may be strengthened in your inner being with power through his Spirit, and that Christ may dwell in your hearts through faith, as you are being rooted and grounded in love.

Ephesians 3:16–17

Christ resides in us, and we reside in Christ by our trust that what God says about himself and us in the person of Jesus Christ is true. By faith we participate in the triune love of God. Paul's prayer is for this divine participation to be increasingly experienced as we are increasingly "rooted and grounded in love."

Through the work of the Spirit in our lives and through the discipline of our minds (Rom. 12:2), the roots of our lives must become firmly planted in the reality of God's love as revealed in Christ. Like the ground from which a tree's roots are nourished, God's love is the one source from which we are to drink and derive nourishment.

When we are empty, we are to drink the fullness of God's love. When we face temptation, we are to drink the strength of God's love. When we catch ourselves feeling superior, we are to drink the mercy of God's love, remembering that we ourselves are forgiven sinners. When we feel condemned, we are to drink the forgiveness of God's love. When we feel despair, we are to drink the hope of God's love. When we feel despondent, we are to drink the joy of God's love. When we feel apathetic, we are to drink the passion of God's love. And when we feel lifeless, we are to drink the abundant life that is God's love. It is all there in Christ. He is the truth and he is the life (John 14:6). We must be rooted in him and in him alone (cf. John 15:4–5).

God's love, as revealed in Christ, is also the source of our grounding, our stability, in life. Trees with deep roots bend when strong winds come, but they are not uprooted like trees with shallow roots. So too, our stability in life depends on our being firmly grounded in the reality of God's love as it is revealed in Christ. If our lives are grounded in idols from which we try to get life, we are building our house on sinking sand. But if our lives are grounded in Christ as "the source of [our] life" (1 Cor. 1:30), our house is built upon an immovable rock (Matt. 7:24–27).

This point is crucial, for we live in a world yet under the influence of the Accuser, who roams about as a lion seeking whom he may devour (1 Peter 5:8). He is continually accusing God before us, just as he is perpetually accusing us before God, ourselves, and each other. The Genesis narrative is replayed in our lives every day. If we are not rooted and grounded in God's love, we will invariably find ourselves unconsciously or consciously bringing God, and then ourselves and each other, before the tribunal of our own knowledge of good and evil. We will live in judgment, and the flow of love from God to us and through us will be suppressed.

Trusting God

In this fallen, Satan-oppressed world we live in, there will certainly be many occasions for us to doubt God. For this reason we must be rooted and grounded in God's love as revealed in Jesus Christ, and *in nothing else.*

We may see glimmers of the glory of God in the starry night, beautiful sunsets, and majestic mountains. But our view of God and our trust in him must not be rooted in such things, for the fallen world is also full of tornadoes, disease, famines, earthquakes, and the like. We may thank God for our health, financial blessing, and intimate friends. But if our trust is based on these things, it can be no more stable than they are—and, sorry to say, *these things are not stable!* Friends may betray you, your boss may fire you, and your health may quickly leave you. If we are not rooted and grounded in the revelation of God's love in Jesus Christ, the Accuser will rise up whenever misfortune strikes to turn us into accusers of God, and thus of ourselves and other people.

We have to honestly acknowledge that there are times when God may appear other than he is in Jesus Christ. In this war zone in which we live, it is easy to wonder where God is and what he is up to. When the cancer we thought had been cured returns, when the newborn baby of a beloved friend is diagnosed with an incurable disease, when our spouse dies, when we lose all our possessions in a fire, or when we fall once again into our destructive addiction, we wonder where God is. Is God's character really such as is revealed in Jesus Christ?

Perhaps even more troubling, many of us find it challenging to trust God simply because we read the Bible! How can the same God who is decisively revealed on the cross of Calvary have anything to do with the slaughtering of the Canaanites, including the women and children? Why does God sometimes appear so hot tempered and so extreme in his punishments in the Old Testament? Did he really have to kill every firstborn Egyptian child?

Here is where it is crucial to know what you can know and what you can't know. We *can* know God's character is decisively revealed in Jesus Christ. We shouldn't seek to see God outside of Christ (John 14:7–10). What we *can't* know—what we can at best only guess at—is what it's like to be God running this universe. We can't judge God on the basis of his behavior—or what we might suspect is his behavior—outside of Christ because we don't know all the variables with which he has to contend. We must simply trust that God's character and purpose are what he reveals them to be in Christ and then try to imagine what possible circumstances might have required God to engage in behavior that seems contrary to this character and purpose, such as ordering the slaughter of the Canaanites.

We cannot judge God for the same reason we cannot judge others: We have no divine right or omniscient capacity to do so. And we have to trust God's revelation of himself in Christ for the same reason we have to trust God's revelation about other people in Christ: We have no other reliable knowledge on which to depend. Our assessment of God and our assessment of all others, therefore, must be solidly rooted in the One who reveals God's love and reveals all humans to be condemned sinners who are nevertheless loved by God. All thoughts we might entertain about God or about others must be assessed in the light of this one criterion: Jesus Christ. Every thought must be made captive to Christ (2 Cor. 10:5).

Living in Ambiguity

The Fallen Impulse to Reject Ambiguity

Trusting that Jesus Christ is the definitive revelation of God and humanity requires that we accept our vast ignorance of God and the world outside of Christ. In our fallen state we find this very difficult to do, and this fact reveals another fundamental feature of the illegitimate knowledge we seized from the forbidden tree. By its very nature, the divine knowledge of good and evil rejects ambiguity, for this knowledge rightfully belongs only to an omniscient God for whom nothing is ambiguous.

The vast complexity of the world is no problem for God. With perfect clarity and perfect character, God knows good and evil. When we seize the divine prerogative of knowing good and evil, we appropriate the *impulse* to be omniscient without possessing the divine *capacity* to be omniscient. We are thus inclined to act like God in pronouncing judgment, but we do it without God's perfect clarity and character. We also do it without God's fullness. Indeed, we pronounce judgment out of emptiness and as a strategy for getting full. Hence, the exercise of our knowledge of good and evil is invariably self-serving.

The fact is that for nonomniscient, severely limited beings such as us, reality is mostly ambiguous. The cosmos is incomprehensibly complex. Humans can't know the innumerable variables that influence us and condition what God does in any particular situation.[8] We thus can't legitimately draw definitive conclusions about good and evil. Yet, under the deception of the Enemy and operating with forbidden knowledge, we have a sinful impulse to ignore this vast ignorance and unfathomable complexity and act as though we *do* have clarity and *can* draw such conclusions. We have an impulse to fit people and situations into the Procrustean bed of our categories, lopping off all ambiguity as though it were irrelevant.[9]

What is more, because of this same impulse, we often convince ourselves that people and situations would be fixed if only they would conform to our Procrustean bed. Our forbidden knowledge resists the humbling truth that some problems are simply beyond the capacity of humans to fix and some questions beyond our capacity to answer. Hence, when the world resists our fixing, we are inclined to blame it on the fact that it doesn't conform to our judgments. If only everyone thought like *we* think all would be well with the world. We feed our empty selves with the illusion that we are fixers rather than ones who need fixing.

Ironically, few mindsets have inflicted more suffering and problems on the world than this arrogant mindset. In the name of fixing the world, religious and political ideologues have murdered millions. Even more ironic, however, is the fact that Jesus systematically evaded attempts to engage him in the numerous ethical, social, and political problems of his day (e.g., Matt. 22:15–22; Luke 12:13–14). As we noted in chapter 5, his concern was not to bring clarity to ambiguous ethical, religious, and political dilemmas but to provide people with a relationship with God that would transform their perspective on all ambiguous dilemmas and on all of life.[10] Jesus' dominant concern was to call us to surrender ourselves completely to him and to walk in obedience to his Spirit within us.[11]

Suffering and the Complexity of Creation

Perhaps nowhere is the fallen impulse to reject ambiguity more evident than in the way religious people tend to interpret suffering. We live in a morally ambiguous world in which fortune and misfortune come upon people in an arbitrary fashion. Yet the fallen, moralistic impulse to reject ambiguity inclines many to insist that those who suffer misfortune deserve it or that their suffering is morally justified because it serves a higher cosmic purpose. Indeed, these have been the two dominant explanations for evil within the Christian tradition.

It is significant that Jesus never embraced either explanation. Never once did Jesus suggest that any of the multitudes of suffering people to whom he ministered were being punished or disciplined by God through their suffering. Though he constantly ministered to "the dregs of society," never once did he ask an ethical question of them or raise an ethical suspicion about them. Nor did he ever suggest that they were suffering for a greater good. Instead, he uniformly attributed their afflictions to demonic forces (e.g., Mark 9:25; Luke 11:14; 13:11–16; cf. Acts 10:38). And his only concern was to manifest the will of his Father by healing and delivering those he confronted.[12]

When his disciples wondered whose sin caused a man to be born blind, Jesus rejected the question. The only thing that mattered was that God be glorified by healing the man (John 9:1–5).[13] When others assumed that people who had been killed by a falling tower or massacred by Pilate were being punished by God, Jesus explicitly rejected the judgment. The only thing such speculators should be concerned about, he insisted, was their own relationship with God (Luke 13:1–5).

Jesus and the authors of the New Testament assumed that the cosmos was much more complex and ambiguous than allowed for by the traditional explanations for evil. They saw the world as under siege by the Accuser, whom they called "the ruler of this world," "the god of this world," and "the ruler of the power of the air" (John 12:31; 14:30; 16:11; 2 Cor. 4:4; Eph. 2:2). While they assumed that every aspect of creation that didn't align itself with the will of God was directly or indirectly the result of fallen human or angelic wills, they never speculated about why things unfold just the way they do. They did not pretend to know much about the virtually infinite chain of influences that lie behind each and every event that takes place. They thus didn't try to penetrate the ambiguity of the world and explain why one person was afflicted, another demonized, another crushed by a falling tower, and another untouched altogether. They did not try to reject the ambiguity of the world by *finding* God's will *in* suffering. They rather worked in the midst of the ambiguity of the world to *apply* God's will *to* suffering.

Ambiguity and the Book of Job

The book of Job is all about humans acknowledging the ambiguity of the world. It seeks to expose the sinfulness and foolishness of humans trying to cross the boundary between humans and God by claiming to know what they cannot know. It thereby exposes the illegitimacy of our illegitimately seized knowledge of good and evil.

The work begins with Satan accusing God of running a Machiavellian universe. No one serves God simply because he's God, Satan claims. They serve him because of the benefits they receive (Job 1:8–10). In the context of this narrative, the charge can only be refuted by being put to the test. Hence, the protective fence around Job and his family is lifted, and Job is allowed to come under the power of Satan (1:12). Consequently, Job loses all that he had and suffers incredibly.

Throughout this book, Job's "friends" assume that all that has happened to Job is God's doing and it is just. They impose their self-serving knowledge of good and evil on the world and insist, against all the evidence, that innocent people don't suffer (e.g., 4:7–9). Throughout the narrative of this work, the friends insist that the universe is not morally ambiguous. Hence, if Job is suffering, it can only be because he deserves it and/or that God is teaching him a lesson.

Job also assumes that all that is happening to him is God's doing, but he insists that it is not just. He thus concludes that God is an arbitrary tyrant. He says, for example, "[God] mocks at the calamity of the innocent. The earth is given into the hand of the wicked; he covers the eyes of its judges—if it is not he, who then is it?" (9:23–24; cf. 21:17–26, 30–32; 24:1–12).

Similarly, Job insists that God ignores those who pray (24:12) and is a cruel adversary who delights in Job's torment (e.g., 10:8–9, 20; 16:7–17; 30:18–21). For Job, the world looks arbitrary and unjust because God is arbitrary and unjust. Job's speeches in the narrative of this work are filled with these sorts of harsh accusations.[14]

When God finally speaks up, he refutes the judgmental perspectives of *both* Job and his friends. And he does it by demonstrating how arrogant it is for humans to judge God or one another *because they know next to nothing about the world*. There are three aspects to God's rebuttal.

First, and most importantly, the Lord reminds Job of the boundary between God and humans. He is God; Job is not. He is judge; Job is not. He is omniscient; Job is not. Hence, the Lord chides Job, "Shall a faultfinder contend with the Almighty? . . . Will you even put me in the wrong? Will you condemn me that you may be justified?" (40:2, 8).

Second, as a way of driving home this boundary, the Lord reminds Job of his massive ignorance about the cosmos. "Who is this that darkens counsel by words without knowledge?" the Lord asks. "Where were you when I laid the foundation of the earth? Tell me, if you have understanding. Who determined its measurements—surely you know! Or who stretched the line upon it?" (Job 38:2, 4–5). The Lord then proceeds to expound upon the complexity, expansiveness, and mystery of the universe he has created, none of which Job or his friends can even begin to understand (38:1–40:14).

Third, the Lord reminds Job of the evil cosmic forces with which God must contend. He reminds him of the spiritual war that engulfs the cosmos. In the ancient Near East, these evil forces were typically depicted as sea monsters that encompassed and threatened the world. In the book of Job their names are Leviathan and Behemoth. The Lord reminds Job of how powerful and ferocious these cosmic beasts are and how incapable humans are of withstanding them (40:15–41:34). Unless Job thinks he could do a better job at contending with these cosmic forces, the Lord is saying, he is in no position to criticize God.

The point of God's climactic monologue is that we finite humans don't see the big picture of the cosmos that God sees. Indeed, it is significant that neither Job nor his friends are ever told about the challenge of Satan to God in the prologue that was behind Job's misfortune. They remain in their ignorance, even after the encounter with God—*and that is the central point* of the prologue in the context of this book.

Unless it is divinely revealed to us, we humans have no way of knowing what goes on behind the scenes. We know very little about the complexity of creation, and we have little knowledge of the activities of forces of evil that engulf the cosmos. For all we know, the answer to a prayer may be delayed because of an interfering spiritual agent behind the scenes (Dan. 10:12–13)! This is why we can't judge others and why we can't judge God. We are ignorant, fallen, finite creatures who have no business pretending to know what God alone knows.

Whenever we give in to the fallen impulse to reject ambiguity, we end up blaming God and/or hurting people. The Accuser has succeeded in making us accusers. If we are going to respond to suffering as God would have us respond, we must accept the impenetrable ambiguity of creation and the glorious clarity of God's revelation in Christ. We must fix our eyes upon Jesus both as our model and as our only reliable guide to the truth about who God is and the truth about who we are because of what Christ has done.

Conclusion

We have a tremendous advantage neither Job nor his friends had; we have the revelation of God in Christ. God's character and purposes have been revealed to us in a way neither Job nor his friends could have imagined. In Christ, the Accuser's deception has been expelled, the true God has been uncovered, the separation of God and humanity has been bridged, and the proper boundary between God and humanity has been restored. By grace we are reunited with God and empowered to obey his command to walk in love.

This can only be experienced, however, if we remain rooted and grounded in Christ. In the face of the impenetrable ambiguity of the world, we must view everything in life, and even everything else in the Bible, from this perspective. Christ must be the interpretative lens through which we view God, ourselves, other people, and the world. If we allow *anything* to qualify this revelation, our trust in God and therefore our union with God will be compromised, and the flow of perfect, triune love from God to us and through us will consequently be to some degree blocked. We will to some degree be trying to get life from idols and judging matters as good or evil based on the strategy for getting life that our idol requires.

When our minds and hearts are rooted and grounded in the love of God as revealed in Christ, when doubt is replaced with trusting intimacy with God, the river of life that is already flowing within us begins to spring forth (John 7:38–39). When we abandon our false view of ultimate reality—whether it be that no god exists or that the god we believe does exist is untrustworthy—and resolve that the true God is uncovered in the crucified Messiah, the serpent's accusation is overcome and the life-giving love of God is allowed to flow to us, abide in us, and pour out from us. When we accept the finitude and fallenness of our human condition and thus accept the ambiguity of the world around us, we can refrain from judgment and live in love. When we are by God's grace freed from our addiction to the Tree of the Knowledge of Good and Evil, we are empowered to live in the blessed garden in which God always intended us to live.

Only then do we experience the fullness of life and love that is fellowship with the triune God. Only then do we begin to be transformed into radical Christlike lovers. Only then does God's purpose for creation, for the church, and for our lives begin to be recovered.

chapter 8

The Lie about Us

"For God knows that when you eat of it your eyes will be opened, and you will be like God, knowing good and evil." So when the woman saw that the tree was good for food, and that it was a delight to the eyes, and that the tree was to be desired to make one wise, she took of its fruit and ate; and she also gave some to her husband, who was with her, and he ate.

Genesis 3:5–6

Whatever does not proceed from faith is sin.

Romans 14:23

Originally man was made in the image of God, but now his likeness to God is a stolen one. . . . What God had given man to be, man now desired to be through himself.

Dietrich Bonhoeffer

In Christ, there was re-created the form of man before God.

Dietrich Bonhoeffer

The Lie: You Must Become

The Shifting Centers

In chapter 3 we saw that we cannot know and love the truth about God without knowing and loving the truth about ourselves and our neighbors. Loving our neighbors as ourselves is part of *what it means* to love God. In the same way, we cannot reject the truth about God without thereby rejecting the truth about ourselves and our neighbors. And we cannot refrain from loving God without thereby refraining from loving ourselves and our neighbors.

It's not surprising, therefore, that in Genesis 3 the very act that brought a false judgment about God also brought a false judgment about Adam and Eve, and thus about all of humanity. The serpent's accusation that God isn't a reliable source of life involved an accusation that God's creatures weren't adequately alive. The heart of the lie about us is that we humans are not okay simply living in union with God. Our lives cannot simply revolve around enjoying God's provision—the Tree of Life—and honoring God's prohibition—the Tree of Knowledge. We can, and we must, provide for ourselves.

This lie follows directly from believing the lie about God. If God is in fact unloving, untrustworthy, and threatened by what he forbids, as the serpent suggested, Adam and Eve must be on their own to find life. The serpent convinced Eve that she and Adam had been duped by God in their previous innocence. The fullness of life she and Adam had enjoyed simply living in fellowship with their Creator was actually the ploy of a threatened deity securing his position on top. Their eyes were not yet opened, the serpent said, for the threatened Creator was keeping them shut (Gen. 3:4–5). Adam and Eve were seduced into believing that there was something they could get that would improve their lot in life, something the Creator was holding back from them out of fear. This presupposed that something was lacking in their lives up to this point and that it was up to them and them alone to get it.

In reality, the moment Eve entertained the possibility that she lacked something, she *did* lack something—but not what she thought. Eve was in the process of turning from God, breaking fellowship with God, and thus creating a vacuum in her heart where there previously had been fullness. The lie she accepted about God and about herself was creating its own truth. The very act of *believing* she was on her own was causing Eve *to be* on her own. The very act of believing she was deficient was creating a deficiency.

By accepting the serpent's lie, Eve was beginning to create her own alternate, godless reality. It is a rebelliously motivated, idolatrous, illusory reality that opposes reality as it is defined by God. The reality God wills is that of an eternal fullness overflowing to, in, and through everyone and everything. The reality Eve was in the process of creating—the reality we humans have been creating ever since—was the reality of a vacuum in which she attempted to get life by having everything flow into it. Instead of reality being centered on the fullness of God, reality for Eve became centered on her own, now empty, self.

The Vicious Cycle

The lure that brought Eve—and us—into this self-centered reality traps us in a vicious cycle. The Enemy still uses this same strategy. He plants a lie in our minds that creates a vacuum in our hearts, giving the world an illusory, idolatrous appearance that confirms the lie. Out of a hunger the lie itself created, Eve suddenly saw that "the tree was good for food, and that it was a delight to the eyes, and that the tree was to be desired to make one wise" (Gen. 3:6). Her perception of the tree as "desired to make one wise" confirmed that she needed something to be full. Yet, as we noted in chapter 7, she never would have viewed the prospect of disobeying God as desirable if she hadn't already believed she was deficient—which is to say, if she hadn't already accepted the serpent's lie about herself and God.

The vicious cycle is repeated in every lie we believe that underlies every sin we commit. And it is this cycle that keeps our empty selves rather than the fullness of God in the center of our world. Believing a lie, we *judge* God to be untrustworthy or inadequate to fill us with life. Our judgment then blocks God's fullness and makes us *feel* empty and on our own. Our emptiness in turn makes other things *seem* like viable candidates to fill us. Things like religion, sexual pleasure, fame, riches, and power take on an illusory god-like attractiveness to us when viewed with the hungry eyes of our vacuous souls.

Indeed, our emptiness often makes it *seem* as though these candidates *actually fill us*. Because of the power of the delusion, these idols can at times create a momentary sense of fullness, life, and worth. But they are never truly satisfying and are never permanent. Hence, the cycle has to perpetually repeat itself, and it will do so until the lie about God and about us is broken and our hearts are freed from their idolatrous cravings.

Trying to Acquire What We Already Have

The lie about God and about Eve made eating from the forbidden tree look desirable. This in turn provided Eve with a perceived solution to her emptiness—a solution that didn't involve depending on God, who was now judged as being untrustworthy. There was something *she could do about her hunger*. The viability of the forbidden tree as a source of fullness gave viability to her embryonic autonomy.

Just like Eve, we believe we can fill our emptiness by *doing* something and acquiring things. We believe we can give ourselves fulfilling worth apart from God by performing. We believe we can become self-sufficient through our efforts. We believe we can fix ourselves as well as other people. All of this is to say, we believe we can and should become wise, like God, knowing good and evil.

It's important to notice that the serpent didn't promise Eve something she didn't already have. This too is an aspect of all that blocks love and thus constitutes sin. The serpent promised Eve that she could be "like God." Yet she and Adam were *already* made in the very image and likeness of God (Gen. 1:26–27). The craftiness of the serpent is found in his cunning ability to make Eve think she *had to become what she in fact already was*. How else could he tempt a person who already had all she would ever need? The serpent convinced Eve that her life had to be found in *doing* rather than simply *being*. He convinced her to break fellowship with God in order to possess the very thing God had already given her for free: her being in "the image and likeness of God."

Had Eve remained in union with God, had she rejected the Accuser's lie about God, the serpent's promise that she could become like God would have been utterly vacuous. She would have remained in the peace of knowing that she already reflected God's image and was full because of the unsurpassable worth

God continually poured into her. Going beyond the "No Trespassing" sign would not have seemed desirable to her.

Only when she accepted the lie and forgot who she was did the promise of becoming like God take on any significance. Rejecting the truth that she was already in God's likeness, she blocked out the love that made her in his likeness. Then, instead of living life out of the fullness of who she already was, dependent upon God, Eve chose to try to become in God's likeness by acting out of her emptiness, independent of God. Her life, and the life of her descendants, would from that time on consist of futilely chasing what we God had always intended to give us for free.

From Full Human Being *to Empty Human* Doing

It is also important to notice that there is an element of truth in the serpent's lie to Eve. (The most powerful lies always contain some truth.) In a sense, the tree *really did* make Eve like God in knowing good and evil. She was now like God in a way she wasn't before. The serpent's lie wasn't about the *nature* of the forbidden tree and what it would do; it was in the implication that this was *desirable* for her. In fact, for finite beings like ourselves, this kind of knowledge is a curse because it blocks the unconditional and unsurpassable life-giving love of God flowing to us, abiding in us, and flowing through us to others.

If Adam and Eve had continued in their union with God, they would never have known good or evil; they would have remained innocent. Loving obedience in all things would have been enough. God would have led in this or that direction, and that would have settled the matter. There would have been no need to make decisions on the basis of our own independent assessment of how good or evil the outcomes of our decisions would be.[1] God alone would know good and evil and direct us accordingly. Nor would Adam and Eve or their descendants have analyzed their experience in terms of good or evil. They would only have known the unsurpassable fullness and joy of living in fellowship with a God who is unsurpassable love and joy.

Had Adam and Eve resisted the serpent's lie about God, and therefore about themselves, the forbidden tree would have remained a helpful "No Trespassing" sign placed in the garden by a God who had their best interest in mind. It would have been a boundary that freed them to focus on the one thing God called them to do: love as God is love.

However, everything changed when Eve allowed the lie about God and about herself to enter into her heart. She began to see the world through her own eyes, separate from God. Now things started to appear good and evil. God was "evil," she became empty, and eating of the tree became "good." So she ate the fruit of the forbidden tree.[2]

The moment she ate the fruit, Eve essentially ceased being the wonderful, God-centered, God-dependent human *being* the Creator intended her to be and became an empty human *doing*—perpetually trying to get life on her own, apart from God. Like Adam and Eve, the human race now lives life illegitimately trying to become what God had already made us to be. The world has become a stage upon which we perpetually assess things and people as good or evil, depending on how we think they can or can't fill the vacuum in our hearts. We thus use everything and everyone in the world as surrogate gods, trying to get from people, deeds, and things what only God can give—what God has already given—for free.

The Nature of False Gods

Many factors influence which particular idols we choose to derive life from. Social context, genetics, family upbringing, and life experiences all play a part. Historically, most people in most cultures choose religious idols. But other people choose secular idols such as ethical behavior, wealth, recognition, pleasure, and so forth. Indeed, there are few things in the world and few behaviors in which humans engage that can't in certain contexts be given a god-like status.

Yet all these diverse gods are fundamentally alike in that they attain their status only because people are striving to become god-like on the basis of a lie that they are not already like God. These false gods are the result of humans illegitimately taking "wisdom" for ourselves in order to know good and evil, and these false gods help sustain us in this forbidden knowledge. The false gods seem potentially filling only because we live in desperate hunger. They promise fulfillment but create only further striving.

This is the original sin and the essence of all sin. It is the root of all evil, for it keeps us from experiencing God's love to us and from having this love flow through us. In short, it suppresses the purpose for which God created the world.

Now, instead of ascribing unsurpassable worth to others out of a fullness of unsurpassable worth we freely receive from God, we strive to derive worth from other people, other things, and our own performance in a futile attempt to fill a vacuum created by God's absence in our lives. So long as the vacuum is there, the striving after false gods will continue, the judgment of good and evil will be present, and hence the love that God wants to give to us, abide in us, and flow through us will be absent. In this fallen state, we cannot love as God is love. We can only ascribe unsurpassable worth to others when we no longer need to use others to acquire worth for ourselves.

The Truth about Us: We Are Condemned

Fully God and Fully Human

God's answer to the lie about us is the same as God's answer to the lie about himself: It is Jesus Christ. In chapter 7 we saw that Jesus is the truth who uncovers the real God, over against every variation of the serpent's lie about God that had previously concealed him from us. For the same reason, Jesus uncovers the truth about us. In revealing the true God, Christ reveals the true human. For in uncovering the God of unsurpassable love, Christ uncovers humanity as the object of God's unsurpassable love.

This is one of the central reasons "the Word became flesh" (John 1:14). In the words of the Chalcedonian creed, the Son of God is "fully God and fully man." God reveals humanity in the very act of revealing deity. Jesus is said to be the image of God both as perfect human and as the perfect expression of God (1 Cor. 15:49; 2 Cor. 3:18; 4:4; Col. 1:15). Christ is both *God before us* as well as *us before God*. Just as all we need to know about *God* is found in Christ, as we saw in chapter 7, so too all we need to know about *humanity* is found in Jesus Christ.

Jesus is who God always intended humanity to be and who humanity truly is—if only we will yield to God's Spirit and relinquish the illusory reality of the serpent's lie. As Bonhoeffer put it: "Jesus is not *a* man. He is *man*. Whatever happens to Him happens to man. It happens to all men, and therefore it happens also to us. The name Jesus contains within itself the whole of humanity and the whole of God."[3]

What Christ reveals about humanity is just as unexpected as what he reveals about God. Nothing about Christ fits easily with our ordinary, fallen preconceptions, for they are polluted with the serpent's lie. Christ uncovers the truth that, as we are now, humanity is in a desperate state of sin. He also uncovers the truth that despite this sin, God loves us with an unsurpassable love. I shall discuss each of these inseparable truths.

The Radical Cure

By dying for us on the cross, Christ revealed the depth of human sinfulness. Most people have a deep, gnawing sense that something is missing in their lives, that something is "off" with themselves and the world, and perhaps even that they are guilty of something, though they can't quite identify what it is.[4] All such intuitions bear witness to the sin-created, God-shaped vacuum in the hearts of humans. Still, very few people, especially in modern Western culture, naturally think of themselves as being as desperate as the cross reveals them to be.

The seriousness of an illness can be assessed by how radical the cure is that is required to overcome it. If a woman goes to the doctor because of a minor headache and, after examining her, the doctor informs her that she needs immediate brain surgery, she clearly understands that her problem is much more serious than a simple headache. So it is with our sin. One symptom of our fallen condition is that we usually don't feel our situation is very grave. On the contrary, owing to the vicious cycle discussed earlier, we usually feel that our lives are going quite well. Our lies *feel like truth*. Our false gods *feel like life*. Yes, there may be a gnawing emptiness that keeps creeping back, but it's nothing our diet of idols can't temporarily suppress if we work hard at it.

It is only when we look at the cross, God's "cure" for our sin, that the full gravity of our condition becomes apparent. If God had to go to the furthest extreme imaginable to save us—Jesus' death on the cross—then our situation must have indeed been desperate.

The Horror of Sin

We see the gravity of our condition in how radical the cure is. But the cure itself includes exposing the seriousness of the sickness it heals. Indeed, exposing sin's horror is a crucial element in its healing. The cross functions like a mirror held up before our eyes in which we see the full gravity of our sin.

Hundreds of years before Jesus was executed, the prophet Isaiah wrote:

> But he was wounded for our transgressions,
>   crushed for our iniquities;
> upon him was the punishment that made us whole,
>   and by his bruises we are healed.
> All we like sheep have gone astray;
>   we have all turned to our own way,
> and the LORD has laid on him
>   the iniquity of us all.
>
> Isaiah 53:5–6

On Christ was laid "the iniquity of us all." "He himself bore our sins in his body on the cross" (1 Peter 2:24; cf. Heb. 9:28). Indeed, Paul dared to say that God "made him to be sin who knew no sin" (2 Cor. 5:21). In the crucified Messiah we see the full horror of our act of violating the boundary between us and God and making ourselves the center.

We also see the consequences of our sin, for on the cross we see God's punishment of sin. This is why Jesus was "wounded" and "crushed." In the words of Paul, "God put [Jesus] forward as a sacrifice of atonement by his blood. . . . He did this to show his righteousness, because in his divine forbearance he had passed over the sins previously committed." God's judgment of Jesus was "to prove at the present time that he himself is righteous" (Rom. 3:25–26). In short, in the God-forsaken death of Jesus on the cross, we see the wrath of God condemning sin. The wages of sin is death—physical as well as spiritual—and we see this death sentence carried out against all humanity on the cross (Rom. 6:23).

Other passages in the New Testament describe what the cross reveals. Nowhere is our desperate situation depicted more starkly than in Romans 3.

> There is no one who is righteous, not even one;
>> there is no one who has understanding,
>>> there is no one who seeks God.
> All have turned aside, together they have become worthless. . . .
> Their feet are swift to shed blood;
>> ruin and misery are in their paths,
> and the way of peace they have not known.
>> There is no fear of God before their eyes.
>
> Romans 3:10–12,15–18

For this reason, Paul concludes that "no human being will be justified in [God's] sight" by their own works (Rom. 3:20). For "all have sinned and fall short of the glory of God" (Rom. 3:23). As for our ability to live consistently with God's character, we are completely dead (Eph. 2:1).

Measuring Up against the True Standard

As mentioned earlier, we usually have difficulty accepting this assessment, for we evaluate ourselves by our own standards over against other people. This judgment is not only false, it is the essence of the very sin from which we need to be freed. We acquire idolatrous worth through the filter of our self-serving knowledge of good and evil. To free us from this false, sinful judgment, Scripture frequently reminds us of the true standard we are up against: God himself.

What God demands is nothing less than perfect union with himself, for this is the purpose for which God created the world. Anything that disrupts this union misses the mark, which is the definition of sin (*hamartia*). Hence, Paul says that *every act* that does not flow out of faith is sin (Rom. 14:23). Every act and every thought that does not flow out of trust (faith) that God is who he reveals himself to be—everything that is inconsistent with the purpose for which God created the world—is sin. The standard, in other words, is perfection, as God is perfect (Matt. 5:48). Next to this standard, every careless word and every idle thought is held against us, for it is evidence of our separation from God (Matt. 12:37).

Along the same lines, Jesus taught that any pledges we make to secure our authority, anything more than a simple yes or no, "comes from the evil one" (Matt. 5:37). If we were in union with God, we would not need or want to appeal to external things to give our words credibility. So too, Jesus taught that it is not enough to refrain from murder; if we ever harbor anger toward our brother or sister, we are already "liable to judgment." And if we judge our brother or sister as a "fool," we are "liable to the hell of fire" (Matt. 5:22). Indeed, any judgment we make about others, in word or in thought, is the judgment that will be held against us, according to Jesus (Matt. 7:1–5). In the same vein, it is not enough to refrain from adultery; if we ever look at someone with lust, we have already committed adultery in God's eyes (Matt. 5:27–28). And there is no such thing as "just cause" for divorce, according to Jesus. All divorce and remarriage involves adultery, for it is a break from God's ideal (Matt. 5:32).[5]

Everything we do, think, or say that is not perfectly consistent with the character of God condemns us. Whenever we fail to love God with all our heart, mind, and body, we stand condemned. Whenever we fail to ascribe to our neighbors or to ourselves the worth God ascribes to us, we stand condemned. Anything and everything we have done that has not proceeded from a faith-filled union with God has missed the mark.

While various religious groups may ascribe righteousness to themselves by separating themselves and coming down on certain sins they happen to avoid while minimizing or ignoring the sins they routinely commit, the Bible forces upon us a much more severe conclusion: *We all stand equally condemned!* Any attempt to feel holy because one does not commit certain arbitrarily selected sins trivializes both sin and holiness.

The Severe Message That Liberates

We stand utterly condemned. This message is crushingly severe. But for just this reason it is also liberating. "It is only as one who is sentenced by God," Bonhoeffer wrote, "that man can live before God."[6] For only by becoming hopeless about our ability to live in perfect union with God *on our own efforts* can we begin to recover perfect union with God by simply *being* who God created us and died for us to be. Only by appreciating the full depth of our own sinfulness and the full horror of our condemnation can we be set free from trying to be wise like God, judging God, ourselves, and others according to our own stolen knowledge of good and evil. Only by accepting that the gulf between us and God is unbridgeable through our own efforts can we stop trying to be good, religious, or ethical as a way of getting life and simply accept the union God has sacrificially established with us in Christ.

In other words, the unsurpassable severity of our condemnation in Christ frees us to live in the unsurpassable love God has for us in Christ. The cursed tree on which Christ hung destroys the forbidden tree from which we ate.

The Truth about Us: We Are Forgiven and Loved

We Are Forgiven

This brings us to the second aspect of the revelation of who we truly are in Jesus Christ. The same act that exposes our hopelessness before God uncovers our hopefulness in God, for it reveals the unsurpassable worth we are mercifully given by God. The very act that exposes the horror of our rejection of God reveals the beauty of God's acceptance of us. The very act of exposing our sin accomplishes our salvation. The act that reveals the disease accomplishes its cure.

The crucified Messiah is simultaneously the full expression of God's judgment and mercy. He bore our judgment that we might receive God's mercy. In doing this, Christ revealed the truth about God—that he is unfathomable love—and the truth about us—that our sin is damnable, that it has been judged, and that we are nonetheless loved, forgiven, and reconciled to God.

Paul summed up the matter: "For our sake [God] made him to be sin who knew no sin, so that in him we might become the righteousness of God" (2 Cor. 5:21). Christ took upon himself all that belonged to us so that all that belonged to him might be given to us by grace. He became our sin so we might become his righteousness. In Christ, we are freely given *the righteousness of God himself.*

In other words, in becoming our sin and bearing the wrath of God against all sin, Christ has opened the way for us once again to participate in the fellowship of the triune God despite our sin. As we discussed in chapter 2, this is the reality Scripture describes as being "in Christ." We become the recipients of and the participants in God's eternal, perfect love. Despite our estrangement, we are reconciled to God.

This message of reconciliation frees us from the curse for the same reason the message of condemnation frees us from the curse. Indeed, they are one and the same message. For if all we are and ever shall be before God is given to us freely in Christ, there is no need or possibility for us to live any longer from the Tree of the Knowledge of Good and Evil. In Christ, both our ability and our need to live off our illegitimate knowledge of good and evil is exposed as a lie. For in Christ we are condemned, and, if we accept it, in Christ we are made alive and reunited with the one true source of life.

The Center

Because of the cross, we are now free to abide (take up permanent residence) in God and God in us (John 15:4–10; Rom. 8:9–10; Col. 3:3; 1 John 2:27–28; 4:13–16). When we live in God and God lives in us, we live in love, for God is love (1 John 4:7–12). This is what it means to live *in Christ.* Instead of living in a lie about God and ourselves, we live in the trust that God's life toward us is God's life toward Christ, and our life toward God is Christ's life toward God. And we must aspire toward *living* here. It is not enough to understand abiding in Christ intellectually as a fact; we must yield continually to it in order to know it experientially and transformationally. We are to *live* in faith and *live* in love (Eph. 5:2).

We are called to live in love and in Christ because this is our true home. It is the garden in which God always wanted us to live. Union with Christ is to be the center around which everything else in our lives revolves and the center out of which everything we do flows. We live in this place when, because of our faith in who God is and who we are (uncovered in Christ), we relinquish every echo of living off of the Tree of the Knowledge of Good and Evil. We honor the prohibition in the middle of the garden (Gen. 2:9; 3:3) and are given access to the provision. As we do this, as we live in our true source center, we begin to experience the unsurpassable worth God ascribes to himself, to ourselves, and to all others. We experientially participate in the divine nature (2 Peter 1:4).

The goal of the Christian life is to increasingly let go of the alien and illusory world "in Adam" and to live in this center, our true home, "in Christ." As we live out of this center, we see past all the external appearances—things that our judgment normally latches on to—and we ascribe unsurpassable worth to people before God. In this place, ambiguity is no longer a reality to be resisted. Rather, it is something to be embraced, for it frees us to do the one thing we are created to do: love without judgment.

To live in this place is to live in the purpose for which God created the world. It is to live right now in the eternal, abundant life that Christ came to give us (John 10:10; 11:25–26). It is to begin to live right now in the ecstatic dance that shall never end. It is to finally live as God intended us to live. It is to cease living in the endless judgments of the knowledge of good and evil and to begin living in the simplicity and freedom of the will of God.[7]

chapter 9

The Curse

Then the eyes of both were opened, and they knew that they were naked; and they sewed fig leaves together and made loincloths for themselves. They heard the sound of the LORD God walking in the garden at the time of the evening breeze, and the man and his wife hid themselves from the presence of the LORD God among the trees of the garden.

Genesis 3:7–8

Instead of seeing God man sees himself. "Their eyes were opened" (Gen. 3:7). Man perceives himself in his disunion with God and other men. He perceives that he is naked. . . . [he] covers himself, conceals himself from men and from God.

Dietrich Bonhoeffer

Man now lives only out of his own self, out of his knowledge of good and evil, and in this he is dead.

Dietrich Bonhoeffer

As we are slowly unwrapping the dynamic between the truth and the lie in the Genesis narrative of the fall, we have found that the lie about God and the lie about us is overcome by the revelation of God in Jesus Christ. We also have found that the lie that we can be "the center" is overcome in Christ, experienced as we die to our old self and manifest our new self. It is time to turn to yet another dimension of the lie that the Accuser imposes upon us to keep us from living the truth of God's love.

The Realm of Death

God warned Adam and Eve that eating the fruit of the Tree of the Knowledge of Good and Evil would bring death. The serpent denied this and claimed that the fruit of the forbidden tree would bring fullness of life. Believing the serpent rather than God, Adam and Eve violated the boundary between humans and their Creator and sought for more life. But in seeking to find life on their own, they lost it (cf. Matt. 10:39).

Adam and Eve passed from the realm of life, which is relationship with God, into the realm of death, which is separation from God. They passed from the realm of innocence into the realm of judgment, where the knowledge of good and evil rather than love of God reigns supreme. In the words of Bonhoeffer,

> Man, knowing of good and evil, has . . . torn himself loose from life. . . . Man knows good and evil, against God, against his origin, godlessly and of his own choice, understanding himself according to his own contrary possibilities; and he is cut off from the unifying, reconciling life in God, and is delivered over to death. The secret which man has stolen from God is bringing about man's downfall.[1]

The Genesis narrative describes what this realm of death looks like in the fate of Adam and Eve. When Adam and Eve abandoned their innocent union with God and were severed from their source, they hid from each other and from God, they deflected their responsibility before God, and they were cursed (while given hope) by God. These are three manifestations of the realm of death Adam and Eve, and all of us, have entered. We shall discuss these three manifestations in this order. This shall set the stage for a discussion in part 4 of how the body of Christ is to overcome these manifestations of death by manifesting life in Christ.

Hiding and Performing

Relating through a Filter

The first manifestation of the realm of judgment and death that Adam and Eve had entered was their shame and hiding. As they came under the lie of the Accuser, they not only accused God, they accused themselves and each other. As is always the case, the judgment they made about God entailed a judgment about themselves and everyone else. Hence, as soon as their eyes were "opened," as soon as they saw the world through their knowledge of good and evil, they judged that their nakedness was not good and that they were guilty before God. The sound of the Lord walking in the "evening breeze" that had been so inviting when they were innocent was now threatening to them (Gen. 3:8). Before each other and before God, they were ashamed. They covered themselves and hid.

This is the story of each and every one of us living in the flesh. We no longer innocently relate to God, ourselves, and each other directly in love. Instead, we relate through the filter of our sinfully acquired knowledge. In this fallen state, we can no longer be naked, open, and vulnerable before each other and before God. We cannot simply walk with God and enjoy his presence as the most relaxing and refreshing part of our day.[2]

Instead, we hide to conceal our emptiness and shame. The innocent and utterly free exchange of overflowing love that God desired humans to experience from him and for each other has been transformed into a strategy for protecting ourselves and for getting life by hiding and performing. We now relate to God, ourselves, and others through the evaluating filter of our knowledge of good and evil.

Nothing in our relationships is direct or innocent; it is all filtered. Which is to say, nothing in our relationships is unconditional. Because we are severed from our source, we do not experience and overflow with the unconditional and unsurpassable worth of God. Instead, the worth we receive, experience, and give is conditioned by our stolen knowledge. We receive and ascribe worth *on the condition* that our knowledge of good and evil approves of it.

Hiding

Because the worth we receive in our fallen state is conditional, our strategies for getting life always require hiding and performing. We were created to receive, experience, and overflow with unconditional worth. It is impossible for us to feel truly fulfilled without this. Whatever momentary satisfaction we may experience in receiving worth conditionally, based on what we do, we are invariably left with a sense that something about us is defective. We experience shame.

Since it is the very absence of unconditional worth that creates this shame, we can't ever rid ourselves of it by any strategy for getting life. We can only hide it. We have to cover our nakedness.

Why do we have to hide our shame? For the same reason we experience the shame. The lie that created our emptiness in the first place leads us to eat of the forbidden tree that now judges our emptiness as defective. Were we not living in our knowledge of good and evil, we would not critically assess ourselves in terms of what we are and are not supposed to be, and we would not experience any emptiness. We thus hide our shame from the very thing that creates the shame: our knowledge of good and evil.

We try to hide our shame from ourselves, from each other, and from God. Because we view God and others through the filter of our knowledge of good and evil, we view them as judges from whom we must hide and before whom we must perform.[3] Because we are empty, we are driven by a strategy to get worth, and this requires avoiding at all costs any judgment that suggests we lack worth. We thus have to hide from the world from which we are trying to get life.

We might say that the world in which we place ourselves in the center as judge becomes a world full of threatening judges. We view everyone, and we assume everyone views us, with the critical eye of the knowledge of good and evil. Our lives of innocence have been replaced by lives of hiding.

Performance

We not only need a strategy for concealing our emptiness, we need a strategy for filling it. As judge, we perpetually try to get life from other judges—the very ones from whom we are hiding our emptiness. Our strategy for getting worth is performance—to display to others what we ourselves judge as "good" while we hide what we assume others will judge as "evil" in us. So we try to conceal our nakedness—who we *really* are—under a covering that hides all that we think is liable to judgment and that displays all that we think is viable as a source of approval.

What particular covering we use, and thus what aspects of our self we hide, depends entirely on which false gods we seek to get life from as well as the particular strategy we adopt for getting this life. If, for example, the god to which we ascribe worth and from which we derive worth is a religious god, then we must display religious attitudes and behaviors and suppress everything about us that is not religious. If, on the other hand, the god to which we ascribe worth and from which we attempt to derive worth is a secular god of success (for example), then we must display success, and everything that might appear unsuccessful in our lives must be concealed.

Something similar could be said of every conceivable god from which we might seek life, whether it be possessions, sexuality, ethics, reputation, pleasure, or security. Living out of our knowledge of good and evil, we display and strive to acquire all we judge as good. And we suppress and strive to avoid all that we judge to be evil. We perform and we hide.

Living by performing and hiding, which is to say, relating to God, ourselves, and others through the filter of our knowledge of good and evil, is not life. The serpent lied. As God warned us, living in a perpetual attempt to get life is death. And it is our very attempt to get life on our own that prevents us from living, for it prevents us from receiving and giving God's unconditional love, which is life itself. We simply cannot receive or give unconditional and unsurpassable love when we are performing before and hiding from the One from whom we are supposed to freely receive love as well as those to whom we are supposed to freely give love.

Futility

Because the realm of death is marked by a perpetual game of performing and hiding, it is also marked by futility. As we have seen, the vacuum we are trying to fill is God-shaped. We are created to experience *unconditional* and *unsurpassable* worth. Our innermost being longs for this love. But the worth we receive from our idols is neither unsurpassable nor unconditional. It is limited in depth and duration, and it is conditioned upon whatever we did to acquire it. For this reason, the limited worth we acquire never attaches to our innermost being, our spirit. Instead, it attaches to whatever we did to get it—our performance. It attaches to our *doing*, not to our *being*. It thus never satisfies our inner being, which was created to be filled with unconditional and unsurpassable worth.

Acquiring worth from our self-created idols is like eating a large meal and having every morsel get stuck in our teeth. The meal might taste good, but it won't nourish us, let alone fill us up. For none of it will reach our stomach. So too we may feast upon the worth our religious or secular idols temporarily give us, but none of it reaches and satisfies our innermost being. It attaches to *what we do*, not to *who we are*. It wasn't given to us for free and thus doesn't feed our inner being. Once the distraction of the good taste is gone—the best our idols can give us is a nice distraction—we are left with our emptiness once again.

This is why the hunger that gnaws at our hearts as we live in Adam never fully goes away and why we cannot simply decide to stop feeding ourselves from the idols of this world. Regardless of how successfully we acquire life from our performance, we are simply never satisfied. We are separated from our true source of life, and our spirit continues to starve. So long as our spirit is starving, we cannot help but try to feed it. Yet so long as we persist in the lie that we *can* satisfy it on our own—if only we can do more, acquire more, perform more good, hide more evil, and so forth—we will continue to starve. We're caught in a self-perpetuating, vicious cycle of futility.

The billionaire who continues to work fourteen hours a day to earn more and the religious ascetic who continues to punish his body to get closer to God reveal one and the same disease.

Only when we yield to God's Spirit and resolve that Jesus Christ uncovers the true God and true humanity, only to the extent that we crucify the old self and live in faith, and only when we stop eating from the forbidden tree do we begin to experience the fullness of life and love God created us and saved us to have.

Only then can we begin to experience freedom from our addiction to idols. Only then is the self-perpetuating cycle of futility broken. Only when our sense of worth, self-esteem, purpose, and life is rooted by faith in who God truly is and who we truly are as revealed in Jesus Christ can we personally experience and overflow with the unsurpassable love that the triune God is.

Blaming

The second manifestation of the realm of death into which Adam and Eve entered followed closely on the heels of the first. Indeed, it is really just a variation of the first manifestation. When our judgment against God turns into a judgment about ourselves, producing shame, we engage in another judgment, this time against others or against God. This is simply another way that we hide. We blame others.

When Adam told the Lord that he was hiding because he was naked and afraid, the Lord asked, "Have you eaten from the tree of which I commanded you not to eat?" (Gen. 3:10–11). Rather than taking responsibility for his action, confessing his sin, and repenting, Adam attempted to protect himself by blaming God and Eve for his actions. He said, "The woman whom *you gave* to be with me, *she* gave me fruit from the tree, and I ate" (Gen. 3:12, emphasis added). When the Lord turned to Eve, she essentially did the same thing: "The serpent tricked me, and I ate" (Gen. 3:13).

This is a manifestation of our stolen knowledge. We employ our knowledge of good and evil in service to ourselves. The statements of Adam and Eve were technically true, but they were intended to conceal rather than reveal. The humans, we see, have begun to take on the craftiness of the serpent. The one who is the Accuser (Rev. 12:10) has made them into crafty accusers. They have lost their innocence. Adam and Eve speak truth, but they speak it to deflect truth—the truth that they are altogether guilty. In deflecting guilt, they accuse. In our fallen state, we point out dust particles in others' eyes in order to deflect attention away from the tree trunks in our own eyes (Matt. 7:3).

The knowledge of good and evil is also at work in the fact that throughout their dialogue with God, Adam and Eve clearly persisted in the judgment that God was untrustworthy. They continued to embrace the serpent's deceptive depiction of God. As a result, they were afraid of him and were not honest with him. If Adam and Eve could have realized that the serpent lied to them, confessed their sin, and returned to their simple confidence that God was good, there would undoubtedly have been consequences to be suffered, but God would have granted them his mercy.

As it happened, Adam and Eve had eaten the forbidden fruit, had placed themselves in the center of the garden, and thus were filtering everything through their self-centered and self-serving knowledge of good and evil. So, instead of returning to trust and vulnerable honesty, they acted out of their own self-interest and continued to judge God rather than humbly letting God be the judge. Hence, they tried to protect themselves by blaming others.

Instead of trusting in God to love them and defend them in their sin, Adam and Eve became their own defense attorneys. They trusted their own knowledge of good and evil to protect them rather than trusting God. They trusted their own ability to justify themselves rather than trusting God. Like Job and his friends, they were willing to accuse God and others to escape condemnation themselves (Job 40:8).[4]

We learn how mistaken Adam and Eve were in taking this judgmental stance when we look at the cross. Here we see what God looks like as our defense attorney, our "advocate" (1 John 2:1–2). To restore union with us, God himself bears the guilt and punishment of our crime. Christ pleads the case of sinners, as it were, before the justice of the Father. In doing this, Christ breaks the Enemy's deception about who God is and reveals himself to be the God of unsurpassable love and mercy. In other words, God is an unsurpassably loving and effective defense attorney. God ascribes infinite worth to us even when we don't deserve it.

But we can never experience this mercy so long as we rely on our own knowledge of good and evil. If we live off the fruit of this stolen knowledge, our lives have to be derived from our estimation of ourselves, which is itself dependent on whatever worth we can suck from people, things, and our deluded conceptions of God. To feed our emptiness, which the knowledge of good and evil itself created, we must rely on our knowledge of good and evil and seek to justify ourselves. We must therefore hide by rationalizing ourselves and blaming others. We judge others harshly in order to judge ourselves with approval.

This is the opposite of love. We simply cannot ascribe unsurpassable worth to those we judge, any more than we can derive unsurpassable worth from God when we judge him as out to get us. Like a computer virus, the Accuser's introduction of accusation in the scheme of things quickly infects everything. It filters and therefore blocks our receiving, experiencing, and giving God's infinite love. It replaces this love with judgment against God, ourselves, and others.

Banishment

Blocking the Way Back

The final manifestation of the realm of death in the Genesis 3 narrative is Adam and Eve's banishment from Paradise. Here again we find that the serpent spoke a half-truth to the woman. He had implied that God was threatened by the prospect of Adam and Eve eating from the forbidden tree. God didn't want the man and woman to be like him in the respect that he is wise, knowing good and evil. This was in a sense true, as is clear from God's banishment of the man and woman from the garden.

> Then the LORD God said, "See, the man has become like one of us, knowing good and evil; and now, he might reach out his hand and take also from the tree of life, and eat, and live forever"—therefore the LORD God sent him forth from the garden of Eden, to till the ground from which he was taken. He drove out the man; and at the east of the garden of Eden he placed the cherubim, and a sword flaming and turning to guard the way to the tree of life.
>
> Genesis 3:22–24

Now that the man and woman had become like God, knowing good and evil, God ensured they would not become like him in living forever, which would have condemned them to an eternity in their fallen state. It is significant that God had not previously forbidden the man and woman from eating of the Tree of Life as he had the Tree of the Knowledge of Good and Evil. If Adam and Eve had chosen to respect the boundary between them and God that was at the center of Paradise, they could have freely eaten from God's provision for deathless life that also was at the center of Paradise. But to enjoy God's provision at the center, they had to respect the prohibition at the center.

It seems that in their innocent union with God, Adam and Eve were in no hurry to acquire everlasting life, for the narrative suggests they hadn't eaten of the Tree of Life yet. Indeed, God banished Adam from the garden precisely because he thought he "might reach out his hand and take also from the tree of life, and eat, and live forever" (Gen. 3:22). Until that time, it seems Adam and Eve had no concern with death and no hunger for more life. They weren't hungry for more than what they already had in union with God. When it was time for them to eat from the tree, they would have done so out of simple loving obedience to a Creator who always had their best interest in mind.

When the couple thrust themselves into the center, however, and saw the world through the critical filters of good and evil, God suspected they would now want to seize what the Tree of Life offered. They would try to fill their vacuum with endless life. But in their fallen state, even endless life would not have filled their vacuum, any more than our endless attempts to fight off aging in modern times fulfill us. Endless life is only a blessing when accompanied by the quality of life only God can give. Eating from the Tree of Life in their fallen condition would have simply resulted in endless futility; it would have eternalized the vacuum. Hence, God mercifully banished humanity from Paradise and blocked the way back to the Tree of Life.

The half-truth of the serpent's lie is that God was indeed threatened when Adam and Eve acquired their forbidden knowledge, but he was not threatened *for himself*, he was threatened *for us*. His goal of replicating his triune love to and through humanity was threatened. If humanity became immortal in their state of separation from God, in the prison of knowing good and evil, it would have quite literally been eternal hell.

So as an act of mercy as well as judgment, the couple was banished from Eden, and the path to the Tree of Life was blocked. Eating from the forbidden tree now required that they be forbidden from the permitted tree. Though we still persist in the lie that life is to be found in acquiring what we judge as good and avoiding what we judge as evil, God knows that this is, in fact, a living death. Since we have violated the proper boundary God first established between himself and us, God mercifully and justly established another boundary between us and the Tree of Life: Our physical life must come to an end.

Bondage and the Persistence of Love

Out of the fullness of life we were to receive from God, humans were given the authority and responsibility to mediate God's providence on the earth. Our task was to apply God's will "on earth as it is in heaven" (Matt. 6:10). We were created in the image of God to rule (Gen. 1:26). As a race, we surrendered this authority over to Satan, God's adversary, when we accepted his lie (Luke 4:6). Hence, Satan is now described as the god of this present world system (2 Cor. 4:4), the principality and power of the air (Eph. 2:2), the ruler who exercises his destructive influence on everyone and everything (John 12:31; 14:30; 16:11; 1 John 5:19). The entire creation is subjected to futility (Rom. 8:20). Our sin opened the floodgates for powers of destruction to corrupt everything.

This is our curse. Whereas we were supposed to be under the loving lordship of our Creator, applying his will "on earth as it is in heaven," we are now under the cruel lordship of the destroyer (Rev. 9:11; cf. Luke 4:5–8; John 10:10; 2 Cor. 4:4; Eph. 2:2; 1 John 5:19). Whereas we were created to participate in the ecstatic love of our Creator, in Adam we participate in the destructive accusations of the Accuser. Even nature is corrupted by the diabolical powers that now rule. Nature resists our rule and brings us fatigue, pain, and ultimately death (Gen. 3:17–18; Heb. 2:14). Even the animal kingdom, which the Genesis narrative suggests was originally designed to reflect God's loving and peaceful character, now reflects the ruthless character of a ruler who is a predator (Gen. 1:31; 1 Peter 5:8).[5]

Despite the fall and its consequent curse, however, God's love was not deterred. God *is* love. God doesn't stop being God simply because the humans he created have rebelled against him. God does not abandon his goal of having others share in the eternal, ecstatic dance of the Father, Son, and Holy Spirit. The world changed dramatically with the fall, to be sure, but God did not change (Mal. 3:6). The cross reveals the immutability of God's love.

Although God's goal of inviting others into his eternal dance of love did not change, the path to achieving this goal would now have to be long and arduous. God would have to exercise much patience, express a good deal of anger and even more mercy, and suffer unspeakable pain. Indeed, the Son of God would have to go to Golgotha and experience nothing less than hellish separation from the Father to accomplish what God's love had set out to accomplish. But God was willing to do this. Indeed, despite the anguish, he considered it joy (Heb. 12:2).

Mercy in the Midst of the Curse

The fall did not change God's love, but it did necessarily change its form. Corresponding to the Tree of the Knowledge of Good and Evil from which humanity now eats, God's love took the form of judgment and mercy.[6] God's judgment is evident in the Genesis 3 narrative in the curse he allowed to come upon the humans. But God's mercy is evident as well, even in the midst of the curse.

For one thing, as noted above, the physical death that the curse brought is in its own way an act of mercy. God blocked the way back to the Tree of Life out of love for us. It is merciful because this is the only way our bondage to our stolen knowledge, our participation in the realm of death, will end. To be sure, to the extent that we persist in placing ourselves in the center and living out of our knowledge of good and evil, this act of mercy is experienced only as a curse. But our lives as judges have a termination point, and this is, in fact, a blessed thing.

God's mercy is also evident in his willingness to work with Adam and Eve after their fall. God meets us in mercy in the midst of our shame. "The LORD God made garments of skins for the man and for his wife, and clothed them" (Gen. 3:21). Though it was their own fault they felt the need to hide, for they now judged their own nakedness, God tenderly accommodated this felt need. An animal was sacrificed—the first blood sacrifice for sin—and God tenderly helped conceal the shame of his children. God's love "covers a multitude of sins" (1 Peter 4:8).

Most significantly, however, God's relentless mercy is evident even while pronouncing the curse. God cryptically announced that this curse itself shall one day be overcome.

> ·I will put enmity between you [the serpent] and the woman,
> and between your offspring and hers;
> he will strike your head,
> and you will strike his heel.
>
> Genesis 3:15

The natural repulsion people have toward snakes is used to illustrate a cosmic-historical reality. Satan shall always be striking at our heel, but the offspring of Eve shall strike his head. The New Testament sees this promise as fulfilled in Christ (Rev. 12:13–17). Through his death and resurrection, Christ dealt a fatal blow to the Accuser who makes us accusers (Rev. 12:10–11). In allowing himself to be struck down by the oppressive powers of this age, Christ defeated the oppressive powers of this age (Eph. 2:6–8). In becoming a curse, Christ in principle broke the curse (Gal. 3:13). In the words of Paul to believers at Colossae:

> When you were dead in trespasses and the uncircumcision of your flesh, God made you alive together with him, when he forgave us all our trespasses, erasing the record that stood against us with its legal demands. He set this aside, nailing it to the cross. He disarmed the rulers and authorities and made a public example of them, triumphing over them in it.
>
> Colossians 2:13–15

The record of our sin "that stood against us" was nailed to the cross, and thus the "rulers and authorities" have been "disarmed," conquered, and made into a mockery. For the only weapon the powers ever had to use against us was our own sin. On the cross we were judged and crucified, and through the resurrection we have been set free. "Because of Christ," the Accuser has nothing to accuse us of any longer!

The Old Testament as a whole points toward this moment, beginning here in Genesis 3 as God pronounces his curse on the world. God's love has to take the form of judgment and mercy now that we filter everything through the prison bars of our knowledge of good and evil. But for all who will accept it, his mercy always triumphs over judgment (James 2:13).

As the body of Christ, the church is called and empowered to live out God's triumphant mercy in the midst of the curse. In part 4 of this work, to which we now turn, we will discuss what this looks like. We shall begin this discussion in the next chapter by analyzing how all three of the manifestations of the realm of death are overcome by mercy in the body of Christ as we learn to place love above our knowledge of good and evil.

Living in Love

chapter 10

Reversing the Curse

Above all, maintain constant love for one another, for love covers a multitude of sins.

1 Peter 4:8

In the world between curse and promise, between . . . good and evil, God deals with man in his own way. "He made them garments," says the Bible. That means that God accepts men as they are, as fallen.

Dietrich Bonhoeffer

Discipleship does not afford us a point of vantage from which to attack others; we come to them with an unconditional offer of fellowship, with the single-mindedness of the love of Jesus.

Dietrich Bonhoeffer

In the last chapter we saw that the three manifestations of the realm of death and judgment in the Genesis narrative were that Adam and Eve fell into a life of performing and hiding, they deflected responsibility by blaming others, and they were banished from the garden. In this chapter we shall first review God's accommodating mercy to Adam and Eve and to all humanity as we dwell under the curse in this realm of death. We shall then discuss how the three manifestations of death are in the process of being reversed in the collective body of those who receive and walk in this mercy.

The God Who Accommodates and Covers

Love over Ethical Ideals

As we saw in the last chapter, God expresses mercy in the midst of the curse. God's curse and mercy are not equally balanced realities, however, for God's mercy is not just present in the curse—it has the last word and ultimately triumphs over the curse (James 2:13). Indeed, the curse itself is just a stepping-stone God uses in accomplishing his goal of expressing the perfect love that he is to us, in us, and through us. God takes our curse upon himself in order to extend his mercy to us.

The church is the body of those who have said yes to this mercy and are thus called to live in the light of God's mercy within the curse. As with Adam and Eve, whom God tenderly clothed to conceal their nakedness, we too are called to proclaim that God's love "covers a multitude of sins" (1 Peter 4:8). God tenderly clothes us in our nakedness, our vulnerability to judgment, and our shameful depravity. In his mercy, the all-holy God works with us. When we fail in his plan A, he tenderly works with us on a plan B, and then a plan C, and then a plan D. For most of us, he's gone through the entire alphabet many times! "The steadfast love of the LORD never ceases, his mercies never come to an end" (Lam. 3:22).

God's accommodating love is displayed throughout the biblical narrative. When God's ideal for monogamy was not working in ancient Israel because many men were killed in wars, for example, God accommodated his will and allowed for polygamy and concubines. This was an act of mercy toward women, who in ancient times would often be left without a husband and thus without a means of support. Similarly, when the Israelites rebelliously wanted a king like other nations, God reluctantly gave them one, even though this was not his ideal (1 Sam. 8:4–22).

Along the same lines, when divorce became inevitable because of the hardness of our hearts, God worked with us to make this sinful occurrence as humane as possible (Deut. 24:1–4; cf. Matt.

19:7–8). This too was an act of mercy toward women who were being abandoned by husbands without due process. Although it was a break from God's ideal of having one sexual partner throughout a lifetime, and in this sense involved adultery (Mark 10:11–12), God nevertheless allowed for divorced people to be remarried. Jesus assumes divorced women, at least, will get remarried: "Anyone who divorces his wife . . . *causes her* to commit adultery" (Matt. 5:32, emphasis added).

This concession was, and is, an act of love toward divorced people who are not given the gift of celibacy (Matt. 19:11–12; cf. 1 Cor. 7:9). God certainly hates divorce, and remarriage involves a departure from his ideal (Mal. 2:16), but in the fallen world, some failed marriage relationships become worse than divorce. God himself commanded certain marriages to terminate (Ezra 9–10). Indeed, it seems he was himself willing to divorce Israel at one point (Jer. 3:8)!

Another example of God's willingness to accommodate himself to our fallen condition is found in Matthew's account of Christ's birth. Though God despises all forms of astrology and divination (Deut. 4:19; 17:2–5; 18:10), he calls a number of professional astrologers and diviners from the East—the "Magi"—to honor his son (Matt. 2:1–14). Indeed, he uses an astrological sign to do it, for this is the language they understand. Not only this, but he accepts gifts purchased by the Magi occult practices as acts of worship (Matt. 2:11). As much as God hates astrology and divination, he apparently loves astrologers and diviners who have a genuine hunger for him. Hence, he's not above suspending his own judgment of their practices to use a star to bring them to Christ, and he's not above accepting offerings from their occult practices as expressions of worshiping hearts.

God has always shown that he is a God who is willing to work with us in our fallen condition. Even the giving of the law in the Old Testament was an accommodation on God's part. Many of the laws in the Old Testament were not remotely close to God's ideal (e.g., laws about women, slavery, war), but they reflect God's accommodating love as he works to inch us forward, out of our barbarism, closer to his ideal.[1]

Even more fundamentally, the very structure of the law reveals God's loving accommodation. God's love takes the form of judgment and mercy, corresponding to our knowledge of good and evil. More fundamentally, the central purpose of this law was to drive us beyond it to Christ. By condemning us, the law exposes the impossibility of our ever living in union with God so long as our relationship is filtered by our knowledge of good and evil. The law thereby prepares us to receive God's judgment of our rebellious knowledge in Christ and opens us up to being reconciled with God in Jesus Christ.[2]

Though God banished us from the garden and the Tree of Life, and though we yet live under the curse, God has not abandoned us, and he promises that he never will (Matt. 28:20). God's mercy permeates his judgment and ultimately triumphs over it. God does not impose his own perfect standard of good and evil on us in an inflexible manner. If he did, we would all be hopelessly lost. Rather, God lovingly works with us in the midst of our fallenness, while we still struggle under the curse. Though the principles of God's character are absolute, God accommodates his perfect moral principles to our fallen reality as he patiently leads us toward his ideal.

We might say that God chooses perfect love over perfect ethics, and this very accommodating choice expresses the essence of who God is. God is a God of love whose love covers a multitude of sins.

The Ultimate Accommodation

As with all things that pertain to the heart of God, his willingness to clothe us in our shameful nakedness is most clearly seen on the cross. God not only accommodates us in our fallen condition, *he becomes one of us* in the midst of our fallen condition. God not only accommodates us in the midst of our sin, *he becomes our sin* (2 Cor. 5:21). God not only works with us in our banishment from Paradise, *he becomes our banishment from Paradise*. God not only works with us in our separation from God, *he becomes our separation from God*. He not only continues to love us within the curse under which we live, *he becomes our curse*.

Nothing could be further from God's ideal than to become *the opposite* of his ideal—to become sin, banishment, separation, the curse. Yet this is precisely what the Lord does for us. And in doing this, God clothes us with his righteousness in the midst of our shame. God covers a great multitude of sins—in principle, all sin—with his love.

The Church as God's Vehicle of Mercy

The church is called to represent this God, just as Christ did. Indeed, the church *is* Christ continuing to manifest the true God. As Bonhoeffer said, "The Church is not a religious community of worshippers of Christ but is *Christ Himself* who has taken form among men."[3] Hence, the church is called "the body of Christ." Living out this truth is the way we testify to a life and a love that is free from bondage to the Tree of the Knowledge of Good and Evil. It is how Christ manifests the reversal of the fall that he achieved on Calvary.

God's love is merciful; so must our love be. If even God does not hold his rightful knowledge of good and evil over us in judgment but rather loves us *where we are*, how much less can we who are sinners hold our stolen and illegitimate knowledge of good and evil over one another, or even over ourselves? How much more (if that were possible) should we rather extend mercy and love to one another and to ourselves? We ourselves live before God only because we have had our shame clothed in mercy and love.

God's love is patient; so must ours be. God's love does not start with an ethical ideal and then pronounce judgment. God doesn't start where he wishes we were, condemning us for what we are not. God starts where we actually are and then pronounces hope and patiently and graciously loves us into becoming what we can be and what we, in fact, already are in Christ.

The body of Christ is to love mercifully and patiently. We are to accept people *wherever* they are and patiently love them and view them with hope. While we cannot ignore practical considerations of safety, we are to embrace people as they are, trusting that the Spirit of God will use our love to lead them to a place closer to where God wants them to be. We are to love like this because this is how we ourselves are loved.

Finally, God's love is accommodating; so must ours be. Unlike ethical principles, which are always abstract, universal, and idealistic, God's love is always perfectly tailored to the complex uniqueness of each individual's nonideal life situation in the present. The covering Adam needed was different from the one Eve needed. When we live out our calling and embody God's triune love, the church does the same thing. We do not live by our knowledge of ethical principles, however good and noble and true they may be. Rather, we live by following the Spirit and by loving people where they are, in the complexity and uniqueness of their nonideal situations. And we do so without judgment.

As we saw in chapter 5, this is the difference between a genuinely loving husband and a merely ethical one. We are called to live out of love, not out of an ethical system. Of course this does not in any sense entail that we relativize ethical truths, but it does mean that we make them subservient to love. Moral principles are absolute, but only love submitted to the will of God can direct us on how they apply in a particular situation.

Only by being acutely aware of our own fallibility and sinfulness and making ethical principles subservient to love do we acquire the freedom and boldness to enter into solidarity with people in radically nonideal situations—as Jesus did with prostitutes and tax collectors.[4] People who live in ethical principles cannot get this close to such people. Their knowledge of good and evil filters their relationships and keeps them from fully entering into the concreteness of another's sinful situation. They can only pronounce what such people *ought* to do and *should* have done.

However, it is only when we enter into solidarity with people as they are that we acquire the wisdom to know how, when, and if various ethical principles apply to their lives. Only then do we learn how to realistically and helpfully adapt ethical principles to the real situations in which people find themselves. Only love, led by the Spirit of God, can discern when (for example) the ideal must be abandoned for a lesser of two evils. And only love, given without hesitation and without conditions, can ever motivate people to trust us enough to invite us to speak into their lives in the first place. This is how God loves us, this is how we are called to love all others, and this is how people are helped in the concrete situations of their lives.

Abolishing Performance and Hiding

Freedom from Performance

When we cease getting life from our knowledge of good and evil and live out the mercy of God in the midst of the fall, we begin to reverse the three manifestations of death depicted in Genesis 3. By living in God's love, we pass from death to life (1 John 3:14). The process of living this out in community is the process of manifesting life arising out of death.

To begin, if we understand and live out who we are in Christ, we are freed from the need to perform and hide. The cross alone defines everything about us. As we noted in chapter 8, on the cross Christ uncovered the full depth of our sin and the full horror of God's judgment of our sin. At the same time, and in fact because of this, the cross reveals the righteousness we have as a gracious gift from God.

The community of those who embody this must therefore be the community that is free from the need to perform. If all of our worth is found in Christ, and if we trust that this worth is unsurpassable, there is simply no *extra worth* to be gotten by such things as looking good, acting religious, or being successful. These things may or may not be true about us. But if they are, they only *express* an unsurpassable value we *already* have in Christ; they don't *add* to it. The body of Christ is called to be the community of people who understand this and live it out. The body of Christ is called to be a community for whom idols of performance have died.

Therefore, in the body of Christ there must be no points given for looking good and no points taken for looking bad. In Christ, the point system with which most social groups—especially religious communities—operate has been utterly abolished. It was nailed to the cross with all our sins (Col. 2:4–15). Hence, in Christ we can no longer view ourselves or others through the lens of our knowledge of good and evil but can only view ourselves and others through the lens of the cross. "In Christ . . . the only thing that counts is faith working through love" (Gal. 5:6). We have faith that God is who God says he is in Christ, and we are who God says we are in Christ. And we express this faith through love. *Nothing else matters!*

Freedom from Hiding

When the pharisaic point system has been abolished, when people no longer derive life from the fruit of their knowledge of good and evil, and thus when performing as a strategy for getting life is abandoned, there is no longer any need to hide. In Christ, we already know the very worst and the very best about each other.

We know that no matter how good we may appear, we are in fact sinners whose depravity was so great the Son of God himself had to die for us. We also know that however messed up our lives may appear, if we have placed our trust in Christ we are redeemed children of the most high God who have inherited the righteousness of God himself as well as "every spiritual blessing in the heavenly places" (Eph. 1:3). We are filled with a life that is not conditioned by our knowledge of good and evil.

There is thus no longer any need to hide. Shame has been swallowed up in mercy. Because of God's love, we are permitted to simply be real people with real struggles who are saved and given a new identity by a real Savior, in the process of being transformed by God's real love.

This of course doesn't mean that every gathering of believers is an appropriate context for people to air all their deepest sins. And it certainly doesn't mean that it is appropriate for people to bring other people out of hiding. Love respects whatever boundaries other people believe they need. But it does mean that the church as a whole must embody the kind of loving atmosphere in which no one feels pressured to pretend. As we shall discuss in chapter 12, it also means that within the body of Christ we should cultivate intimate relationships in which people can speak the truth to one another in love and confess their sins to one another (Eph. 4:15; James 5:16) without fear of judgment.

The body of Christ must be the one fellowship on the planet in which people feel absolutely free to be honest and real, for it is the one fellowship on the planet that shouldn't be structured around people's knowledge of good and evil. There is in this body nothing to hide, for there is nothing to gain and nothing to lose. In Christ, there is only love that accepts where each person is and, in appropriate relationships, patiently loves people to where God knows they can be. Churches, not bars, should have the reputation as being the one place where people can be totally open and honest with others without fear of judgment.

Freedom to Heal

The community in which performance and hiding have ceased is a community in which healing can occur. This is also an essential part of the church's calling. Emotional wounds that are concealed are wounds that can never be healed. Only when people feel safe enough to reveal their innermost pain are they able to begin to deal with it, but this sort of safety requires a context that is free of judgment.

So long as people suspect they will be judged because of (for example) their dishonesty, their abortion, their secret addiction, or their sexual cravings, they will not risk bringing these things out of hiding. So long as a group's collective knowledge of good and evil remains dominant, such people will tend to clothe these issues with a good performance. Indeed, all members of the group will tend to clothe their vulnerable nakedness with a performance. Consequently, it is unlikely that anyone in the group will ever be healed from his or her issues.

Groups in which people relate through the filter of their knowledge of good and evil rather than unconditional love tend to produce people who are profoundly and permanently sick. They may look good, but in fact they are sick. Indeed, they are sick *because* they try to look good. The participants live in secret shame, their wounds fester and often get worse, and, most tragically, they never experience the life-giving, unconditional love of God from him or through his people.

Only when love is placed above everything else, as the Bible commands, can we experience unconditional love, which is the only love that reaches the inner spirit of a person, for it is not based on performance. Only when we resolve that *the only thing that matters* is loving one another unconditionally as an expression of our faith that Christ has loved us and atoned for our sins can we be real *as we are* and thus grow to where God *wants us to be.*

Freedom from Blame

Judging and Explaining

The second manifestation of our lives in the realm of death that we discussed in the previous chapter is that we blame. The Accuser has succeeded in making a race of accusers. Living out of our rebelliously acquired knowledge of good and evil, we have an almost indefatigable drive to assign blame. We blame ourselves, each other, and often God.

Indeed, assigning blame is often our preferred means to explain something. We explain why a man lost his job by blaming his laziness and judging him to be a bum. We explain why a girl got pregnant by blaming her promiscuity and judging her to be a whore. We explain why a man sodomized a boy by blaming his lust and judging him to be an evil pervert.

In all such cases, we leap from an observed behavior to a personalized judgment. Our judgment is not simply an assessment about the rightness or wrongness of a behavior—it's about *the person*. It's about *his or her worth*. And we assign this worth, or lack of worth, by concluding that the person is a bum, a whore, a pervert, a racist, or whatever.

Acting as an explanation of the behavior, our judgment preempts investigation and thus doesn't accomplish anything productive in response to the behavior we observe. Indeed, it is only our addiction to the Tree of the Knowledge of Good and Evil that deludes us into thinking we have explained anything when we judge others. In fact, judgments prevent us from discovering legitimate explanations and thus prevent love from ever helping the person move beyond his or her behavior. As Bonhoeffer repeatedly made clear, judgment is the "gravest impediment" to loving and helpful action. "The irreconcilable opposite of action is judgment."[5]

Judgments only serve the people who make them. They never help the person judged. We eat from the Tree of the Knowledge of Good and Evil to get worth. We feel distinct from and superior to the people we judge. And we feel more secure for having convinced ourselves that the world is neatly divided between good people and bad people, and we are not like *those* bad people.

We have not explained anything or helped anyone other than ourselves with our judgment.

The Story behind the Person

Consider that today's bum was once a young boy full of life, filled with dreams, living with a future of hope. What happened? The whore once wanted to grow up and be someone's lovely princess. What killed that tender dream? The evil pervert once was a mother's precious child who harbored dreams of being a sports star or respected businessman, perhaps like his father. What went wrong?

People don't just decide one day to be socially worthless, sexually promiscuous, or pedophiles. They don't just decide it is in their best interest to live this way. Neither bums nor whores nor perverts really believe their behavior will make them happier and more fulfilled human beings.

In fact, people who engage in destructive behaviors are usually miserable people. They don't benefit from their behavior and they know it. Why, then, do they choose to go down this path? Blaming their character traits and labeling them "bums," "whores," or "evil perverts" does not address this question. Such relabeling accomplishes nothing—except making us feel superior and secure as judges.

In reality, the explanation for a person's behavior is as long and complex as life itself. Without in any way denying our responsibility for our choices, the complete story of a person's life is certainly part of the explanation for why people do what they do. And the only way to understand people's behavior and help them transform it is to *get on the inside* of their stories. This takes a great deal of trust, time, and patience, and it can only be done in love. It can never be accomplished if we are judging them. Indeed, if we draw conclusions about people's inherent worth and think that these conclusions explain their behavior, we will never even see the need or be inclined to get inside their stories.

When we reject self-serving judgments, love people, and empathetically experience their stories from the inside, invariably we begin to understand them better and are moved with compassion toward them. And this understanding gives us a wisdom—the wisdom of love—to know what to do to help them grow out of their destructive behavior.

We readily accept this principle when it comes to *our own* life situations. "If only people understood the complex issues involved in my life," we think, "they wouldn't judge me so harshly." We routinely apply this principle to our children and close friends. Outsiders who judge them harshly simply don't see what we see. Indeed, we may even instinctively apply this principle to people with certain kinds of sins—those that are "religiously sanctioned" within our community (e.g., obesity, divorce and remarriage, greed). But we will never enter into the wisdom of love toward people outside the perimeters of our community's self-definition if we are getting life from the fruit of the forbidden tree.

Jesus and the Woman at the Well

Since the church is called the collective body of Christ, we should note that Jesus consistently demonstrated this sort of wisdom of love. Jesus was moved with empathetic compassion when he faced crowds of people (Matt. 9:36; 14:14). His audiences were composed of ordinary people. They undoubtedly included people who had sex outside of marriage, some who were living together, others who were prostitutes. They included greedy people, deceptive people, demonized people, bigoted people, gay people, self-righteous people, hateful people, and so on. Yet Jesus was moved with compassion, and this compassion gave him wisdom.

A marvelous example of Jesus' wise compassion is his dialogue with the Samaritan woman at the well (John 4:1–42). This was scandalous for a Jewish person—let alone a Jewish rabbi—because first-century Jews typically regarded Samaritans as unclean, worse than the Gentiles (v. 9). More scandalous, however, was that Jesus struck up a conversation with a Samaritan *woman*. Conversing with any woman other than one's wife or daughter was typically frowned upon in first-century Jewish religious culture, and this was a *Samaritan* woman (cf. v. 27).

To top it off, this particular Samaritan woman had a lurid past—and Jesus knew it. She had been married five times and was now living with a man who was not her husband (vv. 17–18)! Yet throughout his dialogue Jesus was concerned about one thing and one thing only: He wanted to express love to this woman. She was a precious creation of God who had unsurpassable worth before her Creator. In fact, within a few years Jesus would give his own life for this priceless woman. Out of love, Jesus wanted to at least plant a seed of understanding in her that she could find all that she had been looking for—working through six relationships in the process—simply by knowing him.

So Jesus asked the woman to give him some water. She was understandably shocked. "You are a Jew and I am a Samaritan woman. How can you ask me for a drink?" she asked. Jesus answered her, "If you knew the gift of God, and who it is that is saying to you, 'Give me a drink,' you would have asked him, and he would have given you living water" (John 4:10). "He *would have given you*," no questions asked. This was Jesus' one desire. He wanted to give this woman *life*. He wanted to quench her thirst. Rather than judge her past or present behavior, Jesus was concerned with filling the emptiness in her soul that was motivating her behavior.

As the conversation unfolded, Jesus revealed that the thirst-quenching water he was speaking of was God's own eternal life, and he was the one who could give it to her. "Those who drink of the water that I will give them," Jesus said, "will never be thirsty. The water that I will give will become in them a spring of water gushing up to eternal life" (v. 14). The woman was still thinking in terms of earthly water, however, and thus responded (perhaps sarcastically), "Sir, give me this water so that I may never be thirsty or have to keep coming here to draw water" (v. 15). If she actually believed Jesus could solve any of her problems, it was only the constant hassle of having to journey to this well all the time. The problem Jesus wanted to fix, however, was much greater than this.

So Jesus gently revealed to the woman that he knew a bit about her story. Up to this point it had been loving for Jesus to hide this woman's multitude of sins, but at this point in the conversation it was loving for Jesus to reveal one of them. He didn't reveal this woman's history to condemn her or to embarrass her in any way. He certainly wasn't trying to shame her into getting her life right. Indeed, Jesus never commented about the information he revealed. Instead, Jesus revealed part of the woman's story solely because he longed for her to know that he was talking about her thirst for life, not just her natural physical thirst. He wanted this thirsty woman to know that he was the Messiah, not just a countercultural man whom she happened to meet at the well. And he wanted her to know that he loved her unconditionally and that his offer of refreshing eternal water stood, despite her past and present life situation.

The woman began to get the point. After Jesus mentioned that the woman had been through five husbands and was now living with a man who was not her husband, she responded, "Sir, I see that you are a prophet" (v. 19). The conversation continued but never returned to the information Jesus brought up about her past.

By the time the conversation ended, the woman apparently believed that Jesus was the Messiah. With excitement and joy—not shame—she ran back to her village and proclaimed to everyone, "Come and see a man who told me everything I have ever done! He cannot be the Messiah, can he?" (v. 29). The story says nothing more about how this woman subsequently worked out the details of her life, for this would undoubtedly be a complex and comparatively irrelevant point. The point of the story is not how Jesus fixes the messiness of people's lives, but how he unconditionally offers the wellspring of God's love *in the midst* of the messiness of people's lives.

The Religious Approach

Pharisees and other people who eat from a religious variety of the fruit of the Tree of the Knowledge of Good and Evil would have had a very different approach to this woman. Their relationship with this woman would not have been unconditionally loving, as was Jesus'. It would have rather been conditioned by their knowledge of good and evil.

If they dared to tarnish their reputations by associating with this woman at all, they would not have viewed her in terms of *her* need but rather in terms of *theirs*. People who get life from religion need to be right and need to try to make other people right or expose them for being wrong. Their attention would have been on the dust particle of this woman's unsavory past rather than on the tree trunks of their own self-righteousness (and whatever other sins were in their lives). If these people had offered this woman any hope at all, it would be on condition that she clean up her act to reconcile it with their knowledge of good and evil.

The Samaritan woman went from being a woman with a scandalous past to an evangelist for Jesus Christ in the span of a short conversation because, thankfully, she did not meet a religious person—she met Jesus Christ. Contemporary "Samaritan women" of ill repute encounter Jesus through the church. The question is, do they really meet *Jesus* when they encounter the church, or do they meet *religious people?*

Loving without Judgment

If we are led by love and by the Spirit of God, there will be times when we are called not only to refrain from judgment but to incarnate ourselves in another person's story to gain understanding and promote healing in his or her life. Most of the time, however, this is not possible. In such cases, love leads us to move past judgment and simply acknowledge that there *is* a story behind a person's behavior that God alone knows fully. In either case, however, there is no judgment; there is only love.

At times we may have to intervene to stop destructive behavior. If it is our place, we may have to hold the person socially responsible for his or her behavior and stipulate consequences. For example, when some members of a family confront another who is an alcoholic because he is destroying himself and his relationship with them, this is loving. But it is never our place to pretend to be God. It is never our place to pronounce in our thoughts, words, or deeds *a conclusion about the person* other than the one God commands us to embrace because of Calvary. It is never our place to serve our own needs by judging others to be evil. When we try to be like God according to the serpent's lie, knowing good and evil, we cease being like God according to God's truth, loving him and loving others as ourselves.

The only thing we need to know is that the other person is, like us, a sinner who has been given unsurpassable worth in Christ Jesus. If we understand ourselves and others as we are in Christ, we will live in the awareness that we are no better than the bum, the whore, the evil pervert, the obese glutton, or the Samaritan woman who failed at five marriages and was now living with a man out of wedlock. Seeing through the lens of the cross, we will live in the understanding that we are all equally condemned and all equally loved. We know the worst and the best about ourselves and every other person ahead of time, and this frees us from the compulsive fallen need to assign blame or make excuses.

What we have in common—our sin and our unsurpass-able worth—dwarfs in significance whatever differences exist among us. This exposes any attempt to separate ourselves from others on the grounds that *we* don't commit *that* sin as nothing more than an idolatrous attempt to acquire worth by sucking it off of others. Whatever particular dust-particle-like sin we see in another can only remind us of our own tree-trunk-like sin that has been nailed to the cross, which in turn must remind us that we have been loved freely and are therefore called to love freely (Luke 6:31–38; 7:47; 1 John 3:16; cf. Matt. 10:8).

This is the life of love that the Lord calls us and empowers us to live. This is our participation in the eternal, triune fellowship. At the center of this participation is the confidence that the Lord will sustain us (Tree of Life) and the awareness that we are not God and must leave to God that which God reserves for himself (the Tree of the Knowledge of Good and Evil). As it was in Eden, so it is now in Christ. Living in right relationship with God and with others revolves around honoring the divine prohibition in the center of the garden. We can only be God-like in the way we are created and saved to be if we refrain from trying to become god-like in the way the Accuser tempts us to be.

As the community of redeemed people who know this, the church must be the community of people who simply love as God loves. We are not to eat from the forbidden tree by assessing people in terms of their relative goodness or evil. *That* job belongs to God alone.

Freedom from Banishment

Reversing the Ban

The final manifestation of death we discussed in the previous chapter was God's banishment of the man and the woman from the garden he had created for them and his blocking the way back to the Tree of Life. God mercifully and justly imposed a death sentence upon us because of our rebellion. Our spiritual death also resulted in a physical death. From this point on, life "in Adam" would not be the Paradise God intended. Our curse is that we live by the fruit of the tree from which we ate and thus outside the beautiful, innocent union with God. Moreover, we live largely under the domination of a world and of a spiritual power we were meant to dominate.

In principle, Christ reversed all this on the cross when he closed the infinite gulf that separated us from God. No gap remains. On the cursed tree on which Christ hung, the forbidden tree from which we ate was abolished. Our judgmental way of life was slain. On the cross, both our goodness and our evil as a strategy for getting life was exposed as sin, and we were given a righteousness that does not and cannot come from our own efforts. There is no further righteousness we can achieve or imagine. On the cross and through the resurrection, the Accuser was disarmed (Col. 2:14–15), for the only weapon he ever had against us—our sin—was annihilated. For all who will accept Christ's sacrifice, not a sin remains. On the cross and through the resurrection, spiritual death, and even physical death, has in principle been overcome. We share the eternal life of Christ.

All of this has *in principle* been accomplished, but of course it has not been fully manifested. We live in the momentary interval between the light going on and the darkness fleeing, between the *already* and *not yet* of the beginning and end of the one event of the cross and resurrection. But we are called to manifest the *already* in the midst of the *not yet* by regarding the event as *fait accompli*. We are called to live in the dying proclamation of the Savior: "It is finished" (John 19:30). The curtain that separated us from the Holy of Holies has been ripped in two (Matt. 27:51). Our banishment from God's presence is over. We are accepted despite our sin.

People can and do continue to reject what Christ has accomplished. They may choose to live in the serpent's lie about God and about themselves. They may refuse to manifest the truth of what Christ has done on Calvary. Hence, they may continue to live in the futility of desperately trying to acquire the life God wants to give them for free. Indeed, they may persist in this futile rebellion to the bitter end, sealing their separation from God for eternity.[6] But the fact that people remain free to deny the truth does not alter the truth. Whether or not they acknowledge and manifest it, in Christ the lie has been exposed, the devil has been defeated, the curse has been cursed, atonement has been made for the sin, and the banishment has ceased.

The job of the church is to proclaim and embody this truth, in the hope that all will acknowledge it, experience it, and be transformed by it. We are thus called to live out the cessation of the ban by demonstrating a love that knows no condition or boundaries.

It's crucial to understand that our all-encompassing acceptance of others is not a shallow form of tolerance, such as people sometimes extend to former enemies. God does not merely tolerate us, as though we must forever bear the shame of a people who once rebelled and now must be grateful for receiving crumbs that fall from the master's table. No, when the prodigal son returns, he is immediately acknowledged as a son, *as though he'd never left.* He is robed with an heir's robe, and a party is thrown for him (Luke 15:11–32). So it is for all who say yes to what God has done in Christ. A party is thrown for them, and God himself sings and claps his hands in jubilation over them (Zeph. 3:17; Luke 15:6, 9–10).

The Outrageous Invitation

In Christ, we who "once were far off have been brought near" (Eph. 2:12–13)—so near, in fact, that we are "in Christ," who is in perfect union with the Father and Spirit. In truth, we could not be nearer than we are when we say yes to the reuniting work of God through Christ on the cross. We once again dance in the fellowship of the triune God, as though we had never left. God's love covers—indeed, it abolishes—our multitude of sins.

God's love—the love that he eternally is—flows to us, abides in us, and flows through us to others.

As the community that dances once again in the triune fellowship, the church must be a people who manifest to all others the cessation of the ban from the garden. Our single task is to ascribe unsurpassable worth to every human being, and the form this takes in our fellowship is that we invite and welcome all to the celebration of the cessation of the ban.

Whoever is hungry—and all are—can come and eat without payment. Whoever is thirsty—and all are—may come and drink from the spring of life for free (Isa. 55:1; Rev. 22:17). Indeed, they can have this eternal spring of refreshing water flowing out from their own innermost being (John 7:37–38). Whoever is weary and carries a heavy burden may come and find rest (Matt. 11:28). Whoever wants life, whoever wants joy, whoever wants peace—whoever wants back into the garden—may come. Samaritan women who have failed in five marriages; tax collectors like Matthew who rip off their own people working for an unjust, oppressive government; zealots like Simon who assassinate tax collectors in the name of their political ideology; people who will tarnish our reputation with their ungodly lifestyles, as they did Jesus' (Matt. 9:10–11; 11:19; Mark 2:15–16; Luke 7:34; 15:2)—all are invited to the celebration of the cessation of the ban. And it is our job to announce it *by how we love.*

When they come, they must not simply be tolerated, for God never merely tolerates anyone. If we eat from the Tree of the Knowledge of Good and Evil, we can at best tolerate the bum, the whore, the sexual pervert, or the messed-up Samaritan woman. Though we may tolerate them for a time—and feel as though we are being gracious while doing it—we will be condemning them in our mind, wanting to fix them with our superior ethical knowledge. But really we will be trying to fix ourselves, for we feed off our presumed superiority and feel as though we're condoning their sin if we don't condemn it. We will believe—and they will certainly sense—that despite our tolerance, we are (at least in our own minds) really a holy club of people who "have arrived." And, if we continue to feast from the forbidden tree, we will fear that our reputation will be tarnished if we do not clean them up quickly.

Of course, all the while we will be unwittingly condemning ourselves as hypocrites. For as a matter of fact, none of us have "arrived." It's just that, for self-serving reasons, we've decided to categorize some sins—*our* sins—as acceptable and other sins—*their* sins—as condemnable.

If we view ourselves and everyone else through the lens of the cross rather than our knowledge of good and evil, we will see that our self-serving categorizations of sin are as unnecessary as they are illegitimate. In Christ, we *all* stand condemned and forgiven and righteous. Hence, the prostitute, the bum, the pervert, the gossiper, the addict, the pedophile, the greedy, the murderer, the obese, the homosexual, the rude, the unbathed, the drunk, the poor—even the Pharisee if he is willing—are to be welcomed back to the garden with enthusiastic celebration.

If we see things through the lens of the cross, our welcome cannot be on the condition that they first clean up their act. Scripture does not say that Jesus fellowshipped with *former* prostitutes, tax collectors, and sinners. The Pharisees would not have found this as objectionable. What outraged them was that "this fellow welcomes *sinners* and eats with them" (Luke 15:2, emphasis added).

The point is all the more important for us because, unlike Jesus, *we* are not entirely cleaned up yet. How can we demand this of others as a condition of fellowship? Indeed, we are not even to welcome them back on condition that they first believe. They will never see the reality of love that *leads* one to repent and believe if we withhold love *until* they repent and believe (Rom. 2:4). Love believes all things, hopes for and sees the best in everyone, and bears what must be borne in order to do so (1 Cor. 13:7).

We must therefore welcome all who are hungry and thirsty simply on the basis of their hunger and thirst, not on the basis that they've already accepted the One who alone can feed their hunger and quench their thirst. We are to embrace them as one of our own, hoping that as God works in their lives, they will eventually come to partake of the life that is offered them in Jesus Christ.

Bonhoeffer stated the matter well:

It is not an approved standard of righteous living that separates a
follower of Christ from the unbeliever, but it is Christ who stands
between them. Christians always see other men as brethren to
whom Christ comes; they meet them only by going to them with
Jesus. . . . The disciple can meet the non-disciple only as a man
to whom Jesus comes. . . . Discipleship does not afford us a point
of vantage from which to attack others; we come to them with
an unconditional offer of fellowship, with the single-mindedness
of the love of Jesus.[7]

It is only when we in love draw all as near to ourselves as God
has drawn us to himself in Christ that they begin to experience
nearness to God. Then the process that is going on in us begins
to go on in them: The love of God begins to lead them to repentance, to constrain them, and to change them, just as it does
us (Rom. 2:4; 2 Cor. 5:14; Eph. 2:4–5). Indeed, the perimeter
between "us" and "them" *loses all significance.* When we love
people *exactly as they are,* which is how we are loved, we invite
them into the possibility of eventually becoming what God knows
they can become when the reconciling work of Christ is fully
manifested in their lives.

None of this can happen, however, if we put the cart before the
horse and hypocritically demand change in people as a condition
for extending God's love to them. The Tree of the Knowledge of
Good and Evil will block the way back to the Tree of Life.

The point is that God does not merely tolerate us, and we
must not simply tolerate each other, even the vilest sinner
(who is, after all, on a par with all of us) who comes into our
fellowship. We must celebrate the cessation of the ban with
each and every person who simply knows he or she is hungry
and thirsty. Our task is to love as God loves, to celebrate as God
celebrates, to embrace others as we have been embraced, and
to draw near to others as we have been brought near. Whatever
sin persists in the prodigal son's life is hidden by the robe of
sonship we wrap around him, for we ourselves dwell in the
garden of God's love only because we have been wrapped in
this very robe.

If we are celebrating the cessation of the ban in this outrageous fashion, we will face two challenges. On the one hand, we
will likely face the wrath of religious people whose entire way of

life is assailed by this model of the church. On the other hand, we must face the legitimate question of how the church can be this open and yet remain faithful to its call to grow in Christ-likeness. We shall discuss the first of these problems in the next chapter and the second of these problems in chapter 12.

chapter 11

Confronting Pharisees

But woe to you, scribes and Pharisees, hypocrites! For you lock people out of the kingdom of heaven. For you do not go in yourselves, and when others are going in, you stop them.

Matthew 23:13

In . . . freedom Jesus leaves all laws beneath Him; and to the Pharisees this freedom necessarily appears as the negation of all order, all piety and all belief. Jesus casts aside all the distinctions which the Pharisee so laboriously maintains. . . . For the Pharisee, He is a nihilist, a man who knows and respects only his own law, an egoist and a blasphemer of God.

Dietrich Bonhoeffer

Love doesn't always take the form of warm and compassionate words. In exceptional circumstances, it involves confrontation and questioning. In these last two chapters we will examine these other forms of love and discuss the important role they play in the body of Christ. In doing this, we will address the two questions posed at the end of the previous chapter: How do we respond to the rage of the Pharisees, and how do we practically grow in Christ-likeness when we are welcoming all into the celebration of the cessation of the ban?

Pharisaical Rage as Evidence We Are Loving Correctly

The Rage of the Pharisees

If we are proclaiming the cessation of the ban faithfully, the Pharisees of our day will be offended. This is not something to be feared. It is rather something to be welcomed.

The church can only be the conduit of God's outrageous love if it stops being concerned about its reputation in the eyes of those who feast on a religious version of the fruit of the Tree of the Knowledge of Good and Evil. Such a concern is clear evidence that we are ourselves still eating from the forbidden tree. The only reputation we need be concerned with is to have the one Jesus had. He was known for his unprecedented love, by those who would receive it, and scorned for his irreligious attitudes, by those who would not. He was the former because he was the latter. So should it be in the church, which is, after all, simply the corporate expression of this very same Jesus.

Jesus' religious reputation was tarnished in the eyes of religious people because he did not honor many of the religious taboos of his day. Walking in unity with God, Jesus possessed a joyful freedom—indeed, a recklessness—that was scandalous to those whose worth was derived from their supposed ability to judge good and evil and their willingness to separate themselves as good apart from those they judged as evil. Jesus hung out with women, some of whom had tarnished reputations (Luke 7:36–50; 8:1–2; 23:27; John 4:7–27). He was a companion to gluttons, though the Bible expressly warns against such friendships (Prov. 28:7). He fellowshipped with tax collectors, drunkards, and other sinners (Matt. 9:10; 11:19; Luke 5:29–30; 15:1). He healed and fellowshipped with lepers (Matt. 11:5; 26:6; Mark 1:40–41; Luke 17:12–13). He didn't require his disciples to fast (Mark 2:18–20). He praised Gentiles, Samaritans, and even prostitutes and tax collectors over respected Jewish religious leaders (Matt. 12:41; 21:31; Luke 10:29–37; 18:10–14). And he healed people and plucked corn on the Sabbath (Mark 2:23–24; 3:2–4; Luke 13:10–16; 14:1–4; John 5:8–16; 9:14–16). All such actions were loving and expressed the will of God. But they constituted "sins against the knowledge of good and evil" as Bonhoeffer put it.[1]

Among the religious, Jesus' reputation was dishonorable. But Jesus wasn't concerned about his reputation. He did what he was called to do and left other matters in the hands of his Father. Jesus came to heal the sick, not to placate the religious sensibilities of those who thought they were healthy (Mark 2:17). To heal the sick, you have to love the sick, which means you have to fellowship with the sick. And this means you have to ignore what those who (mistakenly) think they're healthy think about you!

Jesus loved with reckless abandon. In doing this, he expressed who God is and thus who we are before God. The Creator fellowships with those who crucified his Son—so intimately that he makes us participants in the eternal love he shares with his Son. The singular task of the church is to replicate this eternal, reckless love to the world. One indication that we are doing our job well is that sinners on the fringes of society will be enjoying fellowship with us, as they did with Jesus. Another indication, directly resulting from this, is that those who survive by eating from the Tree of the Knowledge of Good and Evil will judge us.

If, for example, a church treats gays with the same compassion religious judges treat their own overweight people, its leaders will likely be condemned as "compromising the Word of God" by these judges (see chapter 5). Such a church is sinning against the (self-serving) knowledge of good and evil from which the religious judges feed. Consequently, the judges will likely feel as though their god has been assaulted, and, as a matter of fact, *it has!* As idolatrous people often do when their gods are threatened, they may rage. They did so with Jesus, and there's every reason to believe they will do so with communities that look like Jesus.

Hence, a church that celebrates the cessation of the ban effectively and loves as God loves has to be willing to have their reckless love scorned as compromising, relativistic, liberal, soft on doctrine, or antireligious. After all, what kind of church attracts and embraces prostitutes, drunkards, gays, and drug addicts? What kind of church routinely has smokers, drinkers, gamblers, and bums ushering during their services, hanging out in their small groups, singing in their choir, signing up for classes, volunteering for ministry, and so forth—without anyone immediately confronting their sin? What kind of church would accept a woman who was still living with a man out of wedlock after having gone through five marriages? What kind of church blurs the boundary between those who are "in" and those who are "out" to this degree?

The answer, I submit, is a *Jesus kind of church*. It is a church in which the only qualification for fellowship is that the people are spiritually hungry and thirsty and something somewhere down deep tells them that the food and water they are looking for is to be found in the outrageous, reckless love that flows in and through these people. These church people love the seekers without judgment, and they have a gnawing suspicion that *this* is that for which they were created.

The Center and the Perimeter

To love like this, a community has to be freed from an obsession with its perimeter—its ability to know or decide who is "in" and who is "out." It has to be okay with wheat and weeds growing alongside each other. Indeed, it has to surrender to God any attempt to distinguish wheat from weeds (Matt. 13:24–30, 36–43). Such a community will have to be freed from the addiction to the Tree of the Knowledge of Good and Evil to the point that it is willing to live in total ambiguity as to who is "in" and who is "out."

Of course, there are occasions when the destructive nature of a person's unrepentant attitudes and behaviors requires removal from fellowship, as we shall discuss in the next chapter. But so long as the community as a whole is focused on its perimeter rather than its center, it cannot be a community that fully celebrates the cessation of the ban. It will be to some extent getting life from what it is against, as defined by its own self-serving version of the knowledge of good and evil, rather than by what it is for. What is true of all organizations, buildings, individual people, and the whole creation is true of churches: They exhibit life when they are defined by and live out of *a center* rather than when they are defined by and live on *the perimeter* (see chapter 4).

Only when a community of people are centered on and get their life exclusively from God through Jesus Christ can they be empowered to let go of any attempt to get life from their perimeter. They don't need to police the perimeter to ensure that everyone looks and believes exactly as they do. They do not have to worry for a moment about multitudes of people within their fellowship who perhaps look and act radically nonreligious. They know that, unless they have been invited into the complex lives of these people, the only thing they know of them is the one thing that is important to know, namely, that they are sinners like themselves who have been mercifully given unsurpassable worth in Christ Jesus. Hence, they know that their only job is to agree with God and ascribe unsurpassable worth to them as they celebrate the cessation of the ban with them.

This sort of outrageous love is impossible for communities that acquire their sense of worth and identity by their religious self-identity. Their distinctness of life and thought is the fruit of the forbidden tree from which they feast. Hence, however much they may deny it, their primary focus is on their perimeter. They define "standing up for God" as buttressing their perimeter, whether this be defending their version of orthodoxy or their version of what all Christians should look like. In this light, they must consider as compromisers those communities that allow for, let alone celebrate, the ambiguity of the perimeter.

Indeed, as the Pharisees judged Jesus, a community that possesses this kind of freedom to love without judgment will seem to the religious idolater to negate "all order, all piety and all belief," as Bonhoeffer said. They are casting "aside all the distinctions which the Pharisee so laboriously maintains." A person who loves like this must appear as "a nihilist, a man who knows and respects only his own law, an egoist and a blasphemer of God."[2] In truth, such people are simply living from the center, Jesus Christ, rather than from any religious perimeter.

This of course raises the question of how a community that lives from the center rather than the perimeter can corporately grow in Christ-likeness. We shall discuss this in the next chapter. Presently we need only note that however we answer this question, the answer cannot be "by shoring up the perimeter." This is the tactic of the Pharisee, and it expresses the original sin that blocks the one thing that is needful: the unconditional love that God is pouring into us and through us to all people.

A Love That Calls for Explanation

If the church lives from the center and not the perimeter, and if it therefore loves as God loves, it will puzzle the sick and hungry as much as it outrages the religious. How can people love like this? In God's plan, this puzzle is what prepares people to believe that Jesus Christ is Lord and to surrender their lives to him. The evangelistic task of the Christian community, in other words, *is to live and love in a way that draws people and cries out for explanation*. Our proclamation only has as much credibility as our love requires explanation.

This is not because the world is so sinful that people unjustly require an unreasonable demonstration of truth before they believe it. For too long the church has blamed the world for how ineffective it is at attracting people. Evidence that we have been eating from the same tree from which Adam and Eve ate is that we have deflected responsibility for our sin just as they did. In truth, if people aren't being drawn to the Lord by the church's love, this is *the church's fault*. For Jesus taught us from the start that it is by our love, not just by our words, that people will know he is real and be drawn into a relationship with him. Christ convinced *us* of the love of God by demonstrating it while we were yet sinners. We are called to do the same toward others.

By God's own design—a design that recaptures the purpose for which God created the world—hurting and hungry people are to be drawn into the reality of God's love by seeing it demonstrated in his body. Christ did this in his earthly body, which is why sinners were attracted to him. And he longs to do this again through his church body. To the extent that the church embodies the spirit of Jesus, it will be a magnet for prostitutes and tax collectors. To the extent it embodies the spirit of Pharisaism, however, it will repel them.

When we cease getting life from any perimeter, indeed, when we violate all perimeters with our outrageous love, those who are spiritually sick and hungry are drawn, while those who get life by convincing themselves that they are healthy and full—as evidenced (to themselves) by the fortified perimeter that distinguishes them from the sick and hungry—will be repelled and outraged. *This is precisely how it should be*, for this is how it was in the ministry of Jesus.

Jesus and the Pharisees

The Sin of the Pharisees

Far from tiptoeing around them, Jesus sometimes seemed to go out of his way to confront religious leaders who lived from a religious variety of the forbidden fruit. While he demonstrated only compassion toward ordinary folk, and especially toward those ostracized and/or judged by the religious establishment, Jesus publicly expressed anger toward self-righteous religious leaders—the Pharisees, scribes, and Sadducees. Though these people were "the most moral of people, lived the best lives, and [were] perfectly obedient and virtuous," Ellul wrote, they "substituted their own morality for the living and actual Word of God that can never be fixed in commandments."[3] They were experts on eating from the Tree of the Knowledge of Good and Evil.

Jesus aggressively intended to stop these leaders because they shut the door of God's gracious kingdom on people, placed heavy loads on people's shoulders, and lured people down their own religious path of destruction (Matt. 23:4, 13–17). With their highly refined moralism, they incarnated the serpent's lie about how to be God-like. Consequently, Jesus had to publicly confront these religious forbidden-fruit-eaters.

Jesus exposed the self-serving nature of their moral system by calling attention to the fact that they did not practice what they preached and made demands of others that they themselves wouldn't do (Matt. 23:3–4). He exposed the idolatrous nature and shallowness of their moralism by calling attention to their concern to have their works noticed (Matt. 6:1–8, 16; 23:5–7). Their religion was centered on exterior things rather than the heart (Matt. 23:25–26). For example, they obsessed over paying tithes while they "neglected the more important matters of the law—justice, mercy and faithfulness" (Matt. 23:23 NIV). Hence, Jesus warned them, and others, that these leaders were "whitewashed tombs" that "look beautiful on the outside but on the inside are full of dead men's bones and everything unclean" (Matt. 23:27 NIV).

Despite their good appearance, the hearts of these religious leaders were far from God. Indeed, they were so far gone they mistook the power of God for the power of Satan, a fact that led Jesus to warn them about a state of sin that would never be forgiven (Matt. 12:24–32). They were in danger of going to hell (Matt. 23:33–35), and they were endangering others with this same fate.

Jesus' Loving Confrontation

How different are these words from the compassionate, forgiving, accepting words Jesus consistently spoke to tax collectors, prostitutes, and the ordinary, run-of-the-mill sinners he daily engaged. Indeed, how different is Jesus' treatment of these religious leaders from his treatment of other religious leaders who were at least somewhat open to truth, such as Nicodemus (John 3:1–9).

Why is this? Didn't Jesus love the Pharisees, scribes, and Sadducees? Of course he did. Jesus loved them as much as any other sinners. In fact, even while he publicly confronted them, his heart broke for them as well as for those they were harming. On one occasion, he concluded his harsh confrontation of religious leaders by crying out, "O Jerusalem, Jerusalem, you who kill the prophets and stone those sent to you, how often I have longed to gather your children together, as a hen gathers her chicks under her wings, but you were not willing" (Matt. 23:37). We see that Jesus wanted to gather these blind leaders and their followers under his protection! Knowing that these leaders would put him to death within days, Jesus still expressed the loving, longing, and forgiving heart of God for them. And even after they crucified him, Jesus prayed for their forgiveness (Luke 23:34).

Why, then, were Jesus' words to and about these religious leaders so harsh? The answer is that they *had to be*. Whereas love usually requires we affirm worth by showing compassion toward people, in certain cases it requires aggressive confrontation. If a person is in a severe state of blindness and hardness of heart, and especially if a person is in a leadership position and is damaging others with his or her blindness and hardness, intervention may be necessary. Families or groups of friends who have had to deal with loved ones addicted to alcohol, drugs, or pornography know this side of love well. Such was the case with certain religious leaders of Jesus' day. These leaders were in grave danger and were placing others in grave danger. A radical intervention was called for.

Confronting Contemporary Pharisees

We have addressed the church's need to embody Jesus' outrageous love toward all people. But how are we to apply Jesus' confrontation of harmful religious leaders today? Some have mistakenly taken Jesus' confrontation of the Pharisees, scribes, and Sadducees as a justification for overtly confronting sin *wherever* they see it (except in themselves), whether inside or outside the church. Three observations can guide us in a more balanced application of Jesus' approach.

1. The Unique Nature of Pharisaism

First, it is important for us to notice that religious sin is the only sin Jesus publicly confronted. The religious variety of the forbidden fruit is the most addictive and deceptive variety. Instead of acknowledging that the knowledge of good and evil is prohibited, religious idolatry embraces the knowledge of good and evil as divinely sanctioned and mandated. It gives the illusion of being on God's side even while it destroys life and hardens people in direct opposition to God.

Religious sin is the most destructive kind of sickness, for it masquerades as and feeds off the illusion of health. Far from being open to a cure, this kind of sickness thrives on the illusion that it is the epitome of health. By its very nature it resists soft correction. Indeed, because it gets life from the rightness of its beliefs and behavior rather than from love, the religious version of the Tree of the Knowledge of Good and Evil tends to construe all compassion, accommodation, and unconditional acceptance as compromise. People afflicted with religious sin thus tend to disdain compassionate love, even if it is extended toward them. Hence, Jesus' approach to leaders who fed off this illusion could not be to gently offer them a cure. Rather, for their sake and the sake of those who blindly followed them, he had to publicly expose their sickness.

What does this mean for the church? We have seen that the church is called to be the corporate body of Christ that unconditionally loves and embraces all people, regardless of their sin, and invites them into its own celebration of the cessation of the ban. The only exception to this otherwise unconditional embrace is the sin Jesus confronted in the religious leadership of his day. While all sin is equal in the sense that it separates us from God, sins differ in terms of their impact on people and thus differ in how they need to be dealt with. Religious sin is unique in that it is the only sin that can keep a community from fulfilling the commission to unconditionally love and embrace everyone. As we have said, it is a sin that by its very nature resists the cure of God's unconditional love and embrace.

When religious sin infects people, they feed off their judgment rather than love. Where this diabolic delusion is in place in leadership, the kingdom of God is resisted. God's will can't be done "on earth as it is in heaven" (Matt. 6:10), for those enslaved to this delusion think they are bringing the kingdom *in the very act of preaching their delusion*. They preach the fall and think it is salvation. In the name of opening up the kingdom, they "lock people out of the kingdom" (Matt. 23:13).

For this reason, religious sin sabotages the whole enterprise of the church when it is found in leadership. It prevents the church from manifesting the loving unity of the Trinity, which is God's main witness to the world. When a people—especially leaders—gets life from the rightness of their belief and behavior, they will invariably get life by attacking and/or separating from others who don't see things exactly as they do, even within the body of Christ. They focus on the perimeter rather than the center. Feasting on their own particular version of truth—which is, to them, *the* truth—they will form party lines that fragment the church and ostracize people.

Moreover, since idols never satisfy the hunger that drives us to them, leaders who serve an idol of religion tend to believe they are serving the interest of the kingdom by splitting into increasingly well-defined and ever-shrinking groups. Perimeters must constantly be attended to. This is most clearly seen in the phenomenon of ever-dividing, modern fundamentalism. In the name of purity of doctrine or holiness, the bride of Christ is dismembered into many parts, and there is always room for further division! Paul reserved his strongest words of warning for people who destroy the unity of the body of Christ in this way (1 Cor. 3:17; Gal. 1:6–9).

Hence, while most of the time love requires that we hide the sins of others, the sin of leaders who get life from their religion at the expense of others must sometimes be confronted and exposed. It may be the only hope those who are enslaved to this sin have of recognizing it as sin. It may also be the only way of protecting people who would follow these leaders as well as others who might be harmed by these leaders. Precisely to ensure that it remains a community where outrageous love flows, the church must in love be willing to aggressively confront leaders who are enslaved and enslave others to religious idolatry.

2. The Specific Mission of Jesus

It is important to remember that, while God has always intended to reach the whole world, Jesus' original mission was to Israelites (Matt. 15:24). These were the people of the covenant, and the Good News of the kingdom was brought first to them. It was in this covenantal context that Jesus aggressively confronted certain religious leaders. He did not confront religious leaders in other cultures and religions; his concern was only with religious leaders who were thwarting God's will within God's covenant community of that time.

So too, the church must always remember that it has no business confronting people outside the covenant community, even leaders of other religious groups who are leading people astray (1 Cor. 5:12). Unless God explicitly leads in a different direction, therefore, we should assume that our only job is to compassionately reflect God's love to them and leave to God the responsibility of taking care of them and those who naively follow them. The precedent of Jesus confronting the Pharisees, therefore, only warrants our being willing to confront *Christian* leaders who are sabotaging the mission of the church and possibly destroying the unity of the church with their religious spirit.

In this context we should perhaps say a word about God's command to Ezekiel to be a watchman over Israel. The Lord told Ezekiel that if he didn't warn the wicked of God's impending judgment, he would hold him accountable for their sin (Ezek. 33:8). Some Christians have mistakenly understood this passage to mean that if they see sin in anyone's life and do not warn that person of its consequences, they will share the judgment for that sin. This mistaken interpretation leads people to feel guilty for fellowshipping with people engaged in certain kinds of sin (we are always selective) without mentioning early on their disapproval of that sin. In order to fix themselves—rid themselves of guilt—they compromise their responsibility to communicate unsurpassable worth to people. They are rude, at best, and thus unloving (1 Cor. 13:4–5).

This application of Ezekiel's message is not only damaging to the mission of the church to celebrate the cessation of the ban, it also contradicts Jesus' teaching that we are *not* to look for dust particles of sin in other people's eyes (see chapter 6). To prevent this misapplication of this passage, however, we need only notice three things: First, God called *Ezekiel* to watch over Israel; God didn't call every Jew to watch over every other Jew. Second, God called Ezekiel to watch over *Israel*; God didn't call Ezekiel to watch over every nation. Third, we have to understand that Israel was at this time under God's covenant as a nation, and the "watchman" role Ezekiel played had a role only within this covenant. Though they often disobeyed their prophets, Jews understood the role of prophets in their communities. There is, therefore, a world of difference between a Jewish prophet warning a fellow Jew of his or her sin in the sixth century B.C. and a stranger warning someone about his or her sin in the twenty-first century A.D.

As we shall see in the next chapter, there is still something of a "watchman" role each of us is supposed to play in the body of Christ, but it has nothing to do with pointing out the sins of people with whom we are not in covenant. On the contrary, it only applies to intimate relationships with people who have invited us into their lives. Whatever we make of Jesus' precedent of publicly confronting destructive religious leaders, therefore, we mustn't apply it to people in general or even religious leaders in general.

3. The Unique Authority of Jesus

Finally, it is crucial that we always remember that Jesus was the Son of God and thus possessed a radically unique authority and wisdom. He was the Lord God Almighty who had throughout the ages sent the prophets and teachers whom these religious leaders had not only ignored but sometimes put to death (Matt. 23:34–37). He was the one with whom Israel had made a covenant and the one to whom God had entrusted the leadership of his community. Not only this, but as the one perfect man who was united with God, the one who never spoke unless the Father told him to, Jesus had knowledge of the hearts of those he confronted that the rest of us do not ordinarily possess (e.g., John 2:24–25).

I don't believe this means that believers should never publicly intervene and stop leaders who sabotage the mission and destroy the unity of the church. Following the Spirit, and working within whatever proper means have been established in a particular Christian community, this must sometimes be done. But it does mean that if and when we feel called to do so, we must do it with a humble awareness of our own fallibility, sinfulness, and ignorance. Unlike Jesus, our perceptions can be mistaken. Unlike Jesus, we are often mistaken in how we think God is leading. And though we can discern the negative impact sin has, we can't know the hearts of people or the full circumstances of their lives.

When considering confronting religious sin in leadership, therefore, we must always err on the side of mercy. Overt confrontation like Jesus exercised toward the Pharisees, scribes, and Sadducees should be engaged in only in obedience to the Spirit, after much soul-searching, and as a last effort of love when all softer, interpersonal, gracious approaches have failed.

Conclusion

The most damaging and destructive variety of the forbidden fruit is its religious variety. This is why it is the only sin Jesus publicly and harshly confronted. Yet it is arguably the sin most common in the church today. Wherever people eat a religious version of the fruit of the Tree of the Knowledge of Good and Evil, they won't receive, live in, and overflow with unconditional love and unsurpassable worth for other people. The essence of the religious spirit is getting life from being truer and more righteous than others, rather than getting life from God alone. It is living from the perimeter rather than the center.

This religious mindset has the same effect as it had in Jesus' day. It puts conditions on people coming to the celebration and ensures that they won't live by the joy of the celebration even if they do come. It thus shuts the door on the kingdom, for the unconditional and unsurpassable love that defines the kingdom can't be received or spread by people who live in the religious mindset and continue to feed off the forbidden tree. Their worth is found in their doing, not in their being. Though they may sincerely believe in Christ, they won't be empowered to live out of the fullness of life he gives. Their innermost being will still hunger for a love that is unconditional and a worth that is for free—the very thing their religious idolatry prevents them from experiencing.

The celebration of the cessation of the ban is only a *celebration* if it is centered on the life and love God offers to people for free, without conditions. It is only *transforming* if it invites people to graciously participate in God's life and love, which ascribes unsurpassable worth to people's being rather than their doing or their appearance. Such a celebration will undoubtedly enrage, and sometimes require us to confront, religious Pharisees who rightly perceive that their god is being threatened.

If the church is to be the outrageously loving community God calls it to be, however, how can it also grow in becoming the holy community God calls it to be? If all are welcome as they are, how can they ever be motivated to become other than they are? To these questions we turn in our final chapter.

chapter 12

Love, Confession, and Accountability

They devoted themselves to the apostles' teaching and fellowship, to the breaking of bread and the prayers. . . . All who believed were together and had all things in common; they would sell their possessions and goods and distribute the proceeds to all, as any had need. Day by day, as they spent much time together in the temple, they broke bread at home and ate their food with glad and generous hearts, praising God and having the goodwill of all the people.

Acts 2:42, 44–46

Sin wants to remain unknown. It shuns the light. In the darkness of the unexpressed it poisons the whole being of a person. . . . In confession the light of the Gospel breaks into the darkness and seclusion of the heart. Now the fellowship bears the sin of the brother. He is no longer alone with his evil for he has cast off his sin in confession and handed it over to God. . . . Now he stands in the fellowship of sinners who live by the grace of God in the Cross of Jesus Christ.

Dietrich Bonhoeffer

The Call to Holiness

If the church is to be the nonjudgmental, unconditionally loving, corporate body of Christ it is called to be, how will people be motivated and empowered to increasingly grow out of their sin and become more Christ-like? If even prostitutes or drug addicts can freely fellowship with us, how will they ever become convicted of their sin and begin to find the freedom and holiness Christ died to give them? How do we balance a concern to love nonjudgmentally with a concern to become a holy people?

The concern is in one sense natural, and we shall address it. But at the start it must be noted that the concern itself reveals how much trust we have in our power of judgment rather than the power of God and of his love flowing through us. We trust the accuracy of our judgment and trust the power of our disapproval to fix people—to convict them of sin and move them toward holiness. Somehow *those* sinners need to get the message that their appearance, behavior, and/or beliefs are not okay. They need to realize that *we* are not like *them*. So *they* need to become like *us* if they want to be part of *us*.

A disparaging glance might do. If not, an explicit confrontation may be necessary. Either way, what we are really doing is indirectly uninviting them to the celebration of the cessation of the ban. Indeed, with our lack of unconditionally welcoming love—which is what a disparaging glance evidences—we are really declaring that there is no cessation of the ban to celebrate. We are indirectly proclaiming that worth must be acquired by doing things. Though we may deny it, we are in fact presenting salvation as though it were a matter of getting others to conform to our version of the fruit of the Tree of the Knowledge of Good and Evil.

Moreover, in thinking or presenting this conditional gospel, we are ourselves continuing to eat from this forbidden tree. However unconsciously, we are acquiring worth by being judge rather than the judged, the fixer rather than the fixed, and the one on the inside of the holy community rather than on the outside. With each disparaging thought, glance, or word, we separate ourselves from others and serve ourselves rather than others. In other words, our relationship with others is conditioned by our knowledge of good and evil, from which we are still feasting. At the very least, this means we are not loving others outrageously, recklessly, and nonjudgmentally.

Finally, in thinking we can and should fix people, we are being hypocrites, for we ourselves need fixing. When we communicate, however indirectly, that *we* are not like *you*, so *you* need to become like *us*, we impose our own self-serving sin scale. This alone convinces us that their sin of (for example) prostitution or drug addiction is worse than our sin of self-righteousness, obesity, divorce and remarriage, loveless thoughts or words, or private lust. But, in fact, we have no authority to play God and grade sins. It is, in truth, just a fallen strategy religious people use to get life. And we get it at the expense of the very people we are called to love and serve. Instead of *feeding* others, we *feed off* others.

Still, it is absolutely true that God has called us to make *disciples*, not mere believers (Matt. 28:19; cf. Luke 14:25–35). He saved us to walk in good works (Eph. 2:10). In Christ, he predestines us to be conformed to the image of Jesus Christ and to walk holy and blameless before him (Rom. 8:29; Eph. 1:3–5). While few (if any) of us arrive at the point where we are *fully* devoted disciples, doing *only* good works, *completely* conformed to the image of Christ, and walking *blamelessly* and *perfectly holy* before God, this is that to which we are to aspire and to which God draws us. This should be the goal of our lives, both individually and collectively, for these are aspects of growing in love for God. But how can we as a church move in this direction if all are accepted *just as they are?*

The answer, I shall now argue, is that we are to grow in Christ-likeness not by social pressure but by the work of the Holy Spirit in our lives, by the Word of God being preached and modeled by leaders, and by sharing life together with others in intimate relationships.

Trusting the Spirit

The Reality of Christ and the Spirit

The only way any of us grows in conformity with Jesus Christ is by being in Christ through faith and by having Christ in us through his Spirit. As we noted in chapter 2, this happens when a person surrenders to Jesus Christ. He or she becomes a participant in the divine nature (2 Peter 1:4). He or she *really is* in Christ, and Christ *really is* in him or her.

When we assume that people won't change unless we fix them—as if we don't ourselves need fixing—we show that our ultimate trust is in ourselves, not God. When we don't unconditionally accept people because we don't believe they'll change if we do, we admit that our ultimate confidence is in the conditions we place on our acceptance rather than in God. When we don't simply trust God to change others, we effectively claim that our ability to shame, intimidate, or otherwise manipulate people into change is greater than God's transforming Spirit.

The question is, Do we trust God? Do we trust that God is working in the hearts of all people, leading them at their own pace in the same direction God is leading us? Do we trust that people receive the Holy Spirit when they believe (Eph. 1:13–14), whatever their appearance may be and whatever bondage they might continue to experience? Do we really trust that they have received a new nature when they believe, whatever ongoing sin is in their lives? Do we trust that it is the Spirit's job, working in the quiet recesses of a person's heart, to convict him or her of sin in God's own time? And do we, like Paul, trust that the Holy Spirit is competent in his job (Phil. 1:6)?

We have to acknowledge that we usually have no way of discerning how much the Holy Spirit has done and is doing in another's life. Nor is acquiring such knowledge important if our focus is on the center and not the perimeter. Each person starts at a different place and grows at a different pace. On a genetic, social, and spiritual level, each person inherits a different set of issues when he or she comes into the world. Each person has a different story leading up to where he or she is in the present. Most important, everyone answers to his or her own master (Rom. 14:4). Hence, there is no uniform standard by which to measure the progress of a person. In any case, it is never our job to be concerned with such measurements, even if we could.

None of this matters in the least—unless we are living off the forbidden wisdom of the tree that illegitimately enthrones us as judge over such matters. If we abandon this rebellion and simply trust God to do his job, we will focus on our one and only job: to live in God's love and celebrate the cessation of the ban with others.

Obeying, Not Judging

We are to have faith that what God says about himself in Christ is true, what God says about us in Christ is true, and what God says *about others* in Christ is true. So whatever the appearances may be, we are to have faith that God is working in others to do what only God can do. This means that we must never condition our love and acceptance of people with a judgment about how much or how little progress they are making in their relationship with God.

Conditioning our love and acceptance of people on the basis of our judgment reveals that we don't believe what God says about them or that God is working in their lives. Since "whatever does not proceed from faith is sin" (Rom. 14:23), we should in this case be concerned with the tree trunk of sin in our own life rather than trying to fix the sin we think we perceive in others' lives.

James addresses this point when he commands us to be doers of the law and not judges of the law (James 4:11–12). We should focus on what God commands *us* to do rather than speculating about the extent to which others are or are not doing what God has commanded *them* to do. When we try to detach ourselves and critically evaluate the progress of others, we act as though we are their masters, and we thereby disobey God (Matt. 7:1–5; Rom. 14:4). Indeed, we judge God and judge his law, for we are claiming God is incompetent in his role as judge and transformer in the life of the person we are judging (see chapter 6).

This also applies to people in our fellowship who haven't yet surrendered their lives to Christ. They, too, must be unconditionally embraced and invited into the celebration of the cessation of the ban (chapter 10). Indeed, our unconditional, loving embrace is the central way these people are to come to know we are disciples of Jesus Christ. They encounter the reality of Jesus Christ as they experience his love through us (John 17:20–26). Though they cannot see God, they experience his love as it is manifested through us (1 John 4:12). As we said in the last chapter, our outrageous love becomes a puzzle to them for which Jesus Christ is the only adequate explanation.

But doesn't such an unconditionally loving approach to sinners make light of sin? As Bonhoeffer asked, "Does not the evil in the other person make me condemn him just for his own good, for the sake of love?"[1] The answer, according to Bonhoeffer, is a decisive no. Indeed, just the opposite is the case.

We radically trivialize sin when we make it a matter of *more* or *less*. We undermine its absolute seriousness when we allow for supposed "holier" people to love "less holy" people conditionally, based on "holier" people's own judgment and according to their own standards. Sin is only taken seriously when we realize that, apart from Christ, we are all in the same septic tank of condemnation together. It is taken seriously only when we realize that sin has been irrevocably exposed, condemned, and overcome on the cross. And we repeat this condemnation of sin and confess our conviction about its absolute seriousness every time we love others as Christ has loved us—unconditionally, despite our sin. Thus Bonhoeffer concludes:

> The love of Christ for the sinner in itself is the condemnation of sin, is his expression of extreme hatred of sin. The disciples of Christ are to love unconditionally. Thus they may effect what their own divided and judiciously and conditionally offered love never could achieve, namely the radical condemnation of sin.[2]

When we love as Christ loves, we give occasion for the Spirit of God to apply Christ's condemnation and victory over sin on Calvary to other people's lives. The best thing we can do for others, therefore, is to *do* the law and love them, not judge the law and judge them (James 4:11–12). Hence, regardless of whether people are believers or not, and regardless of how things may appear, we are called to unconditionally embrace them with Christ's love and trust that God is at work in their lives, despite their sin, as he is in our own lives. We can believe and trust that we are all moving in the same direction, at our own pace, because the same Spirit is operating in each of us.

The Teaching Ministry—The Anchor of the Community

One of the primary ways the Holy Spirit grows us into conformity with Christ is through the teaching and preaching ministry of the church.[3] In the New Testament, this ministry is foundationally important (1 Cor. 12:28; Eph. 4:11; 1 Tim. 1:13; 4:11;

5:17; 2 Tim. 2:2; James 3:1). The community of Christ is to be centered on the teaching and preaching of God's Word as a means of being centered on Christ. When the Word is taught, the Spirit uses it to motivate us, convict us, enlighten us, transform us, and move us as a community in a common direction (2 Tim. 3:16). As Christ is lifted up through the preaching and teaching of the Word, he draws all people to himself, both to have a relationship with him and to grow into his likeness (John 12:32).

For this reason, a biblical community must have as unqualified a commitment to the Word of God as it does to loving all people without judgment and accepting all people without condition. Indeed, it must have the one precisely because it has the other. There is nothing judgmental, unaccepting, or inappropriate about the Word of God being boldly taught or proclaimed within the Christian community, even to those who don't yet believe. For in their very willingness to hear the Word, people give the teacher or preacher permission to speak into their lives. The teacher or preacher may publicly proclaim and teach things about our lives that would be judgmental for an individual to proclaim to another individual without an invitation to do so.

This of course does not give the teacher or preacher the right or the obligation to go further, without invitation, and directly address personal issues in another person's life. We couldn't barge into the bedroom of a stranger's house simply because he or she once invited us into the foyer! This is rude and thus not loving (1 Cor. 13:4–5). But it does mean that when operating out of one's call as teacher or preacher, one need not and should not be overly concerned about offending people.

True, if a sermon or lesson is presented in love, it will be tailored as much as possible to the needs of the particular congregation or class. But, as has been said before, if the congregation or small group is part of a vibrant community that is loving outrageously, the audience may consist of people in widely different places spiritually. The teacher or preacher must simply trust the Spirit to apply the lesson or sermon to each individual. If a person in the congregation or small group is not willing to hear what is being taught, he or she will simply shut it out and perhaps not return. So it was in Jesus' ministry, and so it should be in ours (John 6:66–67). Biblical teachers or preachers shouldn't go out of their way to offend, of course, but neither should they go far out of their way not to offend. They must simply present the Word of God faithfully and lovingly.

The teaching and preaching ministry of the church isn't limited to those who teach and preach, however. As it was in the ministry of Jesus and of Paul, *modeling* plays a vital role in teaching others within the Christian community (1 Cor. 11:1; Phil. 3:17; 4:9; 2 Thess. 3:7–9; 1 Tim. 4:12; Titus 2:1–8; Heb. 13:7). All who are in leadership within a church, regardless of their particular pastoral role, teach by their example. They lead by being ahead of those who follow. Their character is one of the beacons that keeps a community's spiritual compass intact.

Hence, according to Scripture, maturity in Christ is as much a part of people's qualification for ministry as is their giftedness and/or education (1 Tim. 3:2–12; Titus 1:7–9). Leaders need to be people who are advanced in their love for Christ and for people. They need to be sound in their faith, full of the Holy Spirit, stable in their emotions, and respectable in their personal affairs. Their lives need to be examples of what is explicitly taught and preached in the church. They need to be examples of what it looks like to *do* the will of God rather than just to hear it or judge it (James 1:25; 4:11).

This of course doesn't mean that leaders must be perfect. Indeed, one of the things leaders should model is how God uses imperfect people to accomplish his will. Leaders need to be secure enough in themselves and their relationship with God that they can model transparency to others. They need to be free from the fallen addiction to hide and perform (chapter 9). Yet what people generally see in leaders' vulnerable transparency must be a relative wholeness that sets a mark others can aspire toward as the Spirit works in their lives. Communities will naturally vary in terms of the specific evidences of maturity they look for in various levels of leadership, but the general principle is that leaders lead not just by what they say but even more significantly by *who they are*.

We see, then, that the teaching and preaching ministry of the church, combined with the work of the Holy Spirit in people's lives, keeps a community focused on its center and growing in Christ-likeness. It is this focus, when freed from the knowledge of good and evil, that frees a community to ignore perimeter issues and love outrageously. So long as Jesus is leading the pack, it is no one's concern to police those who follow.

Confession and Accountability

The Early Church Communities

The church grows toward Christ-likeness by the working of the Spirit and the preaching of the Word. But there is a third, vitally important way in which the body of Christ is to grow together in love and into the likeness of Christ.

The members of the body of Christ are to minister *to one another*. The New Testament teaches that members of the body of Christ are to encourage one another (1 Thess. 4:18; 5:11, 14; Heb. 10:24–25), confess sins to one another and pray for one another (James 5:16), speak the truth to one another (Eph. 4:15, 25), care for one another (1 Cor. 12:25; 1 Peter 4:10), admonish one another (Gal. 6:1; Heb. 3:13), and even confront one another. Indeed, we are to be willing to remove a member of our community from fellowship if he or she obstinately persists in sin that destroys him or her and/or threatens the community (Matt. 18:15–18). We are, in short, called to lovingly help each other increasingly manifest our true identity in Jesus Christ. We are to help each other put off the old self and put on the new (Eph. 4:22–25).

How can this be done without judgment? How can we possibly speak truth to others and hold them accountable if we aren't supposed to be looking for dust particles in others' lives? How can we possibly end fellowship with someone if we aren't supposed to judge others?

If the New Testament's teaching on confession and accountability seems to us to stand in tension with its strong teaching against judgment, it is only because the New Testament presupposes an understanding of community that is largely absent in the modern church. Without this understanding of community, we don't have a context to obey in a healthy way the New Testament's teaching on the role of the community in transforming us by holding us accountable. When we try to apply this teaching outside the context of community as understood by the early church, it becomes judgment.

We know from a variety of sources, biblical and otherwise, that the early Christians met frequently—often daily—in each other's houses (Acts 2:46; Rom. 16:5; 1 Cor. 16:19; Col. 4:15; Philem. 2; 2 John 10; cf. Acts 8:3; 12:12).[4] They ate together, worshipped together, studied together, shared resources with one another, and lived life together in small clusters of house churches. Moreover, they frequently gathered in a hostile environment where the outside world could break in at any moment and take away their jobs, their houses, and even their lives. In other words, early Christians lived life in strongly bonded, intimate relationships with one another.

First-century Christians also met in large, citywide gatherings, to whatever degree their circumstances would allow them (Acts 1:13–15; 2:46; 5:12). But the *primary* gatherings (*ecclesia*, "church") in the early period were in people's homes. It wasn't until the fourth century that special religious buildings were devoted to Christians gathering in large groups.

Hence, when Paul or any other New Testament author wrote to "the church at" a certain locale, he was actually writing to various house churches in that region. The letter would be circulated to the various intimate gatherings in that area and eventually to house churches in other regions as well. So far as we can tell, these house churches would ordinarily consist of no more than forty or fifty people. Indeed, the church *as a whole* in any given region wouldn't have been very large when the New Testament was written. Paul's letters reveal that the church largely consisted of people who knew each other personally (e.g., Rom. 16:3–23; 1 Cor. 16:10–20; Col. 4:10–15; 2 Tim. 4:19–21).

The New Testament's teaching about our need to confess sin to one another and to hold each other accountable has to be understood against this background. In fact, the teaching can only be applied in a healthy, loving way in contexts such as a house church. Within contexts such as this, confession and accountability are simply what speaking the truth in love to one another looks like (Eph. 4:15, 25).

In a small-group context, confession is healing, for it is done in trust, without the need to hide or perform. Within this context, accountability is beneficial, for it is carried out in the wisdom of love, which has taken the time to get on the inside of another's story. Feedback is offered not on the basis of abstract, idealistic principles of right and wrong, for the relationship is not conditioned by the knowledge of good and evil. Feedback is rather offered with a personal understanding and empathetic appreciation for the complex uniqueness of the person's concrete situation. For this reason, it is loving and helpful, not judgmental.

Loving and helpful confession and accountability are founded on a Spirit-created trust that grows out of life shared together. It cannot be demanded on the basis of a program or a rule. In intimate contexts, people are freed to be open about their struggles and to ask for help, for they fear no judgment. Nothing is forced; nothing is done with a motive to judge or shame. Each person grows in his or her walk with God with the loving assistance of the other members of the group. This is how the life of a disciple was meant to be lived.[5]

Yet, as with a family that has to deal with a radically dysfunctional member, there were times in the early church, just as there are times in our own lives, when the group was led to intervene and put a stop to the actions of one of its members (Matt. 18:15–18; 1 Cor. 5:1–5; 1 Tim. 1:20). When a person obstinately persisted in choices that could destroy himself or herself and/or others, and after all other avenues had been explored, the group had to in love confront the person with an ultimatum. If the group itself was too immature to do this, as was the case at Corinth, a leader had to do it. In either case, the person would either repent and receive love and support from the group or the group would withdraw fellowship from him or her.

Out of love for the individual and for the integrity of the group, the community leveraged their relationship with the person in order to help the individual wake up to the destructive nature of his or her behavior. The decision to end fellowship with someone was significant in a small-group context, for the relationships meant something. And even when removal from fellowship occurred, its motive was not vengeance but love. For example, Paul instructed the Corinthians to turn a certain unrepentant man "over to Satan . . . so that his spirit may be saved in the day of the Lord" (1 Cor. 5:5).

A Tragic Transposition

While all Christians are commanded to love all people without judgment or condition, the form of love that is appropriate to intimate relationships cannot be practiced generally. It usually takes a good deal of time, energy, and self-sacrificial commitment—as well as an invitation—to enter deeply into another person's life. The sharing of stories and the trust that results from this—the trust that alone makes confession and accountability a healthy, nonjudgmental activity—usually does not come easily or quickly.

While intimate relationships among small clusters of Christians characterized the early church, they are largely absent from the modern church. Today the church is usually associated with a weekly, large-group gathering of people who are mostly strangers to one another. Sadly, relationships have ceased being essential to the definition of *church*. Indeed, today the church is usually identified with the building where people occasionally gather while remaining strangers to one another.

Consequently, many Christians today live out their faith without any deep, meaningful relationships with other believers or seekers. They do not have a small body of people who know them profoundly and whom they know profoundly. They have not entrusted their stories to others. They do not in any significant sense journey with others. There is no one they trust enough to naturally confess sin or ask to be held accountable.

This is one of the greatest deficiencies of the modern church. What is even more tragic, however, is that we often abstract the New Testament's teaching about confession and accountability out of its first-century house-church context and try to apply it *generally*—as though the teaching were a set of rules that could be applied anytime, anyplace, to anyone. The result is that many Christians assume that it is their job to hold others accountable, whether or not they are in intimate relationships with them. We actually think we are doing what Scripture teaches when we police people about whom we know nothing.

The result is that in the name of obeying Scripture, we disobey Scripture. In the name of love, we judge. In the name of serving others, we end up serving ourselves. Indeed, with the consistent misapplication of these scriptural teachings, we become trained specialists in deflecting attention away from the tree trunks in our own eyes and in finding dust particles in other people's eyes (Matt. 7:1–5). We barge into houses where we haven't been invited and offer guidance that hasn't been solicited and is devoid of wisdom, for we haven't taken the time to get involved in other people's stories. Outside of small-group settings, confronting people about issues in their lives is rude, to say the least, and thus is not loving (1 Cor. 13:4–5).

Consequently, instead of being a community that expresses freedom from the fruit of the Tree of the Knowledge of Good and Evil, we become a community of people who vigorously eat of this very tree as we try to "fix" others. Lifting the New Testament's teaching on accountability out of its original context of intimate, small groups and generalizing it in a *carte blanche* way today is not only not helpful, it is positively harmful. It motivates us to judge others and the law rather than doing the law (James 4:11–12). It leads us to act as though we are their masters rather than leaving them to answer to their own master (Rom. 14:4). It distracts our attention from the center and orientates us toward the perimeters.

But it does not stop there. We cannot eat of the Tree of the Knowledge of Good and Evil without becoming addicted to it. Our judgment of other Christians, in the name of love, invariably carries over to a judgment of all others. When we put on the critical grid of judgment, it cannot easily be taken off. Hence, we judge nonbelievers as well. Indeed, though the New Testament specifically prohibits it (1 Cor. 5:12), we *especially* judge nonbelievers, for they have sins *we* don't think we have, sins that supposedly are worse than ours, sins that put them on the outside rather than the inside.

With such an orientation, our minds become polluted with an ongoing, unconscious, judgmental commentary about people's lives, and with every judgmental thought, love is being blocked. We are no longer seeing these people through the lens of the cross. We are seeing them, each other, ourselves, and even God through the filter of our knowledge of good and evil. We become a community of accusers rather than a community of outrageous lovers. We become a community of religious parasites sucking worth off those to whom we are supposed to be ascribing unsurpassable worth. We become a community that lives by its knowledge of good and evil.

The Need for Intimacy

This tragic aberration of Christianity is largely due to the fact that modern Christians generally lack the sort of intimate fellowship upon which the body of Christ is supposed to be built. We cannot live and grow in Christ as we should without a context in which we can confess our sins and hold others accountable for theirs. Hence, every church body today needs to work hard to fight the hyperprivatized, individualistic, self-centered mindset of modern Western culture and provide opportunities and encouragement for people to become bonded in small groups with other people on the journey.

There is no shortcut to the arduous commitment it takes to grow into an intimate community, so there is no shortcut to acquiring the sort of communities in which the New Testament's teachings about confession and accountability apply. When we try to apply the teachings out of context, we merely exchange intimate, nonjudgmental relationships of accountability for ethical principles we use to police people. We fill the vacuum created by our impersonal, large-group, church mindset with our attempts to enforce our knowledge of good and evil. Thus we choke the flow of love from God to us and through us, which is, we have seen, the only thing Christianity is really about.

Conclusion

The model of the church we have been exploring is one that would look very "unchurchy" to say the least, for it would attract and embrace people who would ordinarily never step inside a church building or fellowship with Christians. To outsiders it would be known for its outrageous, puzzling love and unexpected works of service more than for its distinctive beliefs and ethical teachings. In all likelihood it would also be judged as compromising by people who get life from their religion, for it would not conform to the criteria of "good" set up by their own self-serving criteria of good and evil.

In fact, it would not be compromising at all. On the contrary, it is most uncompromising at the very point we are called to be most uncompromising and at the point communities of judgment are very compromising, namely, in loving as God loves, as manifested in Jesus Christ.

What keeps a community of outrageous love moving in the direction of Christ-likeness, despite its lack of clearly defined perimeters, is its strong center. A community of outrageous love is centered on its confidence that the Holy Spirit is at all times and in all people at work to change us into the likeness of Christ. It is centered on the strong commitment of its leaders to teach the Word of God by word and by example. And it is woven together around this center by the intimate relationships its members have with other members in small-group fellowships.

Most of all, the people who form a community of outrageous love can only love like this if they are centered on Christ. For Christ is their one and only source of life and the lens through which they understand everything: God, themselves, and all other people. The community of outrageous love is centered on the tree on which Christ hung rather than on the Tree of the Knowledge of Good and Evil. Consequently, they are a people for whom God's original goal of creation is being restored. They are collectively embodying and revealing the reality of the triune God, for they are participating in the dance of the triune God.

Epilogue

Repenting of Religion

> The Church is nothing but a section of humanity in which Christ has really taken form. . . . She has essentially nothing whatever to do with the so-called religious functions of man. . . . What matters in the Church is not religion but the form of Christ, and its taking form amidst a band of men.
>
> Dietrich Bonhoeffer

There is no freedom like being free to love without judgment. It is what we were made for. If believers consistently discipline themselves to collapse all judgment and simply ascribe unsurpassable worth to every person they encounter, they learn in an experiential way what it is to "abide in Christ" and "walk in the Spirit." It is the experience of God's own abundant life. It is the experience of God's love flowing to you and through you. It is knowing firsthand the truth that sets one absolutely free (John 8:32). It is dancing with the triune God.

People often think that being Christian is about "being religious," but loving without judgment is as far removed from religion as anything could be. Religion, as I have used this term in this work, is a system of beliefs and behaviors one embraces as a means of getting life—whether this be feeling close to God, one with the universe, or righteous before others. As such, it is part of the idolatrous fallen world that is inextricably tied up with our stolen knowledge of good and evil.

While all religions, including the Christian religion, contain much wisdom and do much good in the world, they also can do much harm. The harm is not only in the vast amounts of blood they have spilled advancing their causes and defending the correctness of their positions. It is found in the fact that they may systematically prevent people from experiencing the love and life of God as a free gift flowing to and through them. So long as one is trying to *achieve* a relationship with God, he or she cannot *receive* a relationship with God by grace.

In this light, the religion of Christianity is the most tragic example of the harm religion sometimes causes. It is in some ways the most fundamental denial of the life and message Jesus came to bring. For the fallen idolatrous behavior of the Christian religion is carried out in the name of the One who came to set us free from the need for idolatrous behavior. In the name of Jesus, the church has frequently ostracized, tortured, and put to death the very people we are called to lay down our lives for. Whereas our commission was to live in such a way that our outrageous love pointed to the reality of Jesus Christ, we have frequently given the world every reason to deny the reality of Jesus Christ. In many respects, the words the prophet Nathan spoke to David apply to us: we have acted in such a way that we have given the enemies of God grounds to blaspheme (2 Sam. 12:14 NASB).

In light of this, we who are the body of Christ need to repent, individually and collectively. We need to ask forgiveness from God, and from the world, *for being religious*. We have striven to be religious when we were called to be loving. To a large degree we have preached our own version of the knowledge of good and evil as though it were the message of salvation. We need to confess that we have sinned in the gravest fashion by frequently loving our version of truth and ethics more than people, and even God himself. For one cannot genuinely love God while refusing to love one's neighbor (1 John 4:20).

Collectively we must ask forgiveness from all those we have deemed unworthy to welcome to the celebration of the cessation of the ban. To cite just a few examples, historically, and still today, we have not outrageously loved heretics. To the contrary, the church has often burned them alive. The white church has not outrageously loved blacks: Large segments of the American white church defended slavery and continue to support racist social structures. The white church has not outrageously loved native Americans: In the name of Jesus it helped steal their land and extinguish their culture. The church as a whole has not outrageously loved Jews, Muslims, and other religious groups: We have rather frequently spoken evil of them and warred against them. And we have not outrageously loved large groups of targeted sinners whom we defined as outside our perimeters: prostitutes, gays, drug addicts, murderers, and others. Instead of standing in solidarity with these and all other sinners, we have eaten from the forbidden tree and constructed our own self-serving sin list to determine who's "in" and who's "out." We have judged these people for whom Christ died and, rather than serve him, have often gone out of our way to make their lives miserable.

If we are to be the people God has saved us and empowered us to be, people who live out their true identity in Christ rather than people who live out a religious version of stolen knowledge, we must first repent. Repentance (*metanoia*) is not primarily about feeling remorseful or even personally guilty over something. Feelings have little to do with it. It is about a *decision to turn*. Individually we are called to turn from our self-centered way of living, trying to acquire our own provision while we violate the divine prohibition. And collectively, as the community of faith, we are called to turn from our religion.

We need to repent of our addiction to the Tree of the Knowledge of Good and Evil, from which we have sought life at the expense of others. We need to repent of placing our "rightness" above love. We need to turn from ourselves, collectively as well as individually, and confess that our true identity is to sacrificially serve the world in love, as Christ has sacrificially served us. We need to repent of our Christian religion in order to live fully "in Christ."

Our life is not found in our correct doctrine or in our piety, as important as these are. To get life from these things *is religion*. Our life is rather found in Jesus Christ, and in Jesus Christ alone. When we repent of our religion and commit to seeing God, ourselves, and every person we encounter only as he or she is revealed in Jesus Christ, and as we allow God's Spirit to express this truth through our outrageous sacrificial love, the world will come to acknowledge that Jesus Christ is Lord, as Jesus himself promised.

But it begins with repentance. Acknowledging our failure must be the first evidence that, as a matter of fact, we don't get life from being right. It is the first evidence that we have ceased eating from the Tree of the Knowledge of Good and Evil and begun eating of the tree of life.

To all we have failed to show Calvary-type love to, to all we have looked down on as though we were in a position of moral superiority, to all we have ostracized, treated rudely, cruelly, and even violently—to all these we must ask forgiveness.

We must testify that it is only by the outrageous love and mercy of God that any of us have any hope. And *that*, in the end, is the only message we have ever had to offer anyone.

Notes

Introduction: Waking Up to Judgment

1. The debate on the nature of the Tree of the Knowledge of Good and Evil is long and varied. For a discussion of five common interpretations, see G. J. Wenham, *Genesis* (Waco: Word, 1987), 62–64. In a ground-breaking study, W. Malcolm Clark successfully established that the central issue was that of moral autonomy and the transgression of the divine boundary it represents. Clark writes, "Judgment in the OT is ultimately a matter for God." W. Malcolm Clark, "A Legal Background to the Yahwist's Use of 'Good and Evil' in Genesis 2–3," *Journal of Biblical Literature* 88 (1969), 272; see also 266–78. As noted in the preface, the most profound influence on my own reflections on the knowledge of good and evil has been Dietrich Bonhoeffer in his works *Creation and Fall/Temptation: Two Biblical Studies* (1937; reprint, New York: Simon & Schuster, 1997) and especially *Ethics* (New York: Touchstone, 1995 [1949]). For other discussions, see J. Ellul, *The Subversion of Christianity* (Grand Rapids: Eerdmans, 2001); idem, *To Will and to Do* (Philadelphia: Pilgrim Press, 1969); idem, *The Ethics of Freedom* (Grand Rapids: Eerdmans, 1976); D. J. A. Clines, "The Tree of Knowledge and the Law of Yahweh," *Vetus Testamentum* 24 (1974), 8–14; M. Tsevat, "The Two Trees in the Garden of Eden," *N. Glueck Memorial Volume* (Jerusalem: Israel Exploration Society, 1975), 40–43; P. Watson, "The Tree of Life," *Restoration Quarterly* 23 (1980), 232–38.

Chapter 1: Dancing with the Triune God

1. See C. S. Lewis, *The Four Loves* (Glasgow: Collins, 1960). While it is helpful to distinguish these four words, it is also true that their distinctness should not be overemphasized, for in actual usage they overlapped considerably. See G. D. Badcock, "The Concept of Love: Divine and Human," in *Nothing Greater, Nothing Better: Theological Essays on the Love of God*, ed. K. J. Vanhoozer (Grand Rapids: Eerdmans, 2001), 30–46.

2. Dietrich Bonhoeffer, *Ethics*, trans. N. H. Smith (1949; reprint, New York: Simon & Schuster, 1995), 53.

3. "Love is always God Himself. Love is always the revelation of God in Jesus Christ" (ibid., 54). Bonhoeffer resisted arriving at a general definition of *agape* love, even one centered on God's revelation of Christ. "Love is not what He *does* and what He *suffers*, but what *He* does and what *He* suffers. Love is always He Himself" (ibid.). I concur with his basic point but do not see how an abstract description of what God does denies this. I rather think it helpful to elucidate a general description of what God's love looks like when it flows *through us*. Such a description lifts up the connecting point between Jesus Christ incarnate and Jesus Christ in us. See Bonhoeffer's insightful discussion in *Ethics*, 51–56. With Alan Torrance, Karl Barth, and others, I see the incarnation as the basis for the possibility of our speaking analogically about God's love, or about God at all. See "Is Love the Essence of God?" in Vanhoozer, *Nothing Greater, Nothing Better*, 114–37.

4. Alan Torrance commented, "The love of which the New Testament speaks, *agape*, is that new kind of love revealed in Jesus Christ which gives value to what it loves, even where its object may be degraded and worthless." Torrance, "Is Love the Essence of God?" 132.

5. P. Kreeft, *Knowing the Truth about God's Love: The One Thing We Can't Live Without* (Ann Arbor, Mich.: Servant, 1988), 91.

6. For several insightful discussions on the fellowship of the three divine persons, see L. Boff, *Trinity and Society*, trans. P. Burns (Maryknoll, NY: Orbis, 1988); R. Gruenler, *The Trinity in the Gospel of John: A Thematic Commentary on the Fourth Gospel* (Grand Rapids: Baker, 1986); C. Pinnock and R. Brow, *Unbounded Love* (Downers Grove, Ill.: InterVarsity Press, 1994), 44–54; C. Plantinga, "The Perfect Family," *Christianity Today* (4 March 1988); M. Volf, *After Our Likeness: The Church as the Image of the Trinity* (Grand Rapids: Eerdmans, 1997); and A. Wainwright, *The Trinity in the New Testament* (London: SPCK, 1962).

7. Kreeft, *Knowing the Truth about God's Love*, 95, 97.

8. Dietrich Bonhoeffer, *Letters and Papers from Prison*, ed. E. Bethge, trans. R. H. Fuller (New York: Macmillan, 1953), 224.

9. Jonathan Edwards masterfully described the creation in such terms in "A Dissertation Concerning the End for Which God Created the World," *The Works of Jonathan Edwards*, vol. 1 (Carlisle, Pa.: Banner of Truth Trust, 1974), 94–121. Some theologians have argued that God does not truly love the world unless God in some sense *needs* the world. See, for example, S. McFague, *Models of God: Theology for an Ecological, Nuclear Age* (Philadelphia: Fortress, 1987), 130–35. So long as it is clear that God out *of his fullness* (not neediness) chose to create a world in which God in some sense needs the world (e.g., to get his will done on earth as it is in heaven), there is nothing objectionable about this way of speaking. Indeed, Scripture sometimes speaks this way (e.g., Judg. 5:23).

10. Edwards, "End for Which God Created the World," 119–21.

Chapter 2: Life "in Christ"

1. See Bonhoeffer, *Ethics*, 122.

2. See G. O. Forde, *Justification by Faith: A Matter of Death and Life* (Mifflintown, Pa.: Sigler Press, 1990).

3. Dietrich Bonhoeffer, *Life Together*, trans. J. W. Doberstein (New York: Harper & Row, 1954), 24.

4. For a discussion on how we are programmed according to "the pattern of this world" (Rom. 12:2 NIV) from a neurological perspective, see Gregory A. Boyd and Al Larson, *Escaping the Matrix: Setting the Mind Free to Experience Real Life in Christ* (Grand Rapids: Baker, forthcoming).

5. See Bonhoeffer, *Ethics*, 81–86.

6. On the recent renaissance of a strongly social understanding of the Trinity, see L. Boff, *Holy Trinity: Perfect Community*, trans. P. Berryman (Maryknoll, NY: Orbis, 2000); D. Edwards, "The Discovery of Chaos and the Retrieval of the Trinity," in *Chaos and Complexity: Scientific Perspectives on Divine Action*, ed. R. T. Russell, N. Murphy, and A. R. Peacocke (Berkeley: Center for Theology and the Natural Sciences, 1995), 157–75; A. Okechukwu Ogbonnaya, *On Communitarian Divinity: An African Interpretation of the Trinity* (New York: Paragon House, 1994); and T. R. Thompson, "Trinitarianism Today: Doctrinal Renaissance, Ethical Relevance, Social Redolence," *Calvin Theological Journal* 32 (1997): 9–42.

Chapter 3: The Center Is Love

1. On Wesley's view of love as the essence of holiness, see his sermon, "The Circumcision of the Heart," in *The Works of John Wesley*, vol. 1, ed. Albert C. Ougler (Nashville: Abingdon, 1984), 398–414. My thanks to Allen Pagett for bringing this to my attention.

2. Bonhoeffer, *Ethics*, 53.

3. Kreeft, *Knowing the Truth about God's Love*, 119. Similarly, Emil Brunner argued that while God's wrath is real, it "is not the essential reality of God. In Himself God is love." The cross, he argued, displays "the reality of wrath, which is yet in some way a subordinate reality, and the far more overwhelming reality of the love of God." See Emil Brunner, *The Mediator* (Philadelphia: Westminster, 1947), 519–21. See also K. Barth, *Church Dogmatics*, II:1 (Edinburgh: T. & T. Clark, 1957); C. H. Dodd, *The Epistle of Paul to the Romans*, 2nd ed. (London and Glasgow: Collins, 1959); A. T. Hanson, *The Wrath of the Lamb* (London: SPCK, 1957); Vincent Brümmer, *The Model of Love* (Cambridge: Cambridge University Press, 1993). This general perspective contrasts with the Augustinian and classical Reformed perspective that depicts God's love and wrath as polar attributes, manifested most poignantly in the decree of eternal salvation for some and eternal damnation for others. See, for example, J. Calvin, *Concerning the Eternal Predestination of God*, ed. J. K. S. Reid (Cambridge, England: Clark & Co., 1961); J. Piper, *The Justification of God: An Exegetical and Theological Study of Romans 9:1–23* (Grand Rapids: Baker Books, 1983); J. MacArthur Jr., *The Love of God* (Dallas: Word, 1996); D. A. Carson, *The Difficult Doctrine of the Love of God* (Wheaton: Crossway, 2000). In my estimation, this perspective misses the insight that love constitutes God's essence in a way wrath does not, for it is not adequately Christocentric. The revelation of God in Christ, including his mercy triumphing over judgment, is not allowed to tell the whole story of God's relationship to humanity. The revelation of God in Christ tells the story of God's love *for the elect*, but not the (supposed) story of God's hatred for the reprobate.

Chapter 4: Becoming the Center

1. A host of exegetical and theological issues typically arise, especially in conservative Christian circles, when the story of Adam and Eve in the garden is discussed. To what extent is this story intended to be taken literally? To what extent is it symbolic and/or mythical? How does this account relate to what science tells us about the age of the earth and the biological origin of humankind? Should we attempt to reconcile this account with evolutionary theory, and if so, how? Etc. For the purposes of this work, these issues are altogether irrelevant as long as the passage is regarded as authoritative and paradigmatic. By paradigmatic I mean that the story is at the very least not only a story about our primordial past, it also discloses structural aspects of the fallen human predicament at all times and places. In this sense it is "myth," whether or not one decides it is *also* historical. It is in my opinion unfortunate that peripheral issues so often take center stage in discussing this passage to the point that the profound wisdom of this passage is often missed. In this work, I am concerned only with allowing the paradigmatic wisdom of this passage to have this impact.

2. Dietrich Bonhoeffer, *Creation and Fall/Temptation*, 54.

3. Bonhoeffer argues that humans are confronted by two things with the prohibited tree: our freedom and our "limit" or "creatureliness." Ibid., 57.

4. Christopher Alexander, *The Phenomenon of Life: The Nature of Order* (New York: Oxford, 2001), 79–108.

5. As Bonhoeffer noted, *tob* and *ra* ("good" and "evil") "have a much wider meaning than 'good' and 'evil' in our terminology." They are rather "the categories for the deepest division of human life in every aspect." Bonhoeffer, *Creation and Fall/Temptation*, 58–59.

6. Bonhoeffer, *Ethics*, 34.

7. Bonhoeffer, *Creation and Fall/Temptation*, 62.

Chapter 5: Love and Religion

1. See Bonhoeffer, *Ethics*, 211–32, for an excellent discussion on the inability of abstract ethics to engage reality.

2. Bonhoeffer insightfully noted that the "convulsive clinging to the ethical . . . which takes the form of a moralization of life, arises from fear of the fullness of everyday life and from an awareness of incapacity for life; it is a flight into a position which lies outside real life." Bonhoeffer, *Ethics*, 264. Bonhoeffer believed the only way to be truly ethical is not to rigidly cling to abstract ethical rules but to live in love. Only by engaging in life *concretely* can we ever make truly ethical decisions. See ibid., 259–72. Bonhoeffer poignantly illustrated this principle in his essay, "What Is Meant by 'Telling the Truth'?" in ibid., 358–67.

3. Homosexuality is mentioned three times in the New Testament, and two of the three references possibly refer to sex between men and boys, not homosexuality as such (1 Cor. 6:9–10; 1 Tim. 1:9–11).

4. Bonhoeffer, *Ethics*, 31.

5. There has been a good deal of scholarly discussion surrounding who the "wretched man" represents in Romans 7. In a groundbreaking study, W. G. Kummel argued this person represents the Jew under the law, apart from Christ (*Römer 7 und die Bekehrung des Paulus* [Leipzig: J. D. Hinrichs, 1929]). This

thesis was further substantiated by Stanley Stowers, who argued that Paul is making use of an ancient rhetorical technique known as speech-in-character. Stanley Stowers, "Romans 7.7–25 as a Speech-in-Character (*prosopopoia*)," in *Paul in His Hellenistic Context*, ed. T. Engberg-Pedersen (Minneapolis: Fortress, 1995), 180–202. See also J. Lambrecht, "Man Before and Without Christ: Romans 7 and Pauline Anthropology," *Louvain Studies* 5 (1974): 18–33; and W. Russell, "Insights from Postmodernism's Emphasis on Interpretive Communities in the Interpretation of Romans 7," *Journal of the Evangelical Theological Society* 37 (December 1994): 511–27. Others have defended the more traditional view that the "wretched man" in Romans 7 represents the Christian. See, for example, J. D. G. Dunn, "Romans 7:14–25 in the Theology of Paul," in *Essays on Apostolic Themes: Studies in Honor of Howard M. Erwin*, ed. P. Elbert (Peabody, Mass.: Hendrickson, 1985), 49–70; and J. I. Packer, "The Wretched Man in Romans 7," in *Keep in Step with the Spirit* (Old Tappan, N.J.: Revell, 1984), 263–70.

6. Bonhoeffer, *Ethics*, 217.

7. Bonhoeffer, *Letters and Papers from Prison*, 191.

8. Jacques Ellul, *The Subversion of Christianity* (Grand Rapids: Eerdmans, 1986), 20–21.

9. Bonhoeffer wrote, "Christ teaches no abstract ethics such as must at all costs be put into practice. . . . He was not, like a philosopher, interested in the 'universally valid,' but rather in that which is of help to the real and concrete human being. What worried Him was not, like Kant, whether 'the maxim of an action can become a principle of general legislation,' but whether my action is at this moment helping my neighbor to become a man before God. For indeed it is not written that God became an idea, a principle, a programme, a universally valid proposition or a law, but that God became man." Bonhoeffer, *Ethics*, 86.

Chapter 6: Love and Judgment

1. On the difference between discernment that arises out of union with God and judgment that arises out of the knowledge of good and evil, see Bonhoeffer, *Ethics*, 36–37.

2. Ibid., 34.

3. Dietrich Bonhoeffer, *The Cost of Discipleship*, trans. R. H. Fuller (1949; reprint, New York: Macmillan, 1977), 204.

4. Ibid., 203.

5. See Bonhoeffer, *Ethics*, 30–41.

6. Bonhoeffer, *Cost of Discipleship*, 205. "Knowing good and evil, man is essentially judge," Bonhoeffer wrote. "As a judge he is like God, except that every judgment he delivers falls back upon himself." *Ethics*, 34.

7. Bonhoeffer, *Cost of Discipleship*, 203.

8. Bonhoeffer wrote, "Man cannot live simultaneously in reconciliation and in disunion, in freedom and under the law, in simplicity and in discordance." Bonhoeffer, *Ethics*, 38.

9. Ibid., 112–13.

10. It is worth noting that the issue is not merely whether another Christian disagrees with another's behavior but whether a person's behavior could cause another to stumble (*proskopto*), which implies being "injured" or perhaps even

"ruined" (cf. 1 Cor. 8:11). This passage is thus not mandating that every Christian community must conform to those who have the strictest opinions (whom Paul identifies as the weak). But it does say that each community should live with a view toward not destroying its weakest members. It is also worth noting that Paul is writing to believers who gathered in houses, not large church buildings. First-century Christian communities thus could not ordinarily exceed several dozen people. We shall discuss the significance of this further in chapter 12.

11. Bonhoeffer, *Ethics*, 49.

12. Ibid., 47.

Chapter 7: The Lie about God

1. I cannot follow Bonhoeffer in his interpretation of the serpent as a symbol for the inconceivability of our rebellion. Bonhoeffer, *Creation and Fall/Temptation*, 70–72. His primary concern was that interpreting the serpent as Satan, or a symbol of Satan, undermines our own culpability before God. For my part, I do not see how being *influenced* by another undermines the responsibility of one's choice, whether the influence comes from humans or spirits.

2. Bonhoeffer's argument that the serpent was claiming to know "a greater, nobler God who does not need such a prohibition" finds no support in the Genesis narrative. Bonhoeffer, *Creation and Fall/Temptation*, 72–73. The serpent speaks only of one "God" in the narrative, and it is the God who (he agrees) gave the prohibition and the God who is threatened by it being disobeyed (Gen. 3:4–5).

3. "Love must by its very nature be a relationship of free mutual give and take, otherwise it cannot be love at all." V. Brümmer, *The Model of Love: A Study in Philosophical Theology* (Cambridge, England: Cambridge University Press, 1993), 161. See Gregory Boyd, *Satan and the Problem of Evil: Developing a Warfare Theodicy* (Downers Grove, Ill.: InterVarsity Press, 2001), chapters 2 and 3, where I develop this point into a more thorough explanation for evil in the world. Bonhoeffer seems to mistakenly assume that to explain why evil exists excuses evil. See Bonhoeffer, *Creation and Fall/Temptation*, 84–85. In fact, if one grants that agents are free to choose for or against God's will, the only "why" that needs to be asked is why God gave agents this sort of freedom. And, as Brümmer suggested, there *is* a plausible answer to this question. Without this freedom, genuine love would not be possible. From this perspective, the "why" question does not rule out responsibility—it simply explains why we *are* responsible. This also transfers the mystery of why evil things happen as they do from a mystery about God's character or purposes to a mystery about the unfathomable complexity of creation, as I argue in *Is God to Blame? Moving Beyond Pat Answers to the Problem of Suffering* (Downers Grove, Ill.: InterVarsity, 2003).

4. A primary literary theme that unites Genesis 1–11 is that of the human transgression of divine boundaries. See R. S. Hendel, "Of Demigods and the Deluge: Toward an Interpretation of Genesis 6:1–4," *Journal of Biblical Literature* 106 (1987), 13–26.

5. Irenaeus, *Against Heresies*, vol. 1, *The Ante-Nicene Fathers*, ed. A. Roberts and J. Donaldson (Grand Rapids: Eerdmans, 1979), IV.vi.6, 469. The theme is frequent in Irenaeus. See, for example, ibid., III.xi.5 and IV.xiii.2.

6. As C. S. Lewis argued, one can see pointers to Jesus Christ in much of the world's religious mythology. In response to the fall, Lewis argued, God "sent the human race . . . good dreams . . . queer stories scattered all through the heathen religions about a god who dies and comes to life again and, by his death, has somehow given new life to men." C. S. Lewis, *Mere Christianity* (1943; reprint, New York: Macmillan, 1977), 54. See also C. S. Lewis, "Myth Became Fact," in *God in the Dock: Essays on Theology and Ethics*, ed. W. Hooper (Grand Rapids: Eerdmans, 1979), 63–67. See also D. Richardson, *Eternity in Their Hearts* (Ventura, Calif.: Regal Books, 1981), and Gregory A. Boyd and Paul Eddy, *The Jesus Myth?* (Grand Rapids: Baker Books, forthcoming).

7. The classical tradition defined God's attributes largely in accordance with Stoic and Platonic ideas of perfection and virtue. For example, God was generally thought to be completely unchanging (immutable), devoid of emotions (impassible), and devoid of potentiality (pure actuality), etc. God could not be affected by anything outside of himself. It is difficult, to say the least, to reconcile this perspective with a Christocentric model of God. For critical discussions of the classical tradition vis-à-vis the love of God, see N. Wolterstorff, "Suffering Love," in *Philosophy and the Christian Faith*, ed. T. Morris (Notre Dame, Ind.: University of Notre Dame Press, 1988), 196–237; R. Creel, "Immutability and Impassability," in *A Companion to Philosophy of Religion*, ed. P. L. Quinn and C. Taliaferro (Oxford, England: Blackwell, 1997), 313–19. Brümmer, *The Model of Love;* J. Sanders, *The God Who Risks* (Downers Grove, Ill.: InterVarsity, 1998); C. Pinnock, ed., *The Openness of God* (Downers Grove, Ill.: InterVarsity, 1994); J. Moltmann, *The Crucified God* (London: SCM Press, 1974); P. Fiddes, *The Creative Suffering of God* (Oxford, England: Clarendon Press, 1988).

8. We can surmise variables that affect what comes to pass but cannot usually discern how they apply in any particular situation. For a discussion of some of the variables that condition God's interaction with us, see Boyd, *Is God to Blame?* as well as idem, *Satan and the Problem of Evil*, especially 145–241.

9. In ambiguous moral situations, Bonhoeffer noted, ethics tends to become a dominant theme. With an element of sarcasm, Bonhoeffer wrote, "[Ethics] brings with it a refreshing simplification of the problems of life; it reduces them to broad general principles and it compels men to make clear decisions and to adopt unequivocal attitudes. In such circumstances . . . everything will be reduced to universal principles, that is to say, simplified; interest in principle will largely take the place of interest in the real processes of life with all their various levels of meaning." Bonhoeffer, *Ethics*, 263.

10. See Bonhoeffer, *Ethics*, 350–52. Christ's "word is not an answer to human questions and problems; it is the answer of God to the question of God to man. His word is essentially determined not from below but from above. It is not a solution, but a redemption" (350).

11. Understanding *morality* to be a set of answers to ethical questions, Jacques Ellul wrote, "Love obeys no morality and gives birth to no morality. None of the great categories of revealed truth is relative to morality or can give birth to it; freedom, truth, light, Word, and holiness do not belong at all to the order of morality. What they evoke is a mode of being, a model of life that is very free, that involves constant risks, that is constantly renewed. The Christian life is contrary to morality because it is not repetitive. . . . Morality always

interdicts this mode of being. It is an obstacle to it and implicitly condemns it, just as Jesus is inevitably condemned by moral people." Ellul, *The Subversion of Christianity*, 71.

12. See Gregory Boyd, *God at War: The Bible and Spiritual Conflict* (Downers Grove, Ill.: InterVarsity Press, 1997), 171–214.

13. For a discussion, see ibid., 231–34.

14. Robert Fyall demonstrates that both Job and his friends confuse God with Satan. See his *Now My Eyes Have Seen You: Images of Creation and Evil in the Book of Job* (Downers Grove, Ill.: InterVarsity, 2002). See also Boyd, *Is God to Blame?*, 85–104; idem, *Satan and the Problem of Evil*, 209–26.

Chapter 8: The Lie about Us

1. For this reason, Bonhoeffer argued that "conscience is not the voice of God to sinful man," as many believe. Rather, "it is man's defense against it." Bonhoeffer, *Creation and Fall/Temptation*, 91.

2. Søren Kierkegaard noted that "sin presupposes itself." *The Concept of God*, trans. W. Lowrie (Princeton: Princeton University Press, 1957), 29. This is evident in the fall narrative in so far as it is impossible to understand Adam and Eve being tempted to eat from the forbidden tree without seeing them already participating in the knowledge the forbidden tree offered. This may be further evidence that the forbidden tree is not a magical tree that confers divine knowledge but simply a "No Trespassing" sign that, if violated, would result in Adam and Eve being separated from God, "knowing good and evil." However, one could rather follow Bonhoeffer and hold that this is indeed a magical tree within a mythological narrative. The fact that Adam and Eve participate in the knowledge of good and evil prior to their eating from the Tree of the Knowledge of Good and Evil is simply evidence that we are dealing with a genre that defies literal analysis.

3. Bonhoeffer, *Ethics*, 74. Similarly, "What befell Christ befell all men, for Christ was man. The new man has been created" (80). The theme is found in Paul. "As all die in Adam, so all will be made alive in Christ" (1 Cor. 15:22). "Just as one man's trespass led to condemnation for all, so one man's act of righteousness leads to justification and life for all" (Rom. 5:18). Christ *is the truth* that defines all people, but people still have the capacity to live in rebellion, *as though* this were not true.

4. Almost every theory of humanity, whether religious or naturalistic, contains the assumption that something is fundamentally wrong with, or lacking in, human experience. See P. LeFevre, *Man: Six Modern Interpretations* (Philadelphia: Geneva, 1968), 19.

5. I side with those scholars who argue that the "exception clause" Jesus cites refers to the Jewish betrothal period. See W. Heth, *Jesus and Divorce: The Problem with the Evangelical Consensus* (Nashville: Thomas Nelson, 1984). In teaching that remarriage involves adultery, I do not see that Jesus was thereby doing away with God's former allowance for remarriage. He was simply noting the carnality that required God to give this allowance in the first place. We should no more interpret Jesus to be "tightening the belt" on divorce laws than we should interpret him to be suggesting that everyone who lusts in his or her

heart and thus commits adultery should be stoned (the prescribed punishment for adultery at the time). Entering into more than one marriage covenant is a serious break from God's ideal. But living a life of singleness after divorce, if one does not have the gift and calling to do so, may constitute an even more serious departure from God's ideal (Matt. 19:10–11; 1 Cor. 7:9).

6. Bonhoeffer, *Ethics*, 76.

7. For Bonhoeffer's reflections on living in the simplicity of God's will, see *Ethics*, 41–51.

Chapter 9: The Curse

1. Bonhoeffer, *Ethics*, 23–24.

2. On Bonhoeffer's theological interpretation of nakedness as innocence, see Bonhoeffer, *Creation and Fall/Temptation*, 86–89.

3. Bonhoeffer wrote, "Shame covers me before the other because of my own evil and of his evil, because of the division that has come between us. . . . In the unity of unbroken obedience man is naked in the presence of man, uncovered, revealing both body and soul, and yet he is not ashamed. Shame only comes into existence in the world of division." Bonhoeffer, *Creation and Fall/Temptation*, 69.

4. Bonhoeffer wrote, "[Adam] confesses his sin, but as he confesses, he takes to flight again. . . . Instead of surrendering Adam falls back on one art learned from the serpent, that of correcting the idea of God. That is, he flees again. . . . Adam has not surrendered, he has not confessed. He has appealed to his conscience, to his knowledge of good and evil, and out of this knowledge he has accused his Creator." Bonhoeffer, *Creation and Fall/Temptation*, 92.

5. For a discussion on the significance of Satan and fallen powers for our understanding of natural evil, see Boyd, *Satan and the Problem of Evil*, 242–318.

6. On the correlation between our knowledge of good and evil and God's curse and promise, see Bonhoeffer, *Creation and Fall/Temptation*, 93–97.

Chapter 10: Reversing the Curse

1. For an excellent discussion of this, see W. J. Webb, *Slaves, Women & Homosexuals: Exploring the Hermeneutics of Cultural Analysis* (Downers Grove, Ill.: InterVarsity, 2001).

2. "God preserves the world by affirming the sinful world and directing it into its limits by means of ordinances. But none of these ordinances any longer have any eternal character because they are only there to preserve life. . . . For us [the preservation of life] is directed only towards—Christ. All the orders of our fallen world are God's orders of preservation on the way to Christ." Bonhoeffer, *Creation and Fall/Temptation*, 100–101.

3. Bonhoeffer, *Ethics*, 84, emphasis added. In Bonhoeffer's view, the church is "merely an instrument, merely a means to an end," for it exists solely for the purpose of proclaiming Christ's lordship and inviting others into the salvation he has accomplished on Calvary." Yet, "precisely through its willingness to be merely the instrument and the means to the end, the congregation has become the goal and centre of all God's dealing with the world" (295–96).

4. Bonhoeffer noted that Jesus was willing to break laws for the sake of love. "As the one who loved without sin, He became guilty; He wished to share in the fellowship of human guilt. . . . Thus it is Jesus Christ who sets conscience free from the service of God and of our neighbor; He sets conscience free even and especially when man enters into the fellowship of human guilt. The conscience which has been set free from the law will not be afraid to enter into the guilt of another man for the other man's sake, and indeed precisely in doing this it will show itself in its purity." Bonhoeffer, *Ethics*, 240.

5. Ibid., 47. See also ibid., 35, 46–51.

6. On hell as living an eternal lie, see Boyd, *Satan and the Problem of Evil*, 319–57.

7. Bonhoeffer, *Cost of Discipleship*, 204.

Chapter 11: Confronting Pharisees

1. Bonhoeffer, *Ethics*, 31.

2. Ibid., 33.

3. Ellul, *Subversion of Christianity*, 70.

Chapter 12: Love, Confession, and Accountability

1. Bonhoeffer, *Cost of Discipleship*, 204–5.

2. Ibid.

3. For Bonhoeffer's remarkable emphasis on the role of preaching in the church, see Bonhoeffer, *Ethics*, 287–91.

4. See R. Banks, *Paul's Idea of Community: The Early House Church* (Grand Rapids: Eerdmans, 1980); V. P. Branick, *The House Church in the Writings of Paul* (Wilmington, Del.: Glazier, 1989); F. W. Filson, "The Significance of the Early House Churches," *Journal of Biblical Literature* 58 (1939): 105–12; C. Osiek and D. L. Balch, *Families in the New Testament World: Households and House Churches* (Louisville: Westminster John Knox, 1997).

5. For an insightful analysis of the theological foundation and dynamics of Christian community, see Bonhoeffer, *Life Together*.

Gregory A. Boyd is founder and senior pastor of Woodland Hills Church in St. Paul, Minnesota, and founder and president of Christus Victor Ministries. Boyd graduated from Yale University Divinity School in 1982 (M.Div.) and Princeton Theological Seminary in 1987 (Ph.D.). He has authored twelve previous books, including *Seeing Is Believing* (Baker Books), *God at War* (InterVarsity), *Satan and the Problem of Evil* (InterVarsity), *God of the Possible* (BakerAcademic), *Is God to Blame?* (InterVarsity), and the award-winning *Letters from a Skeptic* (Chariot Victor). He is a nationally and internationally recognized teacher, preacher, debater, and seminar leader. Boyd has been married to Shelley Boyd for twenty-four years, has three children, and lives in St. Paul, Minnesota.

Also by **Gregory A. Boyd**

Break out of spiritual performance into a liberating relationship with Christ through the power of imaginative prayer.

"[Boyd] makes a powerfully persuasive argument for the use of imaginative prayer by Christians, then outlines a method for beginning the practice."
—*Publishers Weekly,* starred review

0-8010-6502-X • $12.99p

"This is one of the most comprehensive books ever written on the subject. It will not only clear away much misunderstanding, but inspire many to experience the healing freedom and deeper relationship with Jesus that comes through imaginative prayer."
—David A. Seamands, author of *Healing for Damaged Emotions*

"So many books on spirituality offer 'pie in the sky' solutions, but not *Seeing Is Believing.* I love the way Boyd explains and helps us to live out the true identity that we have in Jesus Christ."
—Robert E. Webber, author of *The Younger Evangelicals*

AVAILABLE AT YOUR LOCAL BOOKSTORE